Praise for Religion in I...

"The essays in this volume, and the savvy introduction by Hatzopoulos and Petito, inform us of just how vital is religion in international relations today. Well before the events of 9/11, religion was once again—after a long hiatus—on the radar screen of scholars, although many remained unconvinced of its importance. No more. This volume makes a significant contribution to our understanding."

> —*Jean Bethke Elshtain, The Laura Spelman Rockefeller Professor of Social and Political Ethics, The University of Chicago, author of the forthcoming book:* Just War Against Terror. The Burden of American Power.

"When we talk about religion today, what are we really talking about? The concepts that we have on hand for understanding the status and role of religion in current affairs are by and large obsolete. They only made sense in reference to a certain "stability" in which one could believe and make people believe in. The disappearance of the necessary conditions for this belief signals the entrance into a world characterized by the evidence of movement. Hence the necessity to rebuild our intellectual tools. This work constitutes an important contribution for such an enterprise."

> —*Patrick Michel, Research Director at CERI, Sciences Po, Paris.*

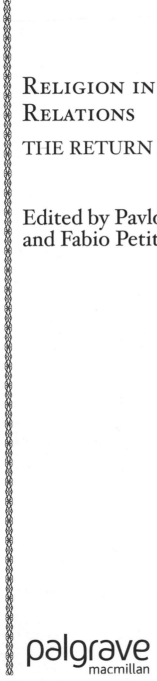

RELIGION IN INTERNATIONAL RELATIONS

THE RETURN FROM EXILE

Edited by Pavlos Hatzopoulos
and Fabio Petito

palgrave
macmillan

RELIGION IN INTERNATIONAL RELATIONS
Copyright © Pavlos Hatzopoulos and Fabio Petito, 2003.

First published in 2003 by PALGRAVE MACMILLAN™
175 Fifth Avenue, New York, N.Y. 10010 and
Houndmills, Basingstoke, Hampshire, England RG21 6XS.
Companies and representatives throughout the world.

PALGRAVE MACMILLAN is the global academic imprint of the Palgrave Macmillan division of St. Martin's Press, LLC and of Palgrave Macmillan Ltd. Macmillan® is a registered trademark in the United States, United Kingdom and other countries. Palgrave is a registered trademark in the European Union and other countries.

1-4039-6206-5 (cl.)   1-4039-6207-3 (pbk.)

Library of Congress Cataloging-in-Publication Data Available from the Library of Congress

A catalogue record for this book is available from the British Library.

Design by Letra Libre, Inc.

First edition: May 2003
10 9 8 7 6 5 4 3 2 1
Printed in the United States of America.

Contents

PART III
POLITICIZING RELIGION:
TOWARD A NEW GLOBAL ETHOS?

CONTRIBUTORS

CARSTEN BAGGE LAUSTSEN PhD candidate in the Department of Political Science, University of Copenhagen, Denmark

FRED DALLMAYR Packey Dee Professor of Government, University of Notre Dame, USA

JOHN L. ESPOSITO Director of the Centre for Muslim-Christian Understanding at Georgetown University, USA

RICHARD FALK Albert G. Milbank Professor of International Law and Practice, Princeton University and currently Visiting Distinguished Professor at the University of California, Santa Barbara, USA

ANDREAS HASENCLEVER Research Fellow at the Peace Research Institute, Frankfurt, Germany

VENDULKA KUBÁLKOVÁ Professor in the School of International Studies, University of Miami, USA

CECILIA LYNCH Associate Professor in the Department of Political Science, University of California, Irvine, USA

TERRY NARDIN Professor of Political Science, University of Wisconsin-Milwaukee, USA

VOLKER RITTBERGER Professor of Political Science and International Relations, University of Tubingen, Germany

SCOTT M. THOMAS Lecturer in International Relations, University of Bath, UK

JOHN O. VOLL Professor of Islamic History at Georgetown University, USA

OLE WÆVER Professor in the Department of Political Science, University of Copenhagen, Denmark

ACKNOWLEDGEMENTS

W e think of Chicago as the place of origin of this project. There, in the International Studies Association conference of 2001, we met Yosef Lapid who encouraged us to submit a book proposal on religion and international relations to the newly born Palgrave Culture, Religion, and International Relations (CRI) series. His encouragements, after all this time, have come into fruition. Then, Yosef had just discussed the papers of a panel on the role of religion in world politics, but already sharply sensed the opportunity to push further this research effort. We want to thank him for having believed that two postgraduate students could accomplish this aim. Most of the chapters included in this volume, however, have a history that predates the Chicago conference. And this history goes back to indefinitely long discussions between us in Grenada House in the Winter 1999, to a conference held at the London School of Economics on May 2000, to a special number of *Millennium: Journal of International Studies* published on December 2000, up to the aforementioned ISA conference where we organised two panels on the subject. We would like to thank all those scholars who participated in one or more of these events but their papers are not to be found in the following pages: Stephen Chan, S. N. Eisenstadt, Andreas Osiander, Bassam Tibi, Charles Jones, Andrea den Boer, Katerina Dalacoura, Fred Halliday, Ali Mazrui, Thomas Uthup and Miroslav Volf. We thank them for their hard work and the inspiration they provided to us.

Finally, we would like, above all, to thank *Millennium: Journal of International Studies* for permission to reprint the following articles from the special issue on Religion and International Relations (vol. 29, no. 3): Scott Thomas, "Taking Religious and Cultural Pluralism Seriously: The Global Resurgence of Religion and the Transformation of International Society," 815–41; Cecilia Lynch, "Dogma, Praxis, and Religious Perspectives on Multiculturalism," 741–59; Vendulka Kubálková, "Towards an International Political Theology," 675–704; Andreas Hasenclever and Volker Rittberger, "Does Religion Make a

Difference? Theoretical Approaches to the Impact of Faith on Political Conflict," 641–74; Carsten Bagge Laustsen and Ole Wæver, "In Defence of Religion: Sacred Referent Objects for Securitization," 705–39; and John L. Esposito and John O. Voll, "Islam and the West: Muslim Voices of Dialogue," 613–39.

All these articles have been revised from their original versions—some substantially, others marginally—to fit the purposes of the book.

—*Pavlos Hatzopoulos and Fabio Petito*

THE RETURN FROM EXILE

An Introduction

Pavlos Hatzopoulos and Fabio Petito

The worldwide resurgence of religion seems nowadays to generate repression—at times through the imposition of religious law upon a community of people; at other times, through the association of religion with "terror," through its supposed inclination to generate extreme—even indiscriminate—political actions; or even in scenarios involving the persecution of members of other religious communities; or, more apocalyptically, as the driving force behind a coming "clash of civilizations."

But what if in order to study the role of religion in international relations we need to reverse this picture? To treat religion not as the generator of repression, but as the "victim"? This reversal should not be understood necessarily in literal terms. Instead, religion is a victim insofar as it was *exiled* from the modern constitution of international relations; religion was the object that needed to vanish for modern international politics to come into being. Religion has been, and largely remains, what the discipline of International Relations (IR) can speak about only as a threat to its own existence. We chose this subtitle— *The Return from Exile*—because we believe that this volume treats this unlikely intellectual reversal as a potent possibility.

The rejection of religion, in other words, seems to be inscribed in the genetic code of the discipline of IR. Arguably, this occurred because the main constitutive elements of the practices of international relations were purposely established in early modern Europe to end the Wars of Religion. At that point in history—paraphrasing the powerful words of Thomas Hobbes—God made space to the great Leviathan (the sovereign state), that mortal God to which the *new modern man* owes his peace and security, religion was privatized, and through the principle of the *cuius regio eius religio* (the ruler determines the religion of his realm) pluralism among states and noninterference were born and worshipped as the new sacred principles of the emerging Westphalian order. As a consequence, politics with reference to religion became the ultimate threat to order, security, and civility, and, could not inhabit both the practices of international relations and, subsequently, the discipline of International Relations.

Having unexpectedly survived the long Westphalian exile, religion is again back to world politics. World politics has changed; religion has changed as well—and perhaps even more radically. The return of religion from the Westphalian exile back to the center of international relations opens up new possibilities and, this book contends, that these cannot be overlooked if the post-Westphalian global coexistence aspires to genuine universality.

Not only that: The return from exile is never a simple return to the "same old ways" of the pre-exile situation, as all the three Abramithic religious traditions know very well. First, the lost home has necessarily changed and, second—and even more fundamentally—the exile can be a deeply transformative experience. The exile opens up the way for what Saint Paul calls a *metanoia,* a drastic "change of mind." But has religion experienced with respect to international politics this *metanoia?* Is religion ready to stand on the side of a "global peaceful ethos" and not of a "global war" as the scenario of a "clash of civilizations" predicts? The future cannot be predicted, but this volume stands on the possibility that the exile has brought a *metanoia* and treats this second reversal as a powerful possibility. But, more of this later on.

This introduction will try to explain how this book reads from our editorial perspective and how it might be read in the light of future research. It will illustrate the coherence and points of incoherence of the book, the utility and futility of its separation into three thematic sections, the contemplated organization and contingency of our editorial decisions. And it will also partially explain why we have paradoxically chosen to include an epilogue that from an argumentative viewpoint attempts to partially defeat the purpose of the book as a whole and from an amicable one to severely limit its aspirations.

This project emanates from a normative reaction toward existing studies on religion in international politics reinforced by the observation of a striking theoretical void in the IR literature. What drives the contributions to the volume is, on a first level, a critical engagement with the "clash of civilizations" thesis and other numerous analyses that all too often associate the resurgence of religion with new Cold War mindsets, the danger of fundamentalist politics, even the threat of global terrorism; or more generally with a novel, disorderly state of international affairs.[1] To say that this association should not be essentialized is almost banal, but the volume attempts to transcend this thin-based critique and to concretely show how an engagement with worldwide religious traditions might lead to creative theoretical and political endeavors.

To pursue this task, it is first of all necessary to grasp theoretically the contemporary interplay between religion and international politics. Against the (always less controversial) sociological background of the "global resurgence of religion" and "desecularization of the world," against the growing concern (among both policymakers and the wider intellectual community) for the role of religions in international politics, IR theory has oddly remained silent.[2] It might be true that theoretically informed discussions on the role of specific religious phenomenologies in contemporary world politics are not missing—it is enough to think of the large number of theoretically sophisticated publications on the international dimensions of Political Islam and other religious fundamentalisms[3]—but the implicit assumption is that the topic of religion does not require a reflection within the realm of IR theory, that is, the elaboration of new interpretative categories and analytical frameworks. It is thought that a policymaking-oriented approach or at most some minor adjustments to the "broader" theoretical frameworks available to deal with the role of ideas, culture, and identity would serve the purpose.[4] This book argues against this assumption and explores new theoretical ways for making sense and interpreting the interplay between religion and world politics.

This void in the literature looks even more serious if we acknowledge that the global resurgence of religion might also hold important implications for thinking about international relations (IR theory) *tout court.* From this standpoint, International Relations theory has not only a problem in dealing with religion but religion has the potential to revolutionize IR theory. In other words, it is a contention of this book that the global resurgence of religion confronts IR theory with a theoretical challenge comparable to that raised by the end of the Cold War or the emergence of globalization. As a consequence, this configures a "critical" meeting for the discipline in the sense of a theory-generative and self-creative reflection—both on an analytical and on a normative level—and not just another ordinary exercise in problem solving. In this respect, the return of religion from the (Westphalian) exile brings with it the promise to emancipate IR from its own theoretical captivities.

The Book

The book is divided into three parts: "International Relations Theory and Religion," "War, Security, and Religion," and "Politicizing Religion: Toward a New Global Ethos?" As is clear from the titles, each part has a specific focus, but the nature of the topic itself makes the borders that separate one part from the other necessarily fuzzy and to some extent artificial. Furthermore, if it is unquestionably true that each chapter stands as an autonomous theoretical inquiry into one aspect of the interplay between religion and international relations, and as such can be read independently, it is also true that this three-way partition was chosen because it reflects the three major arguments that the book as a whole purports to make.

International Relations Theory and Religion

The first part of the book focuses on the implications for International Relations as a discipline in engaging seriously with religion and articulates what we call a "disciplinary" argument in two versions: a weak and strong one. The argument is that International Relations theory hasn't yet developed an adequate theoretical understanding of religion in general and of the recent global resurgence of religions in particular, and as a consequence, in its *weak version,* it calls for the elaboration of new interpretative categories and analytical frameworks. In this respect, all three contributions included in this part explore new theoretical ways for interpreting the interplay between religion and world politics.

Scott Thomas in his contribution argues that if the global resurgence of religion is to be taken seriously, then an earlier *social* understanding of religion, still existent in many parts of the developing world and fundamentally different from Western modernity's invention of religion as a set of *privatized* doctrines and beliefs, needs to be developed and recognized as part of any post-Westphalian international order. For this purpose, he firstly applies Alasdair MacIntyre's social theory and in particular his notion of 'tradition' to the English School's concept of international society, and then argues that MacIntyrean "virtue-ethics" can help us develop a "deeper pluralism" among different communities and states in international society.

In a different but complementary way, Cecelia Lynch argues that theological and religious thinking can contribute considerably to debates about culture in international politics often dominated by Enlightenment worldviews that cast religious belief, thought, and action in overly essentialist terms. Tracing the development of debates about culture in general, and multiculturalism in particular, in contemporary religious thinking, she discusses several theological views on religious pluralism, from exclusivism to syncretism and apologetics, and finally concludes that while much of our political debates over the role of religion remain mirrored in exclusivist analyses, contemporary religious thought provides new ways of thinking about the sociopolitical implications of the multiple systems of belief present in the world.

Vendulka Kubálková's piece pushes further the argument about the inadequacy of contemporary International Relations theory and exemplifies the *strong version* of the disciplinary argument. Following this logic, Kubálková calls for a new subfield of International Relations, what she terms International Political Theology (IPT), in order to battle the fixity of Western social science that remains unwilling (and unable) to treat religions as important social factors on their own terms, on a par with secular forces. IPT wants to correct this systematic omission in the same way that International Political Economy (IPE) was intended at the time of its conception to respond to the neglect of economic factors in international politics. It proposes the systematic study of discourses (and relations among them) concerning world affairs that search for—or claim to have found—a response, transcendental or secular, to the *human need for meaning.*

Traces of the strong version of the disciplinary argument can also be found at least *in nuce* in Lynch's and Thomas' contributions. In Lynch's, this takes the form of an apparently moderate, but in our view far reaching in its consequences, critique of the Enlightenment assumptions—prevalent in contemporary political debates—that associate religion with danger, dogma, or rigid conceptions of otherness. Here, the paradox is that the growing importance of issues of religious identity and alterity in world politics has not corresponded to a growing attention to the multiple understandings of religious belief articulated by religious thinkers themselves, rather the aforementioned Enlightenment assumptions have been *uncritically* reproduced and de facto accepted as *dogma.* Yet—and this is the telling irony—Lynch's detailed discussion of contemporary theological views on the possibilities of religious pluralism and multiculturalism shows that the view of religious identity as uncompromising is today highly *unenlightened* and *unenlightening,* as it is historically inept and ignores significant and lively debates within religious thought itself.

The problem lies, it seems, in International Relations' self-understanding as a party to the Enlightenment project, in its self-conception as a social science that holds a privileged access to knowledge of social phenomena.[5] Firstly, and more broadly, it should not come as a big revelation that religion and the Enlightenment have not always been on "very good terms" either theoretically or politically.[6] Secondly, and more specifically, we have to remember that modern international law, arguably the predecessor of the discipline of International Relations, was born under the auspices of Alberico Gentili's celebrated cry *silete theologi in munere alieno!*—let theologians keep silence about matters outside their province!—which symbolically marked the end of the scholastic world and the advent of a new epoch, the Westphalian era, in which international politics would be examined from a secular rather than a theological standpoint.

This last point brings us to a related exploratory hypothesis that we want to put forward expanding on Thomas' insights. Thomas argues that the "Westphalian presumption"—the notion that religious and cultural pluralism cannot be accommodated in international society but must be privatized, if there is to be international order—is part of the political mythology of liberalism and is based on the "invention of religion" as a set of privately held doctrines or beliefs. Taking this argument further and paraphrasing Carl Schmitt, we could provocatively ask whether all significant concepts of the modern theory of international relations are secularized theological concepts.[7] In this respect, a more careful consideration of religion could problematize some of the secular foundational myths of the discipline, as well as suggest the need to genealogically rewrite some of the *stories* that the discipline tells about the origin and development of essential phenomenologies of international politics—for example, war, international law, the domestic/international nexus, the principle of non-interference, and others—that are today cast within a liberal *weltanschauung* and, as a consequence, result in hermeneutically flawed historical interpretations. This is of critical relevance for the discipline since—quoting from Hedley Bull and Adam Watson—"[International Relations] can be understood only in historical perspective, and without an awareness of the past that generated it, the universal international society of the present can have no meaning."[8]

War, Security, and Religion

The second part of the book, entitled "War, Security, and Religion," tries to shed some light on the complex relationship between religion, war, and security. In other words, it is the most condemning accusation against religion that the contributions of the second section of the book attempt to challenge from two different theoretical standpoints:

the view of the politicization of religion as an inescapable threat to security, as an enabling or mobilizing factor of interstate or intrastate warfare and as inimical to the resolution of conflict.

The common starting point of the two contributions to this part of the volume lies in the recognition that the relationship between political conflicts and religion cannot be grasped either by a "primordialist-essentialist" reading that detects in religious or cultural-ethnic difference the main source of conflict, or by a "modernist-instrumentalist" interpretation that regards religion as nothing more than a malleable, mobilizing device whose political manifestations can be reduced to modern socioeconomic factors. As secular political ideologies, such as nationalism, communism, and, of course, liberalism take the form of "political religion," with their gods, holy texts, and paradises on earth, in the same way does religion, by becoming "political," begin to speak the all-too-modern (and worldly) language of revolution, rights, and the state. This convergence, of course, does not imply that there are not important political differences between secular and religious political ideologies—indeed there are, as there are *within* secular political ideologies—but it works as a warning against any simplistic dismissive or apocalyptic attitude toward the contemporary resurgence of religion in world politics.

Andreas Hasenclever and Volker Rittberger explore some of these themes from a peace research perspective by elaborating what they call a "moderate constructivist" position on the impact of faith on conflicts that is located somewhere between primordialism and instrumentalism. Their contention—in particular against the instrumentalist interpretation—is that religious leaders can "refuse to bless the weapons," and then violence may not occur even if significant socioeconomic and political inequalities exist in or between societies. Their hypothesis is that although differences in religious creed are hardly ever a genuine source of political conflict, under certain conditions they shape conflict behavior decisively in the direction of either escalation or de-escalation. In the final part of the chapter, they focus on a strategy that is devised to initiate a dialogue—or to reinforce the ongoing dialogues—among the world's religions in order to achieve and strengthen an interreligious world ethic. Such a world ethic, often associated with the German theologian Hans Küng, could broaden the space for cooperative forms of conflict management during socioeconomic crises, thus preventing political conflicts from escalating into violent clashes.

Carsten Bagge Laustsen and Ole Wæver then explore the logic of securitization of objects that are of a clearly religious nature and argue for the need to expand securitization studies, the approach of the Copenhagen School, to a new specific religious sector. After showing *why* it is often particularly tempting to securitize religion, *how* it is done, and *what* securitization does, they argue that what is taken to be specific to religion is actually present in many political ideologies. Here, however, they push this insight further by introducing an original set of definitions and distinctions that elucidates the similarities and differences between religion, political religion, and secular ideology. First of all, following Kierkegaard, Laustsen and Wæver put the concept of faith at the heart of their understanding of religion. Citing the title of one of Kierkegaard's most famous books, they claim that religion, because founded on faith, involves "fear and trembling." When mobilized as politics, religion becomes ideology, for it represses the transcendence of the divine. Religious behavior becomes political behavior carried out as though one were God. Fear and trembling is replaced by absolute certainty. This is why ideology, in their reading, becomes a form of quasi-religion, that is, religion securitized and thereby impoverished as religion.

The normative implications of this argument are similar to the dialogue strategy put forward by Hasenclever and Rittberger as a way of delegitimizing the use of violence in the name of religion. In line with the language and general ethics of the Copenhagen School, Laustsen and Wæver stress that the aim is de-securitization, which means that issues should not be lifted above normal politics with an urgency and necessity that often entail antidemocratic effects. But it also means letting religion be *religion*. Respecting religion implies the acceptance of a lack of being, the acceptance of the fact that religious discourse essentially occurs in a transcendental realm.

While rejecting any simplistic interpretation of the relation between religion and security, the second section of the volume also attempts to trace an understanding of religion that is intrinsically other to violence and, although the poststructuralist-inspired IR theorizing of the Copenhagen School marks substantial differences from that of the IR moderate constructivism (with its social-scientific methodology) of Hasenclever and Rittberger, both the contributions find the rejection of primordialist and modernist approaches essential to this attempt.

Politicizing Religion: Toward a New Global Ethos?

The third section has a more exploratory nature but it is here that the normative horizon of the book acquires more distinctly a constructive dimension. It proposes that theoretical and political debates concerning the possibility of a new global ethos cannot be adequate if they lack a thick engagement with worldwide religious traditions. What is effectively at stake here is our view of the world, the very theories and concepts that establish the practice of world politics. A fundamental void looms when these reflect the tenets of liberalism, a political tradition that forecloses the centrality of religion in the everyday practices of "really existing communities."[9] If the normative structure—the global ethos—of future global coexistence is to be genuinely universal, it cannot only be liberal and Western-centric. Genuine universality requires a thick conception of the presence of religion in world affairs; in many ways it must also spring from there. Or, as Vaclav Havel more eloquently puts it:

> It is not enough to take the set of imperatives, principles, or rules produced by the Euro-American world and mechanically declare them binding for all. Different cultures or spheres of civilization can share only what they perceive as genuine common ground, not something that few merely offer to or even force upon others. The tenets of human coexistence on this earth can hold up only if they grow out of the deepest experience of everyone, not just some of us.[10]

The exploratory nature of this argument—made clear in the section's title by the use of the word "toward" and by the interrogative form—required, in the context of our book project, to be creatively pursued from a multiplicity of angles that could provide a platform of insights and research directions for more systematic future inquiries into this key normative issue. As a consequence, the chapters included in this section tackle this question by addressing three rather different issues associated with the role of religious traditions in the creation of a global ethos: the need for a humane global governance, the political meaning of the present global spiritual resurgence, and the (too often forgotten) Islamic voices of dialogue.

In his contribution, Richard Falk argues that the project for a humane global governance—what in other occasions he has defined as "globalization from below"—requires the contribution of inclusive forms of religious traditions. Since secular actors, including states, are presently captive to economic globalization, related above all to the efforts by market forces to coordinate and stabilize their operations on a regional and global basis, they have become threatening to human well-being and to the quality of social and political life. The challenge for religion is to infuse the struggles of the peoples of the world for democracy, equity, and sustainability with a vision of human existence that is human-centered yet conscious of the relevance of our surrounding nature, of the sacred, and of mysteries beyond the grasp of reason and machines. Religion so conceived has the potential of creating some countervailing pressures to neutralize the disruptive societal impacts of the ascendant market forces.

It is interesting to note that Falk's call for a religious orientation to inform the energies of globalization from below has only secondarily a pragmatic function, that is, it does not merely ask for the recruitment of religions as a means of mobilizing and motivating people. Primarily, Falk's argument lies in the substantial belief that religion remains the primary and strongest custodian of a premodern humanistic wisdom that the technological and economy-driven Western societies have almost entirely forgotten. In a similar way, for Havel, a global ethics of responsibility appropriate to the present era needs not only to represent a genuine universality but also to be based on transcendence. It needs, that is, to regain the awareness, peculiar to all great religious traditions, that we are not the creators but mere components of the mysterious order of existence.[11]

Starting from a similar reflection, Fred Dallmayr asks, in the piece included in this volume, which kind of spirituality is most needed in our contemporary globalizing context to foster a peaceful global ethos. While appreciating the unleashing of new spiritual energies in our time, Dallmayr wishes to guard us against their commodification and especially against a possible slippage into "pop" psychology and private self-indulgence. In the effort to avoid or reduce this danger, he turns to the heart of the mystical experience in the two great religious traditions of Christianity and Islam and distinguishes two major forms of spirituality: a gnostic spirituality and a love-based, or *agape*, spirituality.

From the vantage of these traditions, spirituality is not (or not principally) a form of psychic subjectivism, but involves a mode of transcendence and self-transgression—more precisely, an effort to rupture self-centeredness by opening the self toward otherness. In particular, this transformative-transgressive potency, Dallmayr contends, is topically represented by the love-based, or *agape*, form of spirituality (in the examples of John of the Cross and Jalal ad-Din Rumi) that in contrast with gnosticism has a more active and outgoing slant, a slant that potentially ruptures or transgresses all boundaries based on status, race, and ethnic or religious background. This kind of "contemplation in action" is, according to Dallmayr, of great social and political relevance and deserves affirmation today.

The final chapter, by John L. Esposito and John O. Voll, moves, in an apparently sea-change shift, to the discussion of the thought of contemporary Islamic political leaders. It enables, however, the evaluation of the argument for a (also-)religiously inspired global ethos in the post–September 11 context. By reappraising the religious tradition that since this "apocalyptic" date is even more associated with jihadist modes of thought and practice, Esposito and Voll paint a different political reality. In recent years, Islam has been influenced by the emergence of very promising ideas—too easily unnoticed or dismissed in the West—that aim at the creation of a peaceful global ethos.

Esposito and Voll uncover a reality that too often remains hidden in mainstream political and intellectual international relations circles. They show how in the final decades of the twentieth century, an important type of Muslim leader-intellectual became prominent, playing a significant role in Muslim reconceptualizations of religion and international relations. They argue that Muslim activist intellectuals like Anwar Ibrahim in Malaysia, Mohammad Khatami in Iran, and Abdurrahman Wahid in Indonesia had an important role in articulating and sometimes implementing new concepts and paradigms in domestic and international politics. Reacting against the "clash/jihadist view" of the world, they have been active in defining the terms of intercivilizational dialogue from an Islamic perspective that recognize and respond to the realities of global diversity and multiculturalism. As a result of these efforts, issues of democratization, civil society, the rule of law, pluralism, and tolerance have become common themes of the domestic politics and international relations of their countries.

Thanks to this last contribution, it becomes even clearer that if the future global ethos is to represent a genuine universality and not just reinforce a liberal and Western-centric global order, it needs to thickly engage with the great religious traditions. In this respect, the initiative proposed by the president of the Islamic Republic of Iran, Khatami, for a "dialogue of civilizations"—discussed by Esposito and Voll in their piece—points in the right direction. A global ethos cannot be but the result of a multiplicity of dialogical engagements in the form of what Hans-Georg Gadamer has called a "fusion of horizons"—an enriching change from the "pre-judgements" that we carry with us as indispensable and unavoidable starting points in any dialogical engagement.[12]

Prospects of the Book

Leaving behind our editorial position for a moment, we would finally like to suggest another way of reading this book, especially concerning what it proposes in the light of future research. In our reading, the book's advice can be summarized in a sentence. It is not enough to acknowledge the resurgence of religion and then vow to study this phenomenon through the existing categories of International Relations theory.

As to the "resurgence of religion," no serious contention seems to hold: There exists at present a widespread consensus that contemporary international politics are influenced once again by religious forces. One of the debates that have emerged from this observation is whether the concept of 'religion' is appropriate to describe this development. In other words, is religion manifested in the political field really religion? Is the Iranian revolution, or Al-Qaeda, or the American Christian far right truly *religious* phenomena? Or, do religion's current political manifestations involve a distortion of religious character and thus require a conceptual distinction between religion and politicized religion? The predicament of these debates is that they fail to take into account a fundamental mechanism. Political religion has not simply come to the fore as a force mediated by other contemporary developments like globalization or the breakdown of communist regimes. Instead, what should be recognized is that the phenomenon cannot be conceptualized as simply a "return," but that the resurgence of religion marks the "return of the repressed," of what had been banished and sent into exile.

The point to be developed here is not the history of the Westphalian system, or the elucidation of what this system foreclosed. It is not only that the modern system of international relations was established on the binary opposition between the secular and the religious, and the related jettisoning of religion from the political space as codified in the Treaty of Westphalia. What is missing from this account is that the emergence of the modern international system was constituted by a restructuring of international theory. Thus the problem is not simply that we need to tell other, more accurate stories about ourselves and our past, about how modern international relations came into being—rather the problem lies in that we have been telling and can presently tell stories only in a modern way, through the use of distinctively modern concepts. The structure of international thought, our thinking about the international, was imagined as a process based on the suppression of theological concepts and their replacement by new, areligious categories, above all sovereignty.[13] By recognizing this double separation, we can now claim that the contemporary interplay between religion and international politics needs to face the following paradox: How is it possible

to reintegrate the study of religion into our predominantly Westphalian and secular conception of world politics?

If this tension is eschewed, then we necessarily reproduce the modern constitution of international politics. The resurgence of religion
can accordingly be mapped in the preexisting state of affairs without
any fundamental changes. And in the most "tolerant" and optimistic
scenario, one can (cautiously) welcome religion's return but then
strictly confine it within the space of civil society—and not only keep
it there, but also attempt to define what type of religion this should be:
primarily devoid of its notion of the Good; that is, a reflexive version
of religion, at pace and in harmony with modern developments, in
tune with the desires of modern people. George W. Bush's famous
post–September 11 contention, "The enemy is not Islam," coupled
with his repeated visits to American mosques, can be interpreted along
these lines. Far from representing a hypocritical militaristic stance,
Bush's position embodies the liberal attitude *par excellence*. Religion
is not dangerous as long as it remains confined to a marginal political
role, as long as it does not tread beyond the space of civil society.

A contentious point we would like to make here is that this liberal
attitude is correlative with the "clash of civilizations" scenario. To be
more precise, the liberal treatment of religion marks the theoretical
condition of possibility for the present centrality of the clash of civilizations thesis. Taking things strictly anachronistically, the studies on
the peaceful incorporation of religion into the political state of affairs
prepared the space for Huntington's positing of religion qua civilization into the heart of world politics. The "clash of civilizations" func-
tioned as the excessive supplement of the liberal peaceful solution, or
the grave warning of what could happen if the liberal framework were
to be seriously challenged. To put it differently, Huntington's scenario
legitimized even further the "necessity" of restricting religion as much
as possible; it embodied the excess to be avoided through the adoption
of the liberal solution. To claim then that Huntington is wrong says
nothing in itself if we do not first ask the question of what made the
clash of civilizations thesis possible in theoretical terms.

What should not be disavowed in this respect is that religion is
predominantly conceptualized within International Relations theory
in modern terms—"modern" in the sense that it is incorporated into
the modern framework of associations and differences; perceived as
the negation of secular institutions and secular thinking, as the tradition that eschews the principle of rationality. As a consequence, the
contemporary role of religion in world politics can be considered as at
best only supplementary. That is, religion, if God allows, can direct its

energies toward the reproduction of the modern system itself. Religion is thus essentially peripheral, and reflection on international politics is pursued as if it concerned an autonomous space that is not fundamentally disturbed by its presence. These assertions point to a theoretical task: If its resurgence is to have any radical value at all, then 'religion' needs primarily to be unmodernized.

This task is vital but this book cannot claim to fully accomplish it, although it incoherently points in the right direction. Coherence is not possible since this is an edited volume combining writings that come from different positions of enunciation. What disorganizes the contributions is—and here we present our view—that they do not have the same object of analysis. The question here is whether religion as such and its role in world politics should be the object of study. We would take the side of those within the book, and others, who resist this formulation, who regard 'religion' as too general a concept to be of any theoretical use and, more so, are wary of its modern connotations. We agree with those writers who do not engage with religion in general and thus circumvent the prevalent notion of religion as the opposite/supplement of politics.

Maybe in order to unmodernize religion, one needs to sideline the very concept itself. If this advice is followed, then what is at stake in parts of the book is the concept of 'politics,' at the very moment when we begin to emerge into different aspects of religious traditions. Along these lines, it is Fred Dallmayr's inquiry on where the contemporary notion of politics stands in relation to Christian and Islamic spiritualities that is truly radical. We view then the potential of this book, and encourage a similar reading, as a call for the analysis of the concept of politics through an exploration of religious traditions.

Why is this kind of exploration important in the first place? Here again divergences emerge within the book, and we would like in this limited space to consider the dimension that the third section of the volume endorses. These three contributions warn against the danger of limiting the discussion for a new global ethos within a Western and liberal system of thought. Alternatively, they propose that the universality of this endeavor rely on a thick engagement with worldwide religious traditions. This line of argument is clear enough and could be articulated differently through the notion of rootedness. Universality can only emanate from somewhere, and in this respect the liberal tradition is just one of many and rooted in a particular, spatially confined part of the world. What must then come into play is the recognition of the "unspecial" standing of liberalism and then an understanding of what else is out there. But what lies beyond the liberal horizon, and religious traditions can claim that position, potentially challenges the very concepts through which Western ethical life is articulated. Charles Taylor has asked, for example, how the idea of human rights might be transformed through an understanding of the Theravada Buddhist search for selflessness, for self-giving, and *dana* (generosity), or through the Hindu notion of nonviolence, or by resting on the Islamic themes of the mercy and compassion of God.[14]

A similar theoretical direction has been recently emerging in poststructuralist thought—in particular, in the work of Jacques Derrida, Julia Kristeva, and William Connolly.[15] What distinguishes and comments their efforts is not merely their engagement with some of the worldwide religious traditions. Instead, their writings are linked by a common, initial refusal: the denial to conflate the ethical with the spatial limits set by secular concepts. And even more polemically, their writings are bound together by the suggestion that an effective way to transcend the Western liberal horizon would be to draw upon particular aspects of religious thought. These types of undertakings make the reconceptualization of international politics through an exploration of religious traditions valuable.

The implications of this task are far reaching. Primarily, and in contrast to the discussion in the epilogue of this volume, we believe that our notions of theory and morality are at stake—not in the sense of the substitution of the rationality principle in terms of defining 'theory,' or the uncritical acceptance of some religious doctrine as the solid ground of what morality should encompass. The exploration of religious traditions does not imply the substitution of reason with faith or irrationality as the grounding principle of a system of thought. These fears, duly articulated in Terry Nardin's chapter, represent and reproduce the modern notion of religion that we would like to avoid.

In this exaggerated caution, Nardin's piece stands out; in contrast to the rest of the contributors, he clearly articulates a secular and liberal position in relation to religion. His effort is commendable in that he attempts to enter into dialogue with all the other authors of the volume, though this possibility of open dialogue is not what the book aims to accomplish. Nardin's "secular" voice is welcome not simply because we want to appear "open to criticism" or to claim that we have presented in this volume a "balanced" set of perspectives. Instead, Nardin's position functions primarily as the reminder of the intellectual context within which this volume will be asked to operate; it represents the prevalent contemporary theoretical and political stance that seeks to constrain the worldwide religious traditions in an ultimately marginal role. His critique against the thick engagement of social science with religious thought is illuminating, since it embodies the obstacle that all the other contributions need to transcend if they are to have an impact on contemporary thinking.

For our part, we are claiming not that his critical remarks are not legitimate but that they somewhat miss the point.[16] Religion does not pose the challenge of reincorporating morality in its own gulf or of remaking theory in the light of its own method. What is at stake, in theoretical terms, is not the question of method but the potential negation, by religious traditions, of the core of contemporary normative theory: the very terms through which we define what an ethical action is. In one possible reading, religious traditions acknowledge what International Relations theory completely ignores: the fundamental tension between morality and law. The theory of International Relations is primarily concerned with the establishing of laws, or of norms in their nonlegalistic version, and then tackles the question of their grounding. From the perspective of religious traditions, this task is essentially meaningless. Enter Abraham, and other religious figures who performed the ethical as the suspension of law. In this light, the radical provocation of religion is the articulation of the ethical not as correlative to law but as the redefinition of the coordinates that determine law.

At this point, the move from abstract universality to concrete universality is in place. We need to leave behind the abstract notion of religious traditions to show how a particular aspect of a particular religious tradition might embody a universal standpoint. This task is delicate and can begin only from somewhere. Our lack of sufficient knowledge of other than the Christian tradition confines us to trying to develop a possible path taken from there, though of course this is a wholly conscious choice representing our particular predicament. Along these lines—and as an illustration of how this engagement with religion might look—the concept of Paulinian *agape* as interpreted by Slavoj Žižek might present a radical rupture with contemporary predominant notions of a universal morality.

In this reading, *agape* has revolutionary implications for our conception of the ethical. *Agape* primarily asserts the fundamental gap between the ethical and the domain of law; it refuses to articulate universality as the establishment of some type of universal law or as the search for a common ground that can justify such a law. Instead, universality is present in a moment of pure negativity, in the act that suspends the law. Universality arises in Saint Paul's incitement of "dying to the law." Universality lies in the singular position of the individual who lacks his social identity, of that person who has cut himself off from all organic links. The attainment of universality through the path of *agape* urges us toward a violent unplugging from our social background ("if anyone comes to me and does not hate his father and his mother, his wife and children, his brother and sisters—yes, even his own life—he cannot be my disciple"), from what constitutes our conservative identities, fixes our lives within the framework of the community we were born in, and allows for the reproduction of relations of exploitation as the founding stone of this community.[17]

Agape aims thus at the violent destruction of the old order and the birth of something entirely new, a community of the faithful—in Saint Paul's unique expression: "Even though we once knew Christ from a human point of view, we know him no longer in that way. So if anyone is in Christ, there is a new creation: everything old has passed away; see, everything has become new!"[18] *Agape* as the highest expression of the ethical stance involves a militant rejection of the present social order, the cry for the need to transcend the law that sustains this order, and the will to struggle for the construction of an alternative community. *Agape* ultimately demands the birth of a new ethical being, illustrated in Žižek 's reformulation of Thesis 11: "Philosophers have been teaching us only how to discover (remember) our true Self, but the point is to change it."[19]

Agape embodies though, in the context of this text, an illustration, not an ethical pursuit. What is relevant in this respect is that this particular—and brief—exploration of the Christian tradition potentially transforms the parameters of the ethical realm. Christian *agape* redefines the ethical act and the notion of universality; it relocates them away from the domain of law to a position of dislocation, of unplugging. *Agape* represents thus an ethical stance that cannot fit in the contemporary debates of what is termed as normative theory. *Agape* should be disengaged, for instance, from any notion of humanistic love: *Agape* does not merely aim at some harmonious coexistence but involves a fundamentally violent act. One has first to die and destroy what he holds as most precious if he is to be born again in love. And rather than representing a humanistic overflow of compassion through the recognition of the humanity of the Other, *agape* is the product of hard work, a continuous struggle to disengage ourselves from the particular social position we occupy at a given moment. *Agape* is love of the Other not because under the layers of his errors lies a human being, but *because* of his faults.

We stop here and raise some final reservations. This brief elaboration of the notion of *agape* does not speak on behalf of religion as such, but from the particular standpoint of the Christian legacy. Rather than giving guidance on how 'the ethical' or 'universality' should be realized it aims to show that the liberal interpretation of these concepts is suffocating in many respects. Religion in general has no real place in this debate, but the point we want to endorse is that to revisit religious traditions (the Christian in this case, and others for more informed readers than we), is to attempt to break the liberal monopoly on normative theory—to free IR from its self-imposed exile!

Notes

1. See primarily Samuel Huntington, *The Clash of Civilizations and the Remaking of the World Order* (New York: Simon and Schuster, 1996); also Mark Juergensmeyer, *The New Cold War? Religious Nationalism Confronts the Secular State* (Berkeley and Los Angeles: University of California Press, 1993) and *Terror in the Mind of God: The Global Rise of Religious Violence* (Berkeley and Los Angeles: University of California Press, 2000).

2. For sociological studies on the "global resurgence of religion," see the influential volumes by Gilles Kepel, *The Revenge of God: The Resurgence of Islam, Christianity and Judaism in the Modern World* (Cambridge: Polity Press, 1994) and Peter Berger, ed., *The Desecularization of the World: Resurgent Religion and World Politics* (Grand Rapids, WI: Wm. B. Eerdmans/Ethics and Public Policy Center, 1999).

3. As an example of this burgeoning literature, see the five volumes on religious fundamentalism by Martin E. Marty and R. Scott Appleby, eds., *The Fundamentalism Project*, vols. 1–5 (Chicago: University of Chicago Press, 1991–1995).

4. Among the studies with a policymaking orientation, see Douglas Johnston and Cynthia Sampson, eds., *Religion: The Missing Dimension of Statecraft* (Oxford: Oxford University Press, 1994) and Jeff Haynes, *Religion in Global Politics* (London: Longman, 1998). Two studies that announce a more theoretical outlook but at the end fail to seriously engage with IR as a discipline are John L. Esposito and Michael Watson, eds., *Religion and Global Order* (Cardiff: University of Wales Press, 2000) and Ken R. Dark, ed., *Religion and International Relations* (London: Macmillan, 2000). For the now widely accepted "return of culture and identity in International Relations," see Yosef Lapid and Friedrich Kratochwil, *The Return of Culture and Identity in International Relations Theory* (London: Lynne Rienner, 1996).

5. It is interesting here to compare Jacques Derrida's recent call for a new intellectual and political Enlightenment. This requires not an abandonment of rational thought but a willingness to critically reflect on reason's underside in order to avoid the "imperious self-enclosure and ossification of Western modernity." Jacques Derrida, *The Other Heading: Reflections on Today's Europe,* trans. Pascale-Anne Brault

and Michael B. Nass (Bloomington: Indiana University Press, 1992). For a discussion of the implications of this argument for Political Theory, see Fred Dallmayr, *Alternative Visions: Paths in the Global Village* (Lanham, MD: Rowman & Littlefield Publishers, 1998).

6. Here it is useful to underline that at the same time, simplistic generalizations about the opposition between religion and the Enlightenment also need to be avoided.

7. The original quote reads: "All significant concepts of the modern theory of the state are secularized theological concepts." In Carl Schmitt, *Political Theology: Four Chapters on the Concept of Sovereignty,* trans. George Schwab (Cambridge, MA: MIT Press, 1985 [1922]), 1985, 36.

8. Hedley Bull and Adam Watson, Introduction, *The Expansion of International Society* (Oxford: Clarendon Press, 1984), 9.

9. See Jean Bethke Elshtain, "Really Existing Communities," *Review of International Studies* 25, no. 1 (1999): 141–46.

10. Václav Havel, speech at the National Press Club, Canberra, Australia, 29 March 1995, published in *The Art of the Impossible: Politics as Morality in Practice: Speeches and Writings 1990–1996,* trans. Paul Wilson (New York: Alfred A. Knopf, 1997), 195–96. Our argument rests on a version of the hypothesis that culture (and civilization) is significantly shaped by religion, although we are not sure we would go as far as saying that "[t]he moral and spiritual architecture of every civilization is grounded, more than any other factor, in religious commitments that point to a source of normative meaning beyond the political, economic, and cultural structure themselves." In Max L. Stackhouse, Introduction, *God and Globalization,* vol. 3, eds. Max L. Stackhouse and Diane B. Obenchain (Harrisburg, PA: Trinity Press International, 2002), 11. This four-volume project, *God and Globalization: Theological Ethics and the Spheres of Life,* run by Stackhouse and sponsored by the Center of Theological Inquiry in Princeton, well exemplifies the effort by religious studies and theology to engage with the same new dynamics our book looks at from an International Relations perspective.

11. Václav Havel, "The Need of Transcendence in the Postmodern World," speech at the Philadelphia Liberty Medal Award Ceremony, Philadelphia, Pennsylvania, 4 July 1994, published in *The Art of the Impossible,* 165–72.

12. Hans-Georg Gadamer, *Truth and Method,* 2nd rev. ed., trans. Joel Winsheimer and Donald G. Marshall (New York: Crossroad, 1989). See also Fred Dallmayr, "A Gadamerian Perspective on Civilizational Dialogue," *Global Dialogue* 3, no. 1 (2001): 64–75. Along similar lines, see Scott Thomas's notion of "deep pluralism" developed in this volume.

13. The suppression of religion from both political action and political thought with the Treaty of Westphalia reflects MacIntyre's conception of history. "There is a history yet to be written in which the Medici princes, Henry VIII and Thomas Cromwell, Frederick the Great and

Napoleon, Walpole and Wilberforce, Jefferson and Robespierre are understood as expressing in their actions, often partially and in a variety of different ways, the very same conceptual changes which at the level of philosophical theory are articulated by Machiavelli and Hobbes, by Diderot and Condorcet, by Hume and Adam Smith and Kant. There ought not be two histories, one of political and moral action and one of political and moral theorizing, because there were not two pasts, one populated only by actions, the other only by theories. Every action is the bearer and expression of more or less theory-laden beliefs and concepts; every piece of theorizing and every expression of belief is a political and moral action." In Alasdair MacIntyre, *After Virtue,* 2nd ed. (London: Duckworth, 1985), 61.

14. See Charles Taylor, "Conditions for an Unforced Consensus on Human Rights," in *The East Asian Challenge for Human Rights,* eds. J. Bauer and A. D. Bell (Cambridge: Cambridge University Press, 1999), 125–44.

15. See John D. Caputo, *The Prayers and Tears of Jacques Derrida: Religion without Religion* (Bloomington: Indiana University Press, 1997); Julia Kristeva, *Crisis of the European Subject* (New York: Other Press, 2000) and William E. Connolly, *Why I Am Not a Secularist* (Minneapolis: Minnesota University Press, 1999).

16. Nardin's reading of Kubálková's, Falk's, and Laustsen and Wæver's pieces, however, can arguably be criticized for being embedded in a strong version of liberalism.

17. The discussion of the notion of *agape* is based on Slavoj Žižek's recent work. In this case, see Žižek, *The Fragile Absolute—Or Why the Christian Legacy is Worth Fighting For* (London: Verso, 2000), 120–25.

18. Ibid., 127.

19. Slavoj Žižek, *On Belief* (London: Routledge, 2001), 149.

Part I

International Relations Theory and Religion

Chapter 1

Taking Religious and Cultural Pluralism Seriously

The Global Resurgence of Religion and the Transformation of International Society

Scott M. Thomas

People
Are people
Through other people

— *Xhosa proverb from South Africa*

A small circle is quite as infinite as a large circle; but, though it is quite as infinite, it is not so large. . . . A bullet is quite as round as the world, but it is not the world. There is such a thing as a narrow universality; there is such a thing as a small and cramped eternity; you may see it in many modern religions.[1]

— *G. K. Chesterton*

The Western culture of modernity and the institutions of international society embedded in it are being challenged by the global resurgence of religion and cultural pluralism in international relations. This resurgence is part of the larger crisis of modernity. It reflects a deeper and more widespread disillusionment with a "modernity" that reduces the world to what can be perceived and controlled through reason, science, technology, and bureaucratic rationality, and leaves out considerations of the religious, the spiritual, or the sacred. In the second instance, the global resurgence of religion is the result of the failure of the modernizing, secular state to produce both democracy and development in the Third World. This failure became evident by subsequent "political decay"—the decline of politics into authoritarianism, patrimonialism, and corruption since the late 1960s—and by "political collapse"—the disintegration of some states, particularly in Africa, since the late 1980s.[2] Dissatisfaction with the project of the postcolonial secular state and the conflict between religious nationalism and secular nationalism was one of the most important developments in Third World politics in the 1990s.[3]

Finally, the global resurgence of religion is part of the search for authenticity and development in the Third World. The global resurgence of religion in developing countries can be seen as part of the "revolt against the West." Hedley Bull identified what could be called three waves of revolt: the first, from the 1940s through the 1960s, was the anticolonial struggle for independence and sovereign equality; the second, from the 1970s through the 1980s, was the struggle for racial equality and economic justice; and the third—Bull called it the struggle for cultural liberation—was the reassertion of traditional and indigenous cultures in the Third World.[4]

The struggle for cultural liberation, or the global struggle for authenticity, became more powerful in the 1990s. In the Third World, the modernizing, secular state has failed to provide a legitimate basis for political participation and a basic level of economic welfare for its citizens. In many developing countries, secular nationalism and Marxism have failed to produce economic development and extend political participation, and the neoliberal prescription of free markets and open economies has seemingly produced more inequality than development. Because of this situation, "authenticity has begun to rival development as the key to understanding the political aspirations of the non-Western World."[5] The search for authentic identity, meaning, and economic development indicates a new direction in the politics of developing countries: an attempt to indigenize modernity rather than to modernize traditional societies.

For all these reasons, to look at the global resurgence of religion and cultural pluralism through such lenses as the "clash of civilizations," "fundamentalism," or "religious extremism"—as if the global resurgence of religion were an aberration in an otherwise "modern" world— might be extremely misleading. As S. N. Eisenstadt has argued, the global resurgence of religion is not simply a backward-looking return to traditional forms of religion, but involves a forward-looking restructuring of religion given the recognition of "multiple modernities" in a postmodern world.[6] This means that what is happening is that a truly multicultural international society is being formed for the first time.

Therefore, taking cultural and religious pluralism seriously will be an important part of the international politics of the twenty-first century.[7] A new approach to international order is required, which overcomes the Westphalian presumption in International Relations. This is the presumption that religious and cultural pluralism cannot be accommodated in international society, but must be privatized, marginalized, or even overcome—by an ethic of cosmopolitanism—if there is to be international order.

The first part of this chapter attempts a genealogy of religion to show how the Westphalian presumption is based on the "invention of religion" by Western modernity as a set of privately held doctrines or beliefs. It argues that this was a crucial part of the development of the state as well as international society. We risk misunderstanding the global resurgence of religion if we apply a modern concept of religion to non-Western societies where this transition is incomplete, or where it is being resisted as part of their struggle for authenticity and development. If the global resurgence of religion and cultural pluralism are to be taken seriously, then a *social* understanding of religion and its importance to the authenticity and development of communities and states should be recognized as part of any post-Westphalian international order.

To examine what this means and what can be done, the second part of this chapter explores the relevance of the social theory of Alasdair MacIntyre to the concept of international society. The third section suggests that the approach of the English School (ES), which examines the emergence of international society through the prism of historical sociology, is better equipped to deal with religion, culture, and civilization than the more recent constructivist accounts of international society, which reify the assumptions of Western modernity. The final part of the chapter indicates that taking religious and cultural pluralism seriously means developing a "deeper pluralism" among different communities and states in international society. "Virtue-ethics," the approach to ethics that has emerged in the aftermath of MacIntyre's social theory, shows how this can be done by engaging with the social practices of the main world religions in ways that promote order and justice instead of ignoring, marginalizing, or trying to overcome them.

The Westphalian Presumption and the Invention of Religion

The Westphalian presumption is part of the political mythology of liberalism surrounding the Wars of Religion (1550–1650).[8] According to this political myth, what the Wars of Religion unequivocally show is that when religion is brought into international public life, it causes intolerance, war, devastation, political upheaval, and even the collapse of international order. As a consequence, the story goes on to say, liberalism and religious toleration were born out of the cruelty and devastation of these wars. More precisely, the modern state, the privatization of religion, and the secularization of politics arose to limit religion's domestic influence, minimize the effect of religious disagreement, and end the bloody and destructive role of religion in international relations.[9]

Although liberalism accepts the first part of the Westphalian presumption—religious and cultural pluralism cannot be accommodated in international public life—it does not endorse the second part of the Westphalian presumption because it claims that the Westphalian settlement *was a way* of taking seriously religious and cultural pluralism in international society.[10] Both the Peace of Augsburg (1555) and the Congress of Westphalia a century later (1648), by adopting the principle of *cujus regio, ejus religio* (the ruler determines the religion of his realm), made religious toleration and noninterference (on religious grounds) in the domestic affairs of other states—in other words, pluralism among states—one of the main principles of the Westphalian international order.

The ES accepts this account of the Wars of Religion and the Westphalian settlement as part of the common knowledge or, perhaps, even common wisdom of European history. It is what helps locate the Rationalist tradition in international theory as "the broad middle road of European thinking."[11] Through the principles of the Westphalian settlement, state sovereignty, *cujus regio, ejus religio,* and the balance of power, the ability to accommodate religious and cultural pluralism was built into the very framework of international society.[12]

The ES, by endorsing this account of the Wars of Religion and the Westphalian settlement, has underestimated the impact of religious and cultural pluralism in international relations. In contrast, this section shows how the political mythology of liberalism gives a problematic account of the Wars of Religion. First, it explains how the first part of the Westphalian presumption (the notion that religion must be privatized or nationalized in international public life) and the liberal rejection of the second part of the presumption (its belief that the Westphalian settlement *can* take seriously religious and cultural pluralism) are both based on a modern concept of "religion." The modern reading of religion has distorted our understanding of what the Wars of Religion in early modern Europe were all about, and, given the global resurgence of religion, it continues to inhibit our recognition of the religious and cultural pluralism in international relations today.

If we interpret the Wars of Religion as a backward and barbarous period of European history, when people killed each other over clashing religious doctrines, then we would probably also misinterpret the role of religion in the Balkans wars, the Middle East, or anywhere else in the developing world. This does not mean that religion was an unimportant part of the Wars of Religion. At issue is the meaning of religion in early modern Europe, and how we understand religion in international relations today.

Most scholars of early modern Europe now recognize that the confusion over the role of religion and other political or socioeconomic forces in the debate on the Wars of Religion was based on retrospectively applying a modern concept of religion—as a set of privately held doctrines or beliefs—to societies that had yet to make this transition. Scholars have adopted a social definition of religion, which they believe is compatible with how people understood their religious, moral, and social lives at that time. Religion in early modern Europe should be interpreted as a community of believers rather than as a body of doctrines or beliefs, as liberal modernity would have it. Therefore, what was being safeguarded and defended in the Wars of Religion was a sacred notion of the community defined by religion, as each community fought to define, redefine, or defend the boundaries between the sacred and the profane as a whole.[13]

How does this social definition of religion help us to better understand the Westphalian international order and the pressures that the global resurgence of religion has placed upon it? This social definition of religion is the missing element of the work of IR scholars on the origins of the modern state and modern international society. Furthermore, I argue that the invention of religion, as a set of privately held doctrines or beliefs, was necessary for the rise of the modern state as well as the development of modern international society.

If a new concept of religion as well as a new kind of state were required for the emergence of modern international society, how was religion invented? In other words, how did the transition from religion as a community of believers to religion as a set of privately held doctrines and beliefs take place? The story of this transformation has been told elsewhere.[14] What is important here are those elements that help us to recognize the invention of religion as an important part of the development of modern international society, and how this understanding helps us to see the limitations of the Westphalian presumption in international relations prior to the global resurgence of religion.

The transformation of Christianity as a result of the transition from a social to the modern concept of religion has important consequences for our understanding of religion and modern society. During the Middle Ages, the term *religio* referred to the monastic life, or it was used to describe a particular "virtue" supported by practices embedded in the Christian tradition, as part of an ecclesial community (called the Church). In other words, this social definition of religion, as a community of believers, meant that the virtues and practices of the Christian tradition were not separated from the tradition and community in which they were embedded and which sustained them.[15] This social understanding of religion can also be called traditional religion, and this is what Christianity signified for most people in early modern Europe.[16]

As a result of the modern concept of religion, the virtues and practices of the Christian tradition came to be separated from the communities in which they were embedded. The modern concept of religion began to emerge in the late fifteenth century, and first appeared as a universal, inward impulse or feeling toward the divine common to all people. The varieties of pieties and rituals were increasingly called "religions," as representations of the one (more or less) true *religio* common to all, apart from any ecclesial community. A second major change took place in the early sixteenth or seventeenth century, when *religio* began to shift from being representative of various virtues, supported by practices of an ecclesial community embedded in the Christian tradition, to being a system of doctrines or beliefs, which could exist apart from the ecclesial community.[17] Thus, Hugo Grotius could come to write his *De Veritate Religionis Christianae* (1622), and in England, William Chillingworth could write *The Religion of Protestants* (1637) as a defense of what the "Christian religion teaches, rather than simply is, the true worship of God." These writers indicate how Latin Christendom made the transition from a social to a modern concept of religion.[18] What now has to be shown is how this modern concept of religion was necessary for the development of the Westphalian conception of international society.[19]

The rise of the modern state is the other part of the story of the transition from a social to the modern concept of religion, and it is also important for our understanding of the origins of international society. It has been shown how religion was embedded in the practices of power and discipline regulated by the authoritative structure of the ecclesial community. What did the rise of the state mean for this social understanding of religion? Religion had to be made compatible with the power and discipline of the state; religion as a set of moral and theological propositions had to be detached from the virtues and practices embedded in the religious tradition embodied in the ecclesial community. Religious belief, conscience, and sensibility were privatized by the secularization of politics, and the previous discipline (intellectual and social) of religion was taken over by the state, which was given the legitimate monopoly on the use of power and coercion in society. In the words of Thomas Hobbes: "This is the generation of that great Leviathan, or rather (to speak more reverently) of that *Mortal God,* to which we owe under the Immortal God, our peace and defense."[20]

What should be recognized is that the invention of religion—as a body of ideas—is presupposed rather than examined when the Westphalian settlement is discussed in IR as an example of "ideas and foreign policy."[21] Thus, Stephen Krasner, using Clifford Geertz's understanding of religion as a cultural system, examines religion as a menu, a repertoire of ideas and principles, which can be used to justify state policy, since political legitimacy rests on some degree of common understanding in society. This is true, but as Talal Asad explains as part of his criticism of Geertz, this is exactly the way religion is invented as part of the power and discipline of the state. The state has to separate doctrines and beliefs from practices and communities as part of state building and affirmation of its internal sovereignty. Therefore, Krasner's contention that the Westphalian settlement does not constitute an abrupt break with the past underestimates the importance of the invention of religion as an important part of the Westphalian settlement and the origins of modern international society. What Geertz as well as Krasner are missing is the fact that virtues and moral judgements in religion are not "declaratory" propositional, moral statements, to which rational (autonomous) individuals give their intellectual assent. What they mean is shaped by the linguistic conventions of a community, connected to the practices of a religious tradition. They are only intelligible because they are recognized types of behavior (practices) passed on through the narratives that shape the identity of the community.

Thus, the growing civil dominance over the Church by princes and the rise of state power incorporated a transition from a social to a privatized concept of religion. For the state to be born, religion had to become marginalized or privatized. The state used the invention of religion to legitimate the transfer of the ultimate loyalty of people from religion to the state as part of the consolidation of its power, which we have come to term "internal sovereignty." For international society to be born, religion had to be privatized and nationalized by the state, which is what the princes legitimated when they adopted the principle of *cujus religio, ejus religio* as part of the Treaty of Westphalia. This principle, involving the new concept of religion, allowed the state to discipline religion in both domestic and international society, which meant that the principle could also be used (as part of a nonintervention norm) to secure external sovereignty, or the independence of states in international society.

What this section shows is that the pluralist notion, the idea that the Westphalian presumption can take seriously religious and cultural pluralism, is based on the invention of religion as part of the rise of Western modernity. The problem is that many, if not most, non-Western societies and communities have still not entirely made, or are struggling *not* to make, this transition. The privatization or marginalization of religion is not entirely a part of the Orthodox Christian world, nor is it a part of other non-Western societies incorporated (through colonialism and imperialism) into the modern international society. This is why strong religions and weak states still characterize much of the developing world. Communities, and in the developing world this means religious communities, and even states, are being forced more than ever before to define, defend, or redefine their boundaries between the sacred and the profane in the face of globalization.[22] This may explain, as Hasenclever and Rittberger also argue in this volume, why what may appear to be comparatively minor divergences in the understanding of the sacred can become highly significant in the escalation of conflict between communities. What both approaches recognize is that authenticity has come to rival development as the main concern of the developing world. We have a better understanding of this large-scale religious change in international relations by analyzing correctly what took place during the Wars of Religion and the construction of the Westphalian international order. If the global resurgence of religion and cultural pluralism are to be taken seriously, then the social understanding of religion, the contested elements of the social and political boundaries of the sacred, and the importance of this debate, or even the struggle for authenticity of communities and states, should be recognized as part of any post-Westphalian international order. It is the beginning, as the last part of this chapter indicates, of a deeper pluralism between states and communities that make up the international order.

Alasdair MacIntyre: Back to the Future?

How can religious and cultural pluralism become a part of any post-Westphalian international order? Few social theorists have taken other religious, cultural, and social traditions as seriously as has Alasdair MacIntyre. This section explores the relevance of his social theory to IR by examining his thought in the context of the ES's conception of international society. The reason for this effort is that the ES has been concerned about questions of religion, culture, and the nature of international society from the beginning. These concerns emerged in the aftermath of decolonization, as the European international society expanded to cover the globe and thus incurred the "revolt against the West," which highlighted the tension between Western and non-Western values in international society. At this time, mainstream American IR was mainly interested in the role of developing countries as it pertained to the Cold War. The fact that these questions are some of the most important ones in contemporary international relations is why the ES is "on the frontiers of international society."[23]

The English School between Historical Sociology and Constructivism

This section explores the relevance of MacIntyre's social theory by examining the objective and subjective understanding of international society using three sets of concepts he has developed: (1) rationality, culture, and tradition; (2) identity, narrative, and social action; and (3) the rules, institutions, and practices of international relations.

Common to most definitions of society is the notion of a social bond that binds units together with common obligations and common purposes they all recognize. The nature of this social bond in international society—whether it is between states, individuals, or other communities—is behind neorealist and neoliberal debates on the nature of cooperation as well as the debates in the ES on the nature of international society, international ethics, and the moral foundations of international order.[24] The main issues of contention revolve around what is subjective, organic, or traditional about international society, and what is objective, functional, or contractual about it.

The subjectivity of the social bond—the sense of belonging to a society as a member, and of being bound by certain rules and institutions—is crucial to the ES's definition of international society. This is what for them distinguishes a society from a system. The current debates in the ES examine the nature of this subjectivity, and how this question is approached reflects different methodologies employed within the ES.

The first approach asks how this subjectivity *emerges* in international society, and reflects the historical sociological approach of an earlier generation of scholars. It is concerned with defining the idea of international society, determining its origins and boundaries, or whether a common culture is necessary for its emergence. The historical sociological approach brings to the fore the question of the Other—those communities, states, or peoples outside a given historical international society—and asks what should be done about it.[25] This is one of the reasons why the ES's research program since its beginnings has been concerned with the impact of major cultural upheavals—religion, ideology, nationalism, and revolution—on international society.[26]

The second approach asks how this subjectivity is *constructed* in international society, and reflects the growing impact of social theory on the ES. It draws on a growing recognition that the ES, even amidst the critics who dismiss it as traditionalist, empiricist, realist, or even conservative, has an inherent preference for dissent, or even subversion within the discipline of IR. This results today in an increasing recognition that the ES's interpretivist orientation toward the historical sociology of different international societies can be thought of as a form of social constructivism.[27]

Rationality, Culture, and Tradition

The positivist conception of rationality common to the neorealist/neoliberal mainstream of IR is a rationality independent of social and historical context and independent of any specific understanding of human nature or purpose of human flourishing. MacIntyre fiercely criticizes it because of the relationship between rationality and social tradition. This criticism is part of his well-known critique of liberal modernity, which he calls the Enlightenment project.[28]

MacIntyre's explanation for why moral discourse in the societies of Western modernity is characterized by incoherence and ethical pluralism is part of his critique of the Enlightenment project's separation of reason and morality from practice and tradition. According to MacIntyre, the moral problem of modern democratic liberal societies is that the moral concepts and ethical conceptions used in ethical discourse, including debates about war and peace, are fragments of conceptual schemes that have been separated from the historical and social contexts that give them meaning and coherence.

MacIntyre argues that these values and ethical conceptions about the nature of the good, what is just, what is right, and notions of obligation, and the rationality on which they are based, are socially embodied in particular social traditions and communities. There is no rationality independent of tradition, no "view from nowhere," and no set of rules or principles that will commend themselves to all, independent of their conception of the good.[29]

The concept of "social tradition," as MacIntyre understands this term, has to be explained if it is to avoid its conservative and "neoconservative" connotations. He views practices and virtues as part of a wider social and historical context called a social tradition. A set of practices constitutes a tradition. Traditions can be religious or moral (Catholicism, Islam, humanism), economic (a particular craft like basket weaving on the Somerset Levels, a profession, trade union, or guild), aesthetic (types of literature or painting), or geographical (centered on the history or culture of a house, village, or region).

The concept has been ideologically used by conservatives to contrast tradition with reason, and it has been used by liberals—indebted to Max Weber—as well as by modernization theorists, who contrast the concept of bureaucratic authority with that of traditional authority, and compare the backwardness and stability of traditional society with the conflict and social change necessary for the emergence of modern society. For MacIntyre, however, the most important social conflicts take place *within* traditions as well as *between* them. These conflicts are about the various incommensurable goods that members of a particular tradition pursue, and *a viable tradition is one that holds conflicting social, political, and metaphysical claims in a creative way.* It is when traditions begin to break down that modern bureaucratic organizations arise.[30]

Therefore, contrary to the positivist mainstream, MacIntyre argues that rationality, interest, and identity can not be separated in the way the rational choice approach does. What makes it "rational" to act in one way and not in another is the conception of the good embodied in a particular social tradition or community. Individuals, social groups, and even states act not only to gain tangible things—territory or access to resources—but also to establish, protect, or defend a certain conception of who they are. They act not only because there are things they want to have, but also because there is a certain conception of the kind of persons, societies, communities, or even states they want to be in the world. If this is the case, then action in defense of identity and authenticity can be more fundamental than action in defense of interests because what is, or is not, an interest depends on some conception of individual or collective identity. This action cannot be redescribed in "rationalistic" terms as a defense of interests because the calculations about interests make sense only when they are attached to a particular person, social group, community, or state.[31] The rationality associated with the construction of the national interest can not be separated from matters of religion and culture because they shape, inform, and determine the conception of the good among particular social traditions and communities.

MacIntyre's philosophical argument is given anthropological depth and historical support by Adda Bozeman's study of international law in different civilizations (the West, Islam, Africa, India, and China). On the basis of this study, she states: "Differences between cultures and political systems are functions primarily of different modes of perceiving and evaluating reality."[32] Her study also shows, as Bull has pointed out more generally, that religion has been the main basis for order in most times and cultures, for "whether viewed as a set of concepts, norms, or social institutions, law everywhere is linked, explicitly or implicitly, with schemes of social and political organization."[33] This general perspective that political systems are grounded in cultures leads to the recognition that present day international relations are therefore by definition also intercultural relations.[34]

It might appear that MacIntyre's understanding of tradition-dependent rationality separates him from the ES's Rationalist tradition of international thought, but this is not the case, as he himself has indicated. The Rationalist tradition, which Martin Wight associates with the Greeks—especially the Stoics—Aquinas, Vitoria and Suarez, Grotius, and Locke, holds to an older conception of rationalism that predates the epistemological debates of the eighteenth century. These thinkers emphasized that through reason there exists a prepolitical moral order behind international society. Although these early theologians, philosophers, and natural law theorists played an initial role in the tradition's development, Wight points to modern Catholic social thought and the Catholic Church as upholding the Rationalist tradition today.[35] Catholic social thought has developed complex strategies of engagement and a language of the "common good" as a discourse on the basis of which "all persons of good will" who are capable of reason can be appealed to, and not only Catholic Christians explicitly, as Wight has pointed out in relation to Judaism and Islam.[36]

MacIntyre has indicated how his social theory is compatible with the Rationalist tradition of international thought by showing how tradition-based standards of rationality are related to a teleological conception of the moral life, which is also part of the Catholic natural law approach to Rationalism.[37] This conception is closer to the Rationalist tradition, as Wight has expressed it, although some of the ES's recent interpreters have linked the Rationalist tradition to a critical-emancipatory project of liberal modernity.[38] Given MacIntyre's social theory and its compatibility with the natural law tradition of Catholic social thought, it may be time to reexamine some of the debates within the ES over natural law, as well as the hesitancy of Bull, Vincent, and recent interpreters to consider this tradition.[39]

The next section will show why MacIntyre's tradition-dependent concept of rationality does not deny a sense of belonging to the community of humankind, a fundamental concern of the Rationalist tradition, as Andrew Linklater and others have interpreted it. What MacIntyre does contend, however, on the basis of a narrative conception of identity, is that our common humanity is expressed through (rooted in) the culture, tradition, and history of particular communities because this is the way we are constituted as human beings. What he objects to is the interpretation of cosmopolitanism as a universal emancipatory project when in fact it is the project of a particular tradition, liberal modernity.[40]

Identity, Narrative, and Social Action

The ES recognized from the beginning that a deeper and prior agreement—an organic, or intersubjective understanding—among states that form an international society may be necessary for the development of common institutions and for the rationality and interests of states to effectively foment international cooperation. This intersubjective sense of belonging between states *emerged* through a common culture that underpinned different states-systems (Wight) or international societies in history (Watson).

One of the earliest, and most enduring, debates in the ES was whether a common culture was necessary for the existence of international society. The ES's contention that a common culture provides an important foundation for international society was taken in two directions. The first, mainly indebted to Wight, Herbert Butterfield, and to some extent Michael Donelan, with his discussion of "fideism,"[41] has been to recognize more directly the role of religious doctrines in different cultures and civilizations, and to examine the consequences of this for international society. The second, developed in the later writings of Bull, Vincent, and the "solidarist" interpreters of international society, has been to project the common culture of liberal modernity as the foundation of a global international society.[42]

The notion that religion and culture underpin international society was one of the main reasons for an organic conception of international society. It was Wight who believed that a common culture, a degree of cultural unity among states, was necessary for the existence of international society. Why was this the case? What was important to Wight was the degree of subjectivity, or sense of belonging and obligation, that a common culture provides for any meaningful conception of international society. Wight argued that this was the case because a common culture or civilization was one of the most important foundations for past international societies.[43] This was the case even if a prior political hegemony in some instances was responsible for the spread of the common culture that formed the foundation of international society.[44]

Wight recognized that "the greater the cultural unity of a states-system, the greater its sense of distinctness from the surrounding world is likely to be."[45] This led to two interrelated problems, which have become accentuated by the global resurgence of religion. The first problem is the relation with the Other, the outsider, what Wight called "the barbarian problem" in international relations. Although it was less then appreciated at the time, he was clearly on the side of the "barbarians" and vehemently criticized the moral pretensions of European colonialism, or the view that developing countries were outside the moral parameters of international society.

Although the ES was concerned from the beginning with the incorporation of the Other as international society expanded, in the first instance this concern was expressed over the resiliency of the existing institutions of international society. The ES exhibited a conservative concern for international order, and this was why it accepted only a partial accommodation to the demands of developing countries. However, the way the ES accepted some of these demands fits uneasily with their assumption that Third World elites represented the will of their populations.[46]

The first part of this chapter has indicated how tenuous this assumption was. The global spread of democracy has been accompanied by the global resurgence of religion and the demand for cultural authenticity and development, which are at odds with the "modernizing mythology" espoused by Western-educated elites from developing countries.[47] What was less appreciated at the time was the extent to which the "revolt against the West" took place within the discourse of Western modernity. At issue in international relations was not the impact of new values and beliefs, but the way different ideologies (capitalism, socialism, or even nationalism) could legitimate a different distribution of power among states in international society. This explains why the ES, at the time, was relatively sanguine about accommodating some of the demands of developing countries within the existing international order.[48]

The second problem Wight raised was concerning religion, and this was the concept of "holy war," or jihad, since political communities outside the states-system were subject to different rules of war than those within international society. Wight asked, "Have all states-systems entertained some notion of Holy War in their external relations? Or is it a product of the Judeo-Christian Islamic tradition?"[49] He did not think the evidence was clear. Given the global resurgence of religion and the rise of ethnonational conflicts and terrorism, often with religious dimensions, Wight's question is an increasingly important one. Contemporary scholars have reformulated it as a question about the relationship between monotheism, religion, and war, particularly focusing on Christianity and Islam, and have answered in the affirmative.[50]

Another question Wight asked related to the problem of holy war and led him to a distinction between types of states-systems, which may also become more important in the future. He distinguished between states-systems (or societies of states) with a common culture and states-systems he called "secondary," which were characterized by cultural pluralism, indicating to Wight that they should not be classified as states-systems at all. What concerned him about these states-systems was the lack "of a common ethos or ideology," and the limited extension of what he called the "chivalric practices and feudal assumptions" of Latin Christendom to Byzantium and Islam (the Abbasid Caliphate).[51]

These questions about religion and war, practices and religious traditions in international relations have remained a latent concern within the ES's research program. Although Wight's understanding of practices is different from the one used in MacIntyre's social theory, it will be argued below that his early—underdeveloped—recognition of the relationship between practices and religious tradition may be a useful way to proceed. The ES seems to have marginalized the study of religion and the kind of questions Wight raised about religions and civ-ilizations, even when it has accepted the need for a common cultural foundation for international society. The solidarist interpreters of the ES, those with the strongest desire for a "thick" notion of interna-tional society, were the most interested in a cultural underpinning of international society.

As a foundation for international society, they turned to the com-mon culture of liberal modernity. The solidarist interpreters were rightly concerned that the rationalism of the neorealist/neoliberal mainstream accounts of international society overlooked the deeper structure on which it rested, that is, the pluralism of international so-ciety rested on a deeper solidarity.

The solidarist interpreters of the ES construct a thick conception of international society only by adopting a "thin" conception of culture on which to underpin international society. Vincent argues that glob-alization has created what is now called "McWorld," a cosmopolitan ethos of global values and a global consumer culture. As Vincent ac-knowledges, in Edmund Burke's sense, "[n]one of this amounts to the spirit of religion," but there is a global culture, "however shallow."[52] Thus, Vincent accepts the ES's early arguments about the cultural foundations of international society, but only if they are transformed into support for the cosmopolitan culture of liberal modernity as the common culture of global international society.

Like Vincent, Bull transformed the ES's early concern about reli-gion, culture, and civilization into support for liberal modernity as the common culture of a global international society, although with some misgivings. Bull recognizes that European international society is now a global international society, but it lacks the common culture or civilization that characterized the Christian European international society. Because of the importance of culture to the foundations of in-ternational society, Bull speculated on how "the prospects of interna-tional society [were] bound up with the prospects of the cosmopolitan culture," what we would call the culture of Western modernity, which underlies the working of contemporary global in-ternational society.[53]

Bull speculated that there are elements of a "common intellectual culture" in international society, at least at the elite or diplomatic level. However, even at the time of his writing in the 1970s Bull recognized that the elite culture of diplomacy was already eroded by the democ-ratization of diplomacy and the rise of mass democratic politics, which has spread globally since the 1980s. He also pointed to the common in-tellectual culture among the "global elite," whom Peter Berger has identified as the professors, intellectuals, development workers, and policymakers from the West, and their counterparts, the Western-educated, "modernizing elites" of the Third World.[54] Even then, Bull acknowledged that its "roots are shallow in many societies," and he doubted whether the international political culture, even at the diplomatic level, embraced a common moral culture or set of common values. Bull, like Vincent, suggested that the extension of a cosmopolitan culture could provide a global international society with the kind of cultural unity it needed.

Bull, more importantly, speculated that the cosmopolitan culture of Western modernity *would have to absorb non-Western elements to a much greater degree* if it was to provide the basis for a global international society.[55] Apart from appeals for multicultural sensitivity to cultural difference, or the desire for a "dialogue between civilizations," but one determined by the assumptions and values of liberal modernity, Bull's challenge remains unanswered. The problem that solidarist interpreters of international society understandably are trying to overcome is how it is possible to have a thick understanding of global international society—or even a world society—and still allow for a thick understanding of religion and culture in the developing world. In other words, how is it possible to take seriously the resurgence of religion and culture in global international society?

The ES's second approach to understanding the intersubjective sense of belonging among states in international society is indebted more to social theory than to historical sociology. The ES does not view mere compliance with international rules, norms, or laws as proof of the existence of international society. Rather, rules, laws, and the working of common institutions are intellectual and social constructs that states accept as part of the idea of international society.[56] Where does this sense of "commonality" come from? How does it emerge, or how is it constructed in international society?

If the ES's first approach emphasized that the sense of commonality emerged from a common religion, culture, or civilization underlying international society, the second approach explains it as an outcome of social action through the development of common practices or institutions of international society. This second approach reveals the similarity between the ES's early interpretivist understanding of international institutions and the social constructivist approach to international society.

The constructivist approach focuses on the way interests and identity of states are not a given feature of the international order, but are socially constructed through their interaction. What is, or is not, an interest depends on some conception of individual or collective identity. The identity and interests of states are mutually constitutive, that is, the collective identity and interests of states are formed by the intersubjective "social practices" between states in the process of interaction.[57] A normative potential for global transformation is part of this approach. Thus, states have constructed international society in a particular way—giving rise to the security dilemma and the anarchy problematique—and with sufficient political will or imagination they can adopt new forms of interaction (practices), which can change their intersubjective knowledge and understanding of world politics and (potentially) transform an anarchical international society into a cosmopolitan world community.[58] For example, Alexander Wendt thinks, in a way similar to the later work by Bull and Vincent on the global culture of liberal modernity, that this may be already happening. Globalization, rising interdependence, the rise of global consumerism, and the spread of democracy may indicate new ways in which states identify with each other, making international conflict less likely.[59] The first part of this chapter, however, has indicated that the trends Bull speculated on in the 1970s have become more powerful with the global resurgence of religion and the struggle for authenticity in the 1990s, making it perhaps more difficult to absorb non-Western elements into international society.

MacIntyre's social theory has similarities with the ES's interpretivist orientation. Both would acknowledge the distinction Martin Hollis and Steve Smith make between (objectively) explaining events and (subjectively) or interpretatively understanding human actions. Where Hollis and Smith differ is in the way MacIntyre goes on to distinguish the "situated self" of practice, narrative, and tradition from the "atomistic self" of liberal modernity.[60] At a basic level MacIntyre's social theory is also compatible with the ES's interpretivist understanding of the way practices are constitutive of individual and collective identity. In MacIntyre's narrative account of social action, the self has a life story, embedded in the story of a larger community from which the self derives a social and a historical identity. The life stories of members of the community are embedded and intermingled with the stories of others in the story of the communities from which they derive their identity.[61] Thus, it follows from MacIntyre's narrative conception of the self that human actions, such as the construction of state practices, become intelligible only when they are interpreted as part of a larger narrative of the collective life of individuals, communities, and states. This is another way of stating the ES's contention that international institutions, that is, practices, do not make international society—the illusion of idealists—but they indicate that such a society exists, since they have been intersubjectively constructed by those states who are its members with a sense of belonging to it.

What is important to recognize is that MacIntyre contends that these interpretative boundaries are not the same as moral boundaries. His social theory does not deny the existence of the community of humankind, but it recognizes that only by taking our particularity—or pluralism—seriously can we begin to ask the question, how do we formulate a hermeneutic to determine what is universal in our particularity, or what G. K. Chesterton has called our "narrow universality"? In *After Virtue*, MacIntyre effectively states:

> The fact [that] the self has to find its moral identity in and through its membership in communities such as those of the family, the neighborhood, the city, and the tribe does *not* entail that the self has to accept the moral *limitations* of the particularity of those forms of community. Without those moral particularities to begin with there would never be anywhere to begin; but *it is in moving forward from such particularity that the search for the good, the universal, consists.* Yet particularity can never be simply left behind or obliterated. The notion of escaping from it into a realm of entirely universal maxims which belong to man as such . . . is an illusion and an illusion with painful consequences.[62]

Thus, in terms of the Rationalist tradition as Wight has expounded it, there is in MacIntyre's social theory a latent cosmopolitanism, which could appeal to the ES's solidarist interpreters of international society. As the conclusion of this chapter shows, if we can overcome the Westphalian presumption, some of the ways to answer the above question involve the ES's early concerns about religions, doctrines, and civilizations, by identifying similar principles and practices in different religious traditions.

Rules, Institutions, and Practices of International Relations

Although this article has indicated the similarities between MacIntyre's account and the constructivist account of how social practices can be constitutive for individual and communal identity, there is a fundamental difference between them. It is the distinction between those tradition-constitutive practices in which individuals and communities (or maybe even states) are *coparticipants* and those types of practices (to be called procedural rules) that have been intersubjectively constructed. This distinction can be related to the different ways that the ES accounts for the subjectivity of international society, which have already been mentioned: how this subjectivity *emerges* in international society, and how this subjectivity is *constructed* in international society. What this distinction indicates is how the fact that some social practices "emerge" as part of common religious tradition, culture, or civilization is what may make them different from those practices that are intersubjectively "constructed" based on the assumptions of liberal modernity.

The definition of social practices that MacIntyre uses differs significantly from the one adopted in IR to describe what states do or to illustrate the institutions of international society, such as state sovereignty, diplomacy, the balance of power, diplomatic immunity, extraterritorial jurisdiction, or international law. MacIntyre's understanding of practices goes back to his upbringing among the Gaelic-speaking farming and fishing communities in Scotland, which emphasized the importance of particular loyalties and ties of kinship. He has explained that this communal part of his early life taught him that

> to be just was to play one's assigned role in the life of one's local community. Each person's identity derived from the person's place in their community and in the conflicts and arguments that constituted its ongoing . . . history. Its concepts were conveyed through its histories.[63]

MacIntyre indicates that this conception of social practices out of which his understanding of morality, tradition, and community emerges may very well be consistent with the intuitive understanding of social practices and morality still found in most, if not all, parts of the developing world.[64] This indigenous knowledge of morality is increasingly being challenged by a liberal modernity conveyed as much by development practitioners from the West as by the forces of globalization.[65]

MacIntyre's understanding of social practices and traditions is crucial to his conception of tradition-dependent rationality. MacIntyre has recognized that *rules* are only one of the important elements that define a practice, whereas, for the discipline of IR, they are the main element of its definition, even though scholars differ on how they have come about. MacIntyre understands a practice to be a systematic form of cooperative activity through which goods (goals) inherent in performing a particular activity are realized in the course of trying to achieve standards of excellence defined by, and appropriate to, that particular activity. It is not enough to say that obedience (compliance with or adherence) to particular rules, which define a particular activity, make that activity a "practice," for example, chess, cricket, or state sovereignty. This confuses practices with rules, and for MacIntyre they are not the same thing. In order to define a "practice," a number of *additional* questions need to be asked, which effectively define a practice as a craft, i.e., a skill applied to a particular form of systematic activity: What are the standards of excellence relevant or applicable to this particular systematic form of activity? What does it mean to be "good" at this particular activity? and What is the good achieved by performing this particular practice, that is, the good internal, specific, or common to that practice?

These additional elements of MacIntyre's definition are missing from the understanding of practices commonly used in IR. As MacIntyre explains, this is why bricklaying and planting turnips are not practices, but architecture and farming are practices. This is why, as we can now see, state sovereignty, diplomatic immunity, and extraterritorial jurisdiction are not practices of international relations according to MacIntyre's understanding. Regarding these activities, you can not ask the question, What does it mean to be good at sovereign statehood, diplomatic immunity, or extraterritorial jurisdiction? Although they are not "practices" of international relations as MacIntyre understands this term, they may constitute "rules," laws, norms, or principles of international society. Therefore, the practices of international relations may be more limited in MacIntyre's understanding, or we might want to call these "procedural" or "rule-based" practices: the thin practices of international society.

According to MacIntyre's understanding, what international activities might we call the thick practices of international society? It would seem that war (soldiering) and diplomacy (diplomatic statecraft), which represent the ends of the spectrum in relations between states (as conflict and cooperation), are two such defining practices of international society. These practices, in one sense, conform to the functional understanding of practices as procedural rules (or institutions) that "rationally" regulate the relations between states, but in another sense these social activities can be defined as practices as MacIntyre understands this term because in each case the question can be asked, What does it mean to be good at soldiering? What does it mean to be good at diplomatic statecraft? A glimpse of this understanding of soldiering and diplomacy as thick practices of international relations may be evident in the various diplomatic handbooks of early modern Europe, the most famous being Niccolò Machiavelli's *The Art of War* (1521) and Francois de Callières' *The Art of Diplomacy* (1716). Another glimpse of war and diplomacy as practices of international relations in the MacIntyrean sense may also be found in the international societies of ancient Greece, the kingdoms of China, and the diverse states of India, since war and peace are the inevitable ways for independent states to have continual international intercourse.

The practices of war and diplomacy conform, in another sense, to MacIntyre's understanding of the thick practices of international society because states are *coparticipants* in socially established cooperative activities embedded in the religious and moral traditions of their culture or civilization, and it is in this way that the practices are constitutive for communal identity. What did the social embeddedness of war and diplomacy mean for those societies? It meant that the early practices of international relations were part of a teleologically based religious tradition, and so they fulfilled a larger moral purpose for these individuals, communities, or states. This was inevitably the case because the social embeddedness of conceptions of the good is a characteristic of premodern societies. How thick practices "emerged" among states that were coparticipants of a religious tradition, culture, or civilization with common history and collective memory (Anthony Smith's understanding of culture) is what may make them different from those thin practices that are intersubjectively "constructed" within the global culture of liberal modernity.[66]

MacIntrye's social theory may help us tell the story of the expansion of international society in another way. The Westphalian presumption helped reduce the social practices of international relations to rules by separating them from religious tradition, as part of the invention of religion and the secularization of international society. Before this change, the thick practices of international relations—war and diplomacy—were sustained by traditions of warfare and statecraft embedded in the wider religious and cultural traditions of Christendom that lasted until the sixteenth century. Similar practices were also sustained by similar traditions of statecraft and warfare embedded in various religious traditions of non-Western societies and communities until they were destroyed by colonialism and imperialism. Between the fifteenth and seventeenth centuries, these practices became detached from the Christian tradition as Christendom gave way to the invention of religion and religion came under the modern state's power and discipline. The ES has shown how Christendom was transformed into "Europe" as a geographical expression, and a European international society was formed whose religion was still Christianity, but whose culture was increasingly European.[67]

The way the practices of international relations were reduced to rules was assisted by the emerging idea of international law. Practices were detached from Christianity as a social tradition as part of the transition from Christendom to Europe. It was Grotius, and subsequent international lawyers, who contributed to this change by abandoning a teleologically based understanding of morality and tradition in international relations: by shifting from an understanding of religion as a social concept to one of privately held doctrines and beliefs. Grotius, of course, wanted to insulate these procedural rules or laws from religion as part of a wider effort to overcome the conflicts resulting from religious pluralism (Catholicism and Protestantism) among the states of Europe.[68] This separation of theology from ethics is considered to be his great achievement, and contributed to the Grotian conception of international society.[69] What we can now recognize is that the modern concept of religion as well as that of the modern state were required for the development of the Grotian conception of international society.

What MacIntyre's social theory may help us now to see is that the Grotian legacy of the separation of theology from ethics and the reduction of the thick practices of international relations (embedded in the social traditions of world religions and civilizations) to thin practices (as procedural rules) has undermined the basis for the social bond that made them binding in international society. His social theory and tradition-dependent account of rationality may also help us to see that by detaching the practices of international relations from the social traditions of world religions and civilizations, the debates about just war, arms races, or humanitarian intervention have become incommensurable not only within the Western societies of liberal modernity, but among Western and non-Western countries as well.

Conclusion

There have always been people of good will belonging to different faith communities—or to none—who in the past have devised peace plans for relations among states, worked for the abolition of war as an instrument of foreign policy, promoted interfaith dialogue, and in a variety of ways worked for a world without war. What has changed since the international order proposals of the "last modern century," as indicated by both the global resurgence of religion and the rise of postmodernism, is the collapse of confidence in the way Western modernity has understood the world. There is a growing openness in international relations to what different religious perspectives may have to offer to the world.

The place to begin, given the Westphalian presumption, is the social ethics of the main world religions. Christopher G. Weeramantry, the vice president of the International Court of Justice, has indicated that it is now time to identify the common core of ethical principles contained in the main world religions that are meaningful for international relations.[70] The rejection of the study of religion, as Bagge Laustsen and Waever have argued elsewhere in this volume, has been stronger in IR than in most other social sciences. However, a time may be coming when the absence of religion and theology from IR will begin to look like as bizarre a detour as the absence of normative theory from the discipline. Scholars in IR, Christian Ethics, and Religious Studies are already identifying the common ethical principles among the main world religions on war and peace, the just war, pacifism, human rights, and peace building.[71] The International Committee of the Red Cross has demonstrated how its humanitarian principles are consistent with the social ethics of the main world religions. These social ethics are also being examined by various nongovernmental organizations (NGOs), such as Hans Küng's Global Ethics Foundation,[72] the World Conference on Religion and Peace (Amman, Jordan, 1999), and the self-styled Parliament of the World's Religions. The newly established International Center for Religion and Diplomacy is already involved in conflict resolution in a number of countries.[73]

The social ethics of the main world religions is not the only place to begin. If MacIntyre is right about the tradition-dependent nature of rationality, then morality is not detached from the communities and traditions through which most people in the world live out their moral and social lives. This means that the "humanitarian" practices (of charity to the poor and hospitality to strangers), and the "international" practices (of military conventions and fairness to prisoners of war) can be lived out and experienced only in what Jean Bethke Elshtain has called "really existing communities."[74] Humanitarian NGOs, in an effort to demonstrate the universality of their principles, have reduced humanitarian practices, embedded in the social traditions of the main world religions and communities, to abstract moral rules. They have turned a practice-based morality into a rule- or principle-based approach to international ethics. These rules can be appealed to only by a "rationality" detached from religion, culture, and tradition. But as Elshtain has explained, "the vast majority of people in the world surely do not think of themselves as subjects of international duties and rights"; they experience moral life as MacIntyre indicates—within virtues, social practices, and traditions of their communities grounded in the world's main religions, however imperfectly it is lived out.[75]

If this is the case, then taking religious and cultural pluralism seriously means developing what we have called a deeper pluralism among different communities and states in international society. The existing pluralist approach attempts to promote a limited religious and cultural pluralism by recognizing cultural diversity through the procedural, or thin, practices of international society. The approach advocated here, based on MacIntyre's social theory, goes further by engaging the Other, by engaging the thick social practices of the main world religions in ways that promote order and justice, instead of adopting the Westphalian presumption, which ignores, marginalizes, or tries to overcome them by an ethic of cosmopolitanism. This approach may provide another way forward. It purports to use "communitarian" means to achieve "cosmopolitan" ends.

Deep pluralism adopts the approach called "virtue-ethics," which has been developed in the aftermath of MacIntyre's social theory.[76] It focuses on virtues, practices, and the community rather than the individual or a cosmopolitan community of humankind as a whole. It may provide a way to address both Bull's concern about absorbing non-Western elements in international society and the solidarist concern for both a thick understanding of culture and a thick understanding of global society.

The virtue-ethics approach suggests that the most effective way the humanitarian practices of the main world religions can be developed (as noted, charity to the poor, hospitality to strangers, as well as the international practices of military conventions and fairness to prisoners of war) is for them to be discussed, supported, and engaged in the moral life of particular, real, existing communities. Rather than develop a cosmopolitan ethic of global hospitality, taking religious and cultural pluralism seriously means identifying those practices of particular religious and cultural traditions (the virtues necessary to sustain them) and cultivating and supporting them.[77] This is an element of a collective attempt by a particular community—be it Christian, Muslim, Jewish, Buddhist, or Hindu—to live out the moral life according to its religious tradition.

Because of the Westphalian presumption, "virtue-ethics" are contrary to the approach of Western governments and development agencies, which argue that "religion" gets in the way of helping the poor or promoting development. What has to be remembered is that there is a close relationship between religious freedom and political freedom, and religious toleration often has been the beginning of political toleration, civil society, and democracy.[78] A virtue-ethics approach shows how humanitarian practices can help to build up communities in their faith as well as empower them as part of development, for it may be the case that the two should go together if there is to be lasting political stability, democracy, and development. It might even help all of us—Western and non-Western alike—to learn what it means to embrace the Other in international relations.[79] If the Westphalian presumption can be overcome, then this article can only begin to indicate what taking seriously the global resurgence of religion and cultural pluralism might mean in the multicultural international society that has emerged since the end of the Cold War.

Notes

For helpful comments on earlier drafts, the author would like to thank Jean Bethke Elshtain, Steve Casey, Raymond Cohen, Duncan Forrester, Stanley Hauerwas, Charles Jones, Graham Room, Benedict Rosario, Max Stackhouse, Adrian Winnett, and especially Luke Bretherton for many discussions, along with the most helpful comments by the anonymous referees.

1. G. K. Chesterton, *Orthodoxy* (London: Hodder and Stoughton, 1996 [1908]), 17–18.

2. See Samuel P. Huntington, *Political Order and Changing Societies* (Cambridge, MA: Harvard University Press, 1968) and Ira William Zartman, *Collapsed States: The Disintegration and Restoration of Legitimate Authority* (Boulder, CO: Lynne Rienner, 1994).

3. Mark Juergensmeyer, *The New Cold War: Religious Nationalism Confronts the Secular State* (Berkeley and Los Angeles: University of California Press, 1993); Jeff Haynes, *Religion in Third World Politics* (London: Open University Press, 1994); and David Westerlund, ed., *Questioning the Secular State: The Worldwide Resurgence of Religion in Politics* (London: I. B. Tauris, 1996).

4. Hedley Bull, "The Revolt Against the West," in *The Expansion of International Society,* eds. Hedley Bull and Adam Watson (Oxford: Clarendon Press, 1984).

5. Robert Lee, *Overcoming Tradition and Modernity: The Search for Islamic Authenticity* (Boulder, CO: Westview Press, 1997).

6. S. N. Eisenstadt, "The Reconstruction of Religious Arenas in the Framework of 'Multiple Modernities,'" *Millennium: Journal of International Studies* 29, no. 3 (2000): 591–611.

7. John L. Esposito and Michael Watson, eds., *Religion and Global Order* (Cardiff: University of Wales Press, 2000); Ken R. Dark, ed., *Religion and International Relations* (Basingstoke: Macmillan, 2000); and Jeff Haynes, ed., *Religion, Globalization, and Political Culture in the Third World* (Basingstoke: Macmillan, 1999).

8. Thompson defines a political myth as "a tale told about the past to legitimize or discredit a regime." See Leonard Thompson, *The Political Mythology of Apartheid* (New Haven, CT: Yale University Press, 1985), 1.

9. This is the view of theorists of modern liberalism, including John Rawls, Judith Shklar, and Jeffrey Stout, but the rise of toleration in the modern world is a more complicated story than the political mythology of liberalism wants to tell. See Carl J. Nederman and John Christian Laursen, eds., *Difference and Dissent: Theories of Tolerance in Medieval and Early Modern Europe* (London: Rowman and Littlefield, 1996).

10. The provisions laid out in the Treaty of Münster are a striking example (given the contemporary examples of ethnic cleansing in the Balkans) of religious toleration. Not only were the princes and electors unable to impose religious faith in their domain, they had to allow freedom of movement to minorities who resisted the faith of the majority. For a recent review of the treaties, see Klaus Bussmann and Heinz Schilling, eds., *1648: War and Peace in Europe,* vol. 1 (Munich: Bruckmann, 1998).

11. Martin Wight, *International Theory: The Three Traditions* (Leicester: Leicester University Press, 1991), 13–15.

12. Robert H. Jackson, "The Political Theory of International Society," in *International Relations Theory Today,* eds. Ken Booth and Steve Smith (Oxford: Polity Press, 1995) and Robert H. Jackson, "Pluralism in International Political Theory," *Review of International Studies* 18, no. 3 (1992): 271–81.

13. This social definition of religion has increasingly been accepted by scholars of early modern Europe, and the transition to a "modern" understanding of religion is now usually placed in the seventeenth century; see John Bossy, *Christianity in the West, 1400–1700* (Oxford: Oxford University Press, 1985), esp. 170–71; Mack P. Holt, *The French Wars of Religion, 1562–1629* (Cambridge: Cambridge University Press, 1995); and Mack P. Holt, "Putting Religion Back into the Wars of Religion," *French Historical Studies,* no. 18 (1993): 524–51.

14. For an anthropological perspective, see Talal Asad, *Genealogies of Religion: Discipline and Reasons of Power in Christianity and Islam* (Baltimore, MD: Johns Hopkins University Press, 1993), 1–54. Asad criticizes Clifford Geertz's notion of "religion as a cultural system," because it assumes that religion can be examined as a symbolic system separate from religious practices and disciplines. According to Asad, this understanding of "religion" is a construction of Western modernity rather than a universal concept, and it authorizes the politics of a liberal modernity, which defines "politicized religions" as a threat to both reason and liberty.

15. Parts of this section are indebted to William T. Cavanaugh, "A Fire Strong Enough to Consume the House: The Wars of Religion and the Rise of the State," *Modern Theology* 11, no. 4 (1995): 397–420.

16. The focus on the relatively small number of weird and wild groups in early modern Europe, e.g., popular religion, heretics, witches, magic, superstitions, dissidents, etc., has distorted our image of the time. See Eamon Duffy, *The Stripping of the Alters: Traditional Religion in England, 1400–1580* (New Haven, CT: Yale University Press, 1992).

17. MacIntyre's overall argument, in *Three Rival Versions of Moral Inquiry: Encyclopedia, Genealogy, and Tradition* (London: Duckworth, 1990), needs to be recognized here. MacIntyre examines how the medieval anthologies of Thomas Aquinas and works by later commentators separated Aquinas' discussion of law and the natural law from the context of his theology in the *Summa*. This separation contributed to the development of the modern concept of "religion" as a set of privately held doctrines or beliefs as well as it helped legitimate the modern separation of ethics from theology.

18. William T. Cavanaugh relies on Wilfred Cantwell Smith, *The Meaning and End of Religion* (Basingstoke: Macmillan, 1962), for the development of *religio* as a concept. See Cavanaugh, "A Fire Strong Enough," 404.

19. Unlike Bossy and Cavanaugh, Bull's brief discussion of the abovementioned book by Grotius does not recognize the change in the conception of religion that took place during this time. See Hedley Bull, "The Importance of Grotius," in *Hugo Grotius and International Relations,* eds. Hedley Bull, Benedict Kingsbury, and Adam Roberts (Oxford: Clarendon Press, 1990).

20. Thomas Hobbes, "Leviathan," in *Cambridge Texts in the History of Political Thought,* ed. Richard Tuck (Cambridge: Cambridge University Press, 1991), 120, emphasis added.

21. Stephen D. Krasner, "Westphalia and All That," in *Ideas and Foreign Policy,* eds. Judith Goldstein and Robert Keohane (Ithaca, NY: Cornell University Press, 1993).

22. Roland Robertson, "Globalization and the Future of Traditional Religion," in *Religion and the Powers of the Common Life: God and Globalization,* vol. 1, eds. Max L. Stackhouse and Peter J. Paris (Harrisburg, PA: Trinity Press International, 2000).

23. Roger Epp, "The English School on the Frontiers of International Society: A Hermeneutic Recollection," *Review of International Studies* 24, no. 3 (1998): 47–63.

24. David R. Mapel and Terry Nardin, eds., *International Society: Diverse Ethical Perspectives* (Princeton, NJ: Princeton University Press, 1998).

25. Adam Watson, "Hedley Bull, States Systems and International Societies," *Review of International Studies* 13, no. 1 (1987): 147–53.

26. B. A. Roberson, ed., *International Society and the Development of International Relations Theory* (London: Pinter, 1998), and Timothy Dunne, *Inventing International Society: A History of the English School* (Basingstoke: Macmillan, 1998).

27. Timothy Dunne, "The Social Construction of International Society," *European Journal of International Relations* 1, no. 3 (1995): 367–89.
28. MacIntyre's emphasis on social tradition has led to a misunderstanding regarding his political leanings. Kelvin Knight goes so far as to say that the idea that MacIntyre is a "political conservative" is "absurd." This claim is based on a mistaken understanding of his social theory: Those who prioritize tradition are conservatives; MacIntyre prioritizes tradition, therefore he is a conservative. On the contrary, his radical Aristotelian project, rooted in the politics of the local community, is at odds with the "communitarianism" that emerged in the United States in the mid-1980s because MacIntyre believes this critique of liberalism does not go far enough; it is still part of the institutional framework of the modern bureaucratic nation-state and the market in (a structurally unjust) capitalist society. See Kelvin Knight, Introduction, in *MacIntyre Reader,* ed. Kelvin Knight (Cambridge: Polity Press, 1998), 20–24; Kelvin Knight, "Revolutionary Aristotelianism," in *Contemporary Political Studies 1996,* eds. I. Hampshire-Monk and J. Stanyer, vol. 2 (Nottingham: Political Studies Association, 1996), 885–96. Nevertheless, MacIntyre's critique of the Enlightenment project and of liberal modernity has endeared him to religious "neoconservatives" in the United States. They seem to have overlooked his critique of liberal capitalist society; see Edward T. Oakes, "The Achievement of Alasdair MacIntyre," *First Things,* no. 65 (1996): 22–26.
29. Alasdair MacIntyre, *After Virtue: A Study in Moral Theory,* 2d ed. (London: Duckworth, 1985), and *Whose Justice? Which Rationality?* (London: Duckworth, 1988).
30. Alasdair MacIntyre, "Social Science Methodology as the Ideology of Bureaucratic Authority," in *MacIntyre Reader,* 53–68.
31. Erik Ringmar, *Identity, Interest, and Action: A Cultural Explanation of Sweden's Intervention in the Thirty Years War* (Cambridge: Cambridge University Press, 1996).
32. Adda Bozeman, *The Future of Law in a Multicultural World* (Princeton, NJ: Princeton University Press, 1971), ix.
33. Ibid., xii–xiii.
34. *Politics and Culture in International History* (New Brunswick, NS: Transaction Publishers, 1960, 1994).
35. Wight, *International Theory,* 13–15.
36. The seminal role of Pope John Paul II should be mentioned in this regard, including certain important encyclicals, such as *Centesimus Annus* (1991) and *Sollicitudo Rei Socialis* (1987), as part of the emerging debate on democracy and international civil society. See Kenneth L. Grasso, ed., *Catholicism, Liberalism, and Communitarianism: The Catholic Intellectual Tradition and the Moral Foundations of Democracy* (London: Rowman and Littlefield, 1996).

37. Alasdair MacIntyre, "How Can We Learn What *Veritatis Spendor* Has to Teach?" *The Thomist* 58, no. 2 (1994): 171–95.
38. Andrew Linklater, "Rationalism," in *Theories of International Relations,* eds. Scott Burchill and Andrew Linklater (Basingstoke: Macmillan, 1996). Linklater appears to subordinate the role of theologians, natural law theorists, and the Catholic Church in upholding the Rationalist tradition to a more critical-emancipatory project of liberal modernity.
39. For the Bull-Donelan debate in the ES on natural law, and the general status of natural law theory within the ES, see Dunne, *Inventing International Society* and Roberson, *International Society.*
40. MacIntyre, *Whose Justice?,* esp. 326–48.
41. Michael Donelan, *Elements of International Political Theory* (Oxford: Clarendon Press, 1990), 38–55.
42. On the later works of Bull and Vincent, see Dunne, *Inventing International Society;* Nicholas J. Wheeler, "Pluralist or Solidarist Conceptions of International Society," *Millennium: Journal of International Studies* 21, no. 3 (1992): 463–87; and Andrew Linklater, *The Transformation of Political Community* (Cambridge: Polity Press, 1998).
43. Martin Wight, *Systems of States* (Leicester: Leicester University Press, 1977), 21–45.
44. Nicholas J. Rengger, "Culture, Society, and Order in World Politics," in *Dilemmas of World Politics,* eds. John Baylis and Nicholas J. Rengger (Oxford: Oxford University Press, 1992).
45. Wight, *Systems of States,* 34.
46. Epp, "The English School on the Frontiers of International Society."
47. Mayall, "International Theory and International Society."
48. Hedley Bull and Adam Watson, Conclusion, in *The Expansion of International Society,* 425–35.
49. Wight, *Systems of States,* 35.
50. Mark Juergensmeyer, *Terror in the Mind of God: The Global Rise of Religious Violence* (Berkeley and Los Angeles: University of California, 2000); David Martin, *Does Christianity Cause War?* (Oxford: Clarendon Press, 1997); and Regina M. Schwartz, *The Curse of Cain: The Violent Legacy of Monotheism* (Chicago: University of Chicago Press, 1997).
51. Wight, *Systems of States,* 26–34. One of the states-systems Wight had in mind existed during the Amarna period (1440–1220 B.C.). Cohen and Westbrook have recently argued that the ancient Near Eastern empires established a truly "polycultural" international system that cut across religions, languages, and cultures, and it was not until the present global international society that this was repeated. See Raymond Cohen and Raymond Westbrook, eds., *Amarna Diplomacy: The Beginnings of International Relations* (Baltimore, MD: Johns Hopkins University Press, 2000).

52. R. J. Vincent, "Edmund Burke and the Theory of International Relations," *Review of International Studies* 10, no. 2 (1984): 205–18, and R. J. Vincent, "The Cultural Factor in the Global International Order," *The Yearbook of World Affairs* 34 (1980): 252–64.

53. Hedley Bull, *The Anarchical Society: A Study of Order in World Politics* (London: Macmillan, 1977), 315–17.

54. Peter Berger, ed., *The Desecularization of the World: Resurgent Religion and World Politics* (Grand Rapids, WI: Wm. B. Eerdmans/Ethics and Public Policy Center, 1999).

55. Bull, *The Anarchical Society,* 317.

56. Ibid., 38–52.

57. Alexander Wendt, "Collective Identity Formation and the International State," *American Political Science Review* 88, no. 2 (1994): 384–96, and "Constructing International Politics," *International Security* 20, no. 1 (1995): 71–81.

58. Alexander Wendt, "Anarchy Is What States Make of It," in *International Theory: Critical Investigations,* ed. James der Derian (Basingstoke: Macmillan, 1995).

59. Alexander Wendt and Daniel Friedheim, "Hierarchy under Anarchy: Informal Empire and the East German State," *International Organization* 49, no. 3 (1995): 689–721.

60. Martin Hollis and Steve Smith, *Explaining and Understanding International Relations* (Oxford: Clarendon Press, 1991) and MacIntyre, *After Virtue,* 204–25.

61. MacIntyre, *After Virtue,* 205–21.

62. Ibid., 221, emphasis in original.

63. Alasdair MacIntyre, "An Interview with Giovanna Borradori," in *The MacIntyre Reader,* 255.

64. MacIntyre, *Whose Justice?* 354–55.

65. According to MacIntyre, Durkheim described how the breakdown of traditional forms of social relationship increased the incidence of anomie a form of deprivation, a loss of membership in those social institutions in which norms, including the norms of tradition-constituted rationality, are embodied. "What Durkheim did not foresee," MacIntyre explains, "was a time when the same condition of *anomie* would be assigned the status of achievement by and a reward for a self, which had, by separating itself from the social relationships of traditions, succeeded, so it believed, in emancipating itself. . . . What Durkheim saw as social pathology is now presented wearing the masks of philosophical pretension." See *Whose Justice?* 368.

66. Anthony D. Smith, *Nations and Nationalism in a Global Era* (Oxford: Oxford University Press, 1995).

67. The great cartographer Abraham Ortelius wrote in one of the entries of his *Geographical Encyclopaedia* (1578), "For Christians, see Europeans." See John Hale, *The Civilization of Europe in the Rennaissance* (London: Fontana Press, 1993), 5–6.

68. Charles Taylor argues that the political dimension of the shift from what he calls substantive to procedural notions of ethics was anticipated in Grotius' theory of legitimacy and is evident in the rising prominence of social contract theory. Instead of defining the legitimacy of the state in terms of regime type or some conception of the good society, Grotius argued that we should define it by the procedures that led to its creation. Thus, Grotius thought that the regime type did not matter as long as it came about through *consent*. See Charles Taylor, *Sources of the Self* (Cambridge: Cambridge University Press, 1989), 86–87.

69. Hedley Bull, Benedict Kingsbury, and Adam Roberts, eds., *Hugo Grotius and International Relations* (Oxford: Oxford University Press, 1990).

70. Mark W. Janis and Carolyn Evans, eds., *Religion and International Law,* 2d ed. (The Hague: Martinus Nijhoff, 1999).

71. John Witte et al., *Religious Human Rights in Global Perspective* (The Hague: Martinus Nijoff, 1996); Harfiyah Abdel Harleen, Oliver Ramsbotham, et al., *The Crescent and the Cross: Muslim and Christian Approaches to War and Peace* (Basingstoke: Macmillan, 1998); David R. Smock, ed., *Perspectives on Pacifism: Christian, Jewish, and Muslim Views on Nonviolence and International Conflict* (Washington, D.C.: US Institute of Peace, 1995); and Cynthia Sampson, "Religion and Peacebuilding," in *Peacemaking in International Conflict: Methods and Techniques,* eds. I. William Zartman and J. Lewis Rasmussen (Washington, D.C.: US Institute of Peace, 1995).

72. Stephen Chan, "Hans Küng and a Global Ethic," *Review of International Studies* 25, no. 3 (1999): 525–30.

73. The International Center for Religion and Diplomacy (IRCD) (www.icrd.org) was established in Washington, D.C., after the publication of Douglas M. Johnston and Cynthia Sampson, eds., *Religion, the Missing Dimension of Statecraft* (Oxford: Oxford University Press, 1994).

74. Jean Bethke Elshtain, "Really Existing Communities," *Review of International Studies* 25, no. 1 (1999): 141–46.

75. Ibid.

76. This group includes Peter Kreeft, Gilbert Meilander, Stanley Hauerwas, Robert C. Evans, Jonathan Wilson, David W. Gill, and Mary Ann Glendon, the law professor at Harvard who led the Vatican's delegation to the UN Conference on Women (Beijing, 1995). Of course theorists of virtue-ethics are not all the same. See Mary Ann Glendon and David Blankenhorn, eds., *Seedbeds of Virtue* (New York: Madison, 1995) and Nancy Murphy, Brad J. Kallenberg, and Mark Thiessen Nation, *Virtues and Practices in the Christian Tradition: Christian Ethics After MacIntyre* (Harrisburg, PA: Trinity Press, 1997).

77. Michael J. Shapiro, "The Events of Discourse and the Ethics of Global Hospitality," *Millennium: Journal of International Studies* 27, no. 2 (1998): 697–713.

78. Max Maddox, *Religion and the Rise of Democracy* (London: Routledge, 1996).
79. Miroslav Volf, "Forgiveness, Reconciliation, and Justice: A Theological Contribution to a More Peaceful Social Environment," *Millennium: Journal of International Studies* 29, no. 3 (2000): 861–77; Miroslav Volf, *Exclusion and Embrace: A Theological Exploration of Identity, Otherness, and Reconciliation* (Nashville, TN: Abingdon Press, 1996).

CHAPTER 2

DOGMA, PRAXIS, AND RELIGIOUS PERSPECTIVES ON MULTICULTURALISM

Cecelia Lynch

"I am a Muslim," she told us, "but I didn't know that before the war. Before the war, of course, we were all atheists!"[1]

—Amira Muharemović

A couple of days later, I saw the maulana, and I told him I thought some of his students believed that terrorism, under certain circumstances, was Koranically acceptable. "Then you don't understand what we are teaching," he said, frowning for just a moment. "There is a great difference between jihad and terrorism." He invited me to eat with him, to discuss my inability to comprehend the distinction, but I begged off.[2]

—Jeffrey Goldberg

"The Lord rideth," [Father] said, low and threatening, "upon a swift cloud, and shall come into Egypt."

Hurray! They all cheered, but I felt a knot in my stomach. He was getting that look he gets, oh boy, like Here comes Moses tromping down off of Mount Syanide with ten fresh ways to wreck your life.

"Into Egypt," he shouted in his rising singsong preaching voice that goes high and low, then higher and lower, back and forth like a saw ripping into a tree trunk, "and every corner of the earth where His light," Father paused, glaring all about him, "where His light has yet to fall!"[3]

—Barbara Kingsolver

Thef irst of these quotes is from a scholarly treatise on the problem of alterity and violence in allegedly ethnic politics in the
Balkans. It points to the imposition of religious identity from
the outside—not by religious fundamentalists but rather by those (in
this case, some Serbian leaders) for whom fixed notions of alterity rationalize conflict, as well as by others (the Western press and diplomatic corps, the UN) who attempt to mediate and "resolve" violence.
The second quote is a Western journalist's account of an Islamic school
in Pakistan. It demonstrates the distrust of Islamic "fundamentalism"
(itself a controversial label) prevalent in Western media and government circles, and also expresses the author's Orientalist determination
to understand the school's teachings on his terms rather than their
own.[4] The third quote forms part of a fictional narrative about the
neocolonialist clash of power and religion in the Congo. It also highlights the arrogance that accompanied much Christian missionary activity in Africa, even in the second half of the twentieth century. Each
of these quotes, however, also indicates, in different ways, the degree
to which our debates about religion in world politics reflect Enlightenment assumptions. That is to say, each associates religion with danger, dogma, or rigid conceptions of otherness.

While Scott Thomas focuses in his contribution to this volume on
the Westphalian presumption of International Relations theorizing to
analyze our current misunderstanding of the importance of religion in
world politics, here I extend this analysis to the baggage associated
with what I call our Enlightenment assumptions. Enlightenment concerns about religion in world politics are multiple. Most prominent is
the fear that religion, because it addresses such elemental issues as life,
death, salvation, right, and wrong, has the power to create "true believers," who are, at a minimum, psychologically disturbed and, at a
maximum, inciters of intolerance and violence. True believers become
especially dangerous as leaders of mass movements, or when their beliefs are systematized in powerful religious institutions that treat non-
members as heretics, deserving of subjugation and even death.

Conversely, following a certain reading of Karl Marx, many charge
religions, especially those that espouse a belief in a perfect afterlife,
with muting political demands and serving the interests of the powerful by teaching patience and passivity in the face of injustice.[5] Both
Marxists and secular liberals are concerned that religious belief, as evident in the creationist/evolutionist debate in education, can promote
romanticism, ignorance, and backwardness in the face of knowledge
and progress. All of these fears assume that religious belief is dogmatic,
intolerant, and unchanging. The Other, as seen through the prism of

religious belief, in this view, is inevitably inferior, providing the justification for proselytizing, coercion, and violence instead of pluralism and critical thinking. Enlightenment insights were supposed to have overcome these problems, which is at least part of the reason why religion has been for so long overlooked by International Relations thought. But the return to "ethnic" violence and more recently the escalated post–September 11 attention to "terrorist threats" have renewed attention to religious identity and conceptions of the Other, giving them troubling connotations today.

Debates about identity and alterity, including the role of religion, have been rife for several decades in political theory, philosophy, and literary criticism. After Edward Said's shot across the bow, published in 1978, in which he exposed the European representations of Islam as "always a way of controlling the redoubtable Orient,"[6] Tzvetan Todorov in the early 1980s raised the question of whether it was possible for people of different cultures (and religions) "to experience difference in equality."[7] Focusing on the motivations and worldviews of the explorers, conquistadors, and religious leaders who led and justified the conquest of the Americas from the late 1400s through the 1600s, Todorov vividly demonstrates the horrors that resulted from politically and religiously justified notions of alterity. In treating personalities as different as Columbus, Cortés, Las Casas, Sepulveda, Sahagún, and Durán, however, Todorov addresses a range of strategies of inquiry as well as religious stances toward the Other. Nevertheless, he questions whether or not the move toward multicultural recognition, made most notably by Las Casas in his later years, becomes "the first step toward the abandonment of religious discourse itself."[8]

Moving away from these historical/philosophical critiques (and to a degree away from the subject of religion), worries about the problem of alterity in North America coalesced in the early 1990s into a debate about multiculturalism. The primary questions at issue, prompted by Quebecois separatists and Native American communities, were how to accommodate multiple cultural identities in the democratic polity and whether, and to what degree, to satisfy nationalist aspirations.

As Charles Taylor argued in his now classic "Politics of Recognition," cultural groups demand (and deserve) recognition and respect. A significant danger, however, is that those adhering to a given identity will refuse the recognition and respect due to others. Given that most contemporary polities exhibit an increase in cultural identities (or at least an increase in their recognition), such a lack of tolerance can have serious consequences, especially for any polity that presumes to be democratic.⁹ And, according to what became the "communitarian/cosmopolitan" debate, that lack of tolerance can derive from at least two directions: the rigidity of a communal identity that believes itself "authentic" and superior, or the rigidity of a universalist (generally liberal) identity that attempts to subsume all particularities but cannot avoid imposing its own.¹⁰

The "communitarians" in this debate prize cultural identity and want to find room for its expression, seeing it as positive: a good, within and "for" liberalism. Other theorists, however, have recast the relationship between identity and multiculturalism to insist on the contingency and changeability of identity. The problem then becomes not how to accommodate relatively fixed, plural identities, but rather how to provide for multiple *possibilities* of identity and culture. As William Connolly states: "Multiculturalism . . . embodies within itself a quarrel between the national protection of diverse cultural minorities on the same territory and the pluralization of multiple possibilities of being within and across states."¹¹ Drawing on Emmanuel Levinas and Jacques Derrida, David Campbell applies this line of thought to the Bosnian conflict and accuses Western diplomacy of foreclosing instead of fostering such multiple possibilities of being.¹²

But the question remains whether religion should be seen as a special cultural category. Of all the possible categories of culture and identity, including gender, ethnicity, race, and sexuality, religion is often seen as the least permeable and most essentialist, that which requires the greatest degree of adherence to given behavioral and prescriptive rules. K. Anthony Appiah, for example, states that "[r]eligion . . . unlike all the others, entails attachments to creeds or commitments to practices."¹³ Many fear that this type of attachment inhibits thought and blocks critical capacities. Thus, the problem of identity or alterity is believed to assume greater proportions once it takes on a religious cast.

Yet the view of religious identity as uncompromising is historically incomplete and ignores significant and lively debates within religious thought itself. Contemporary theological views on the possibilities of religious pluralism and multiculturalism are enlightening in this regard. Religious thinking has long addressed the problems associated with the existence of multiple forms of belief. Christian, Buddhist, Hindu, Muslim, and Jewish thought, among others, continue to grapple with problems of particularism versus universalism, authenticity versus the complexity of history, and doctrinally oriented versus historically contingent identities. Some contemporary religious thought also moves beyond individualist categories of identity to provide new ways of thinking about the sociopolitical implications of the multiple systems of belief present in the world. While these trends do not form a unified system of thought, religious debates can help point the way toward a nuanced and historically reliable understanding of multiculturalism, and hence, of the role of religion in world politics. Thus, while I agree with many other contributors to this volume that we need to understand the relationships among modernization, secularization, globalization, and religion, I also argue that we must pay attention to the multiple understandings of religious belief articulated by religious thinkers themselves.

In this article I first use recent scholarly, journalistic, and fictional accounts of religion in politics to illustrate dominant attitudes about religion and culture. Second, I articulate the range of attitudes toward interreligious dialogue found in contemporary theological thinking: exclusivism (the position that one's own belief system holds the only possible "truth," hence is superior to others, which in turn are wrong and harmful), inclusivism (the position that "my truth includes your truth," hence that one's own belief system remains superior to others but others contain partial truths), pluralism (the belief that truth itself is multiple, and therefore that other religions must be accepted as equals), and syncretism (the belief that what is true is "life-giving" and invariably takes multiple forms, and hence that it is possible and desirable, as well as inevitable, to merge aspects of different belief systems).[14] I also discuss the concept of apologetics as both a theological attitude and a dialogical process.

These approaches should be seen as heuristic tools that broaden our understanding of religious identity, alterity, and the role of religion in politics, rather than as rigidly bounded categories. I argue that while contemporary political debates continue to regard religion and belief as necessarily exclusivist, theological trends have for some time focused on the boundaries and possibilities of inclusivism and pluralism. While the existence of exclusivism cannot be ignored in the intersection of religious belief and political practice, and certainly the "religious professionals" active in the academy are concerned about the apparent hardening of religious identities in many parts of the world, religious thought also reflects trends toward acknowledging, debating, and legitimizing religious beliefs through, on one hand, apologetical discourse and, on the other, the syncretic blending of beliefs and practices.

Recent Accounts

The conflicts in Bosnia and more recently Kosovo provide telling examples of the construction of religious identity from the outside, especially on the part of the secularist West. Amira Muharemović, for example, "discovers" she is a Muslim when the identity is imposed on her by outsiders: Serbian leaders attempting to justify ethnic cleansing, and even more disturbing, Westerners attempting to make sense of the Bosnian violence by categorizing and reifying her and thousands of others' identities. Her statement implies that nonbelief is cosmopolitan, while being identified as Muslim is anachronistic. Yet she and others also appear to recognize that they cannot escape the religious identity imposed by others, one that alternately makes them intruders, victims, and new subjects of international law.

One of Campbell's primary points in using this quote is not to fault Islam, Eastern Orthodoxy, or any other religion with instigating violence, but rather to point out the variability and contingency of identity, and to emphasize that the rigid perceptions of Balkan ethnic and religious identities that prevail in Western public discourse and diplomacy are in fact particular constructions that subjugate alternative, interdependent, and pluralist identities. As Campbell shows, prewar Muslim identities were ambiguous and complex, "such that a number of the cultural practices of the Muslim community were regarded by their religious instructors as non-Islamic."[15] Indeed, not only Muslims but all faiths exhibited a lack of dogma: "Fluid confessional definitions are widely reported in Bosnia far into the twentieth century. Ethnographic data show a nondoctrinal attitude toward religion by Bosnians of all three confessions."[16] For Campbell, then, the task is to develop "an emancipatory ideal of multiculturalism" that "affirms cultural diversity without situating it" while also recognising when it "suppresses cultural interdependence and plurality."[17]

Jeffrey Goldberg's reporting, conversely, is a recent example of the ongoing Western constructions of identity that lie at the heart of Campbell's critique. Goldberg enrolls in the Haqqania madrasa, an Islamic seminary in Pakistan, "to see from the inside just what this jihad factory was producing."[18] Though Goldberg acknowledges that he never saw a weapon or heard of a military class in the time he spent at the school, he insists that "militant Islam is at the core of most" of the country's 10,000 madrasas, especially Haqqania.[19] Goldberg wishes to understand how groups he labels as terrorist are educated, but his preset identifications make understanding difficult if not impossible. He is convinced that the madrasa teaches intolerance and hatred for other religions and Americans, but he observes only rote learning of the Qur'an and Hadith. He takes as gospel the U.S. State Department's definitions of terrorist organizations, yet appears astonished that Arab students can admire Osama bin Laden. He instructs the students in his own interpretation of Qur'anic teachings, while apparently misconstruing important distinctions.[20] He acknowledges that the term "jihad" has several meanings in Islam, and that there are multiple interpretations of the Qur'an among Muslims, yet he generalizes to all of Islam in asserting "the fact" that "wherever Islam rubs up against other civilizations—Jewish, Christian, Hindu—wars seem to break out."[21] Goldberg's method of attributing meaning to Islamic teaching in particular parts of the world has been replicated over and over since the tragedies of September 11.

Yet if Campbell (consciously) and Goldberg (unconsciously) demonstrate the degree to which Westerners construct the religious identities of others, Barbara Kingsolver openly decries such constructions as neocolonialist. *The Poisonwood Bible* is Kingsolver's novel about a Baptist fundamentalist preacher from Jim Crow Atlanta who undertakes missionary work in an isolated Congolese village, narrated through the voices of the preacher's wife and four daughters. The inability of the preacher, Nathan Price, to bend to the realities of life in Africa, let alone acknowledge the validity of Congolese beliefs, is set against the backdrop of the move to independence and the inability of the Belgians to admit Congolese equality, instead abruptly evacuating the country in 1960.

The novel is impressive in its range of expression (each daughter reacts differently to the cultural clash) as well as its ability to portray the insensitivity and cruelty of Belgian, U.S., and later UN political, economic, and cultural interventions. To its credit, the novel also presents a multifaceted view of religion. Yet the preeminent religious spokesperson, Reverend Price, wears Jesus like the cape of a superhero. For him, the Congo is teeming with unsaved souls, and belief in the Christian God will solve all of their problems. Price's dogmatic beliefs range from the impractical to the absurd and even the dangerous. He decides to plant a garden, but brings seeds from Georgia that cannot pollinate in the jungle. He mispronounces Congolese words, making it unclear whether he advocates baptism or terror (or, according to the obvious implication, both). He insists on baptism by immersion in the nearby river without bothering to find out that it is infested with crocodiles, and that no caring parent would ever permit his/her child to be dunked in it. And he supports Western political authority and economic control, even when that authority is proven bankrupt and he himself is penniless, cut off from all Western sources of funds.

In contrast, the local chief and voodoo priest appear to represent a more pragmatic naturalism. But there are still problems when fundamentalist Christianity and African Traditional Religion come face to face.[22] The chief and local priest welcome Christian practices as long as they siphon off the community's undesirables, but they worry lest too many converts corrupt the village and offend the gods. The primary contrast, therefore, is between uncompromising Christian dogma and unspoiled naturalism. When the daughters lose confidence in the rigid beliefs of their father, they turn instead to faith in nature, agnosticism, or atheism. The one character who represents a more pluralist identity is Brother Fowles, the "papist" Catholic predecessor of Reverend Price. Fowles, who remains in the Congo, combines elements of local religious practices with Christianity, but is dismissed from Western religious institutions as a renegade.

Theological Attitudes and Their Political Correspondents

These recent examples indicate that much of our public discourse assumes that religious attitudes and behavior are inevitably exclusivist. Yet contemporary theological debates range primarily from inclusivism to syncretism.[23] While these categorizations should be seen primarily as heuristic tools, and in practice a given belief system may contain elements of more than one position, it is useful to distinguish among them in thinking through the political implications of contemporary theological debates on multiculturalism and interreligious dialogue.

Exclusivism

The exclusivist position argues in favor of the superiority of one's own system of belief as well as the right to propagate it as widely as possible. The political ramifications of such a position are those most feared—and taken as axiomatic—by students of international politics. In political terms, forms of exclusivism justified the Crusades, the Muslim reaction to them, the conquest of the Americas, the Spanish Inquisition, the Reformation, and colonialism. They also provide a basis for long-standing and seemingly insuperable conflicts in the Middle East, Northern Ireland, India and Pakistan, Nigeria, Sudan, and Indonesia, among others. While many scholars understand these forms of exclusivism—and their violent implications for political behavior—as only partially dependent on religious fanaticism or intolerance (or sometimes as merely a cloak for a more fundamental economic and political power struggle), it is difficult if not impossible to absolve religious motivations for any of these conflicts.[24] Exclusivist positions also appear to be at the root of doomsday cults such as those of

Guyana, Texas, or more recently, Uganda, whose charismatic leaders' insistence on loyalty has led to violent, albeit less politically powerful and widespread, consequences. When imposed by the powerful, we view exclusivism as oppressive and illegitimate; when practiced by the local cult, we see it as tragic.

Goldberg's article both assumes exclusivism by followers of Islam and encourages it on the part of non-Muslims:

> At any given time, there are several hundred Afghan students at the madrasa, along with dozens from such former Soviet republics as Kazakhstan, Tajikistan, and Uzbekistan, and a handful from Chechnya too. To those who see wars like the one in Chechnya as expressions not only of nationalist aspirations but of pan-Islamic ones as well—to those who see a new Islamic revolution on the horizon, a Sunni revolution a generation after the Shia revolution that shook the world—the foreign presence at Haqqania is not comforting.[25]

Campbell highlights the way in which religious exclusivism is assumed and used by Western policymakers to justify ethnic partition. And Kingsolver's novel presents a compelling portrait of both the powerful and the tragic aspects of exclusivism; the character of Nathan Price is an eccentric vestige of colonialist Christian domination, but Price himself becomes increasingly powerless, penniless, and removed from reality. He continues to act ultra-dogmatically at a point when the relationship among the West's military, economic, and religious purposes has broken down, but refuses to see that the previously tight relationship between raw power and exclusivist proselytizing is no longer operable.[26] While such extreme portraits of religion are commonplace, exclusivist thinking is extremely contested among religious scholars, theologians, and the major world religions today. Prominent ecumenical organizations actively discourage participation in exclusivist groups, and even some of Goldberg's maulanas disclaim exclusivist politics.[27]

Inclusivism

Politically, inclusivism also insists on the superiority of one's own belief system. It differs, however, in that it accepts the validity or "right" of other modes of belief to exist. Nevertheless, it views other religious systems as incomplete or unenlightened. Inclusivism in its political ramifications presupposes a kind of liberal tolerance. The belief remains that one's own religion, all other things being equal, "should" be universalized, but given the impracticalities and unethical behavior that imposing a universal belief would necessitate, one must allow, and even acknowledge, the partial truth in other systems of belief.

The missionary movement in the first half of this century vacillated between theological exclusivism and a more inclusivist stance. This fluctuation was manifested in two modes. Some missionaries confronted the Eurocentrism of Christianity and attempted to incorporate their message through various forms of enculturation. These efforts resulted in lively debates about the relationship of the Christian gospel to other religious traditions during the world mission conferences of the 1920s and 1930s, debates that ultimately were left unresolved. More significantly, theological debates in Europe generated by Karl Barth and later Hendrik Kraemer "made a radical separation between God's self-disclosure in the Bible, culminating in the gospel, and all forms of religious life, which were characterized as 'unbelief.'"[28] Barth, in particular, was responding to the failure of Christianity to prevent world war, and so charged Protestantism (along with all other religions) with being bonded to human imperfections, vanity, and sinfulness. Yet, despite their subsequent efforts to engage in dialogue with other faith traditions, some mission leaders continued to interpret Barth and Kraemer's theological stance as a reaffirmation of the gospel message, and hence Christianity, as "truth" while relegating all other faith traditions as merely human, rather than divine, achievements.[29]

Pluralism

This type of inclusivism, even when it attempted to increase interreligious understanding, could irritate non-Western religious leaders. Mohandas Gandhi, for example, complained, "There are some who will not even take my flat denial when I tell them I am not a Christian."[30] After World War II, many of the churches that sponsored missions became members of the newly created World Council of Churches, and an influential set of both Christian and non-Christian postcolonial religious leaders increasingly delegitimized inclusivism in favor of a more pluralistic stance.[31]

Thus the World Council of Churches' guidelines on interreligious dialogue began to state in the 1970s that Christians should not make

> judgements about others as though from a position of superiority; in particular they should avoid using ideas such as "anonymous Christians," "the Christian presence," "the unknown Christ," in ways not intended by those who proposed them for theological purposes or in ways prejudicial to the self-understanding of Christians and others.[32]

These types of statements, along with the academic study of religion, have called for an interreligious dialogue based on a pluralist approach. Pluralism, as in its liberal counterpart, requires an acknowledgement of the multiplicity of truth. This is the belief, as popularly articulated by the later Gandhi or the current Dalai Lama, of the positive similarity of purpose and function of all religions. For Chung Hyun-Kyung, "Pluralism is the most enlightened position among the three in relation to other religions, respecting differences and living side by side with differences."[33] Pluralism, therefore, takes the position that one's own beliefs cannot represent the fulfilment or perfection of the beliefs of others; they can neither engulf nor subsume others as a partial means to one's own religious goals.

While some theologians dispute the pluralist position as untenable (i.e., how can there be multiple religious truths if belief requires adherence to a particular conception of the truth?), other students of religion see exploring pluralist possibilities as necessary. David Gitomer, for instance, distinguishes between the "outside" and the "inside" of a religious tradition. These categories do not denote the institutional versus individual or private manifestations of religion. Rather,

> [t]he "outside" of a tradition is the way the tradition articulates itself in teaching formulas both for its members and for outsiders. The "inside" of the tradition is the collective experience of the reality expressed in those formulas, a reality which . . . cannot be fully expressed in ordinary human language.[34]

Gitomer, an Indologist, unfolds the importance of this distinction for the pluralist attitude:

> As we begin to apprehend the inside of a religious tradition, we begin to understand its power to lay hold of imagination and forge a vision of the world and its meaning. Without necessarily accepting the truth claims formulated by other faiths, we can nevertheless understand the capacity of another tradition to make a total meaning for its followers. Then the specific religious insights of other traditions may contribute to our own. In other words, grasping the *experiential* truth in one's own religious place enables an openness to the quality of compelling meaning in religious places that are not one's own.[35]

Likewise, for the World Council of Churches,

> the aim of dialogue is not reduction of living faiths and ideologies to a lowest common denominator, not only a comparison and discussion of

symbols and concepts, but the enabling of a true encounter between those spiritual insights and experiences which are only found at the deepest levels of human life.[36]

This type of encounter is based on the recognition of the importance of how belief is lived in the everyday experience of different cultures:

> [D]ialogue should proceed in terms of people . . . rather than of theoretical, impersonal systems. This is not to deny the importance of religious traditions and their interrelationships but it is vital to examine how faiths and ideologies have given direction to the daily living of individuals and groups and actually affect dialogue on both sides.[37]

Pluralist sensitivity has been promoted over the past several decades, not only within the academy, but also by postcolonial religious thinkers. Beginning in the 1960s and 1970s, African and Asian theologians became much more vocal in criticizing the legacy of Western missionary activity for its cultural—including religious—imperialism. In the interests of "self-expression," religious thinkers in the Philippines, India, and Kenya demanded moratoriums on Western missions and requested missionaries to leave: "The most missionary service a missionary under the present system can do today in Asia is to go home!"[38]

Apologetics

Yet not all theology is comfortable with the move toward pluralism. For example, Paul Griffiths has resuscitated an argument in favor of apologetics, despite its negative connotations in contemporary theology. Griffiths, a scholar of Buddhism, acknowledges that the notion of apologetics—the defense of the doctrines of a faith tradition—is currently unfashionable in theological circles.[39] Yet, he argues in favor of both negative apologetics (the defense of doctrine when beliefs are challenged from the outside) and positive apologetics (the attempt to demonstrate that the doctrines of one's own belief are consistent and superior to others) as necessary forms of interreligious dialogue. Griffiths criticizes "universalist perspectivalism" (the belief that all religions hold a partial perspective on truth) as elitist and ultimately untenable. What would perspectivalists, for example, have to say about the Jonestown cult in Guyana? They "must construct criteria for separating appropriate affirmations about the ultimate reality from inappropriate ones. They must, in other words, enter into apologetical discourse whether they like it or not."[40]

Griffiths acknowledges the political problems inherent in this project, and proposes specific, noncoercive conditions under which "proper apologetics" can take place.[41] He admits that apologetics always occurs within a political context, yet believes that historical examples of proper apologetics exist despite inevitable political problems.

> The extensive record of Hindu-Buddhist debate in India from the fourth to the eleventh centuries of the Christian era—much of which can properly be called positive apologetics—is, in large part, simply a vital component of the record of the religious and intellectual life of India, and not the record of the oppression of one group by another. . . . And even Peter the Venerable's apologetic against Islam in twelfth-century Europe, developed as it was at the time of the Crusades, is the work of a man who appears to have rejected the idea of the Crusades as a simple adventure in military conquest.[42]

Griffiths' apologetics at first glance appears to be a form of inclusivism in that it rejects exclusivist modes of action while continuing to defend a particular doctrine, though the analogy is incomplete. In this light, the most evident political problem with either apologetics or inclusivism, in general, is whether it can sustain itself without sliding into exclusivist reaction and violence against different modes of belief.

Griffiths' answer is to insist that there is nothing in the belief in the truth of one's own doctrines that requires violence or discrimination against others.[43] But more importantly, we need to recognize the ways in which this form of argument parallels aspects of inclusivism without completely replicating it. Apologetics is primarily a dialogical process, not an ethical endpoint. Thus the process of apologetics can logically result in any ethical standpoint toward other religions, from exclusivism to syncretism. Moreover, in the end, it is the very existence of a political context that, for Griffiths, makes apologetics necessary:

> engagement in apologetics . . . is required for religious communities in some settings . . . to begin to understand, among many other things, why some British Muslims feel impelled to burn anti-Islamic books in Bradford, why some Buddhist monks in Sri Lanka feel called upon to foster and encourage anti-Tamil violence, and why some conservative Catholic Christians in the United States of America are willing to bomb clinics.[44]

Griffiths does not condone such projects as exercises in proper apologetics, but argues that it is only through active engagement and argument about the validity of doctrine that the beliefs underlying such actions (and one's own beliefs to the contrary) can be understood. His project thus points the way toward a new approach to understanding doctrine, including what is generally labeled fundamentalism.

Syncretism

Struggles to find legitimacy for precolonial practices and beliefs in the context of world religions have also pushed theology beyond simple pluralism to notions of indigenization, enculturation, and syncretism. These concepts indicate that, contrary to the dominant portraits painted by Kingsolver, postcolonial religious thought has absorbed, challenged, and changed religious dogma in significant ways.[45]

Syncretism acknowledges and embraces the multiplicity of religious traditions that exist not only within a multicultural society, but also within the individual. The very existence of this syncretism, of course, is often the result of exclusivist politics such as those carried out through colonialism. Nonetheless, the legacy of exclusivism in the Third World has not necessarily been the wholesale adoption of an essentialist understanding of Christianity or Islam. Rather, the very practice of world religions in other contexts has challenged and in some cases revised doctrine. For example, Jean-Marc Ela, a Cameroonian theologian, published *African Cry* in 1970 to expose the "crisis in the local churches of black Africa," calling into question not only the history of Christian missionaries and the practice of Christianity, but also the central doctrine of the Eucharist.[46] In Africa, this challenge developed into a debate over whether enculturation or liberation should be the central task of the churches.[47] But enculturation, especially, implied not only a pluralist stance toward other systems of belief, but also the incorporation of elements of African Traditional Religion (and also, at times, Islam) into Christianity. Yet, while indigenization became increasingly validated in theological circles, the term "syncretism" continued to have negative connotations into the 1990s.

The World Council of Churches worried about the "risks" of syncretism at the same time that demands for enculturation were on the rise, and asked in the late 1970s, "Is syncretism a danger for which Christians must be alert?"[48] If syncretism means "conscious or unconscious human attempts to create a new religion composed of elements taken from different religions," then it can, according to its critics, give rise to two dangers: first, that of going "too far and compromis[ing] the authenticity of Christian faith and life," and second, that of interpreting a living faith not in its own terms but in terms of another faith or ideology. This is illegitimate on the principles of both scholarship and dialogue. In this way Christianity may be "syncretized" by seeing it as only a variant of some other approach to God, or another faith may be wrongly "syncretized" by seeing it only as partial understanding of what Christians believe that they know in full.[49]

Likewise, Pope John Paul II has striven during his tenure to contain what he believes to be the dangers of syncretism, arguing against it on the grounds that it both confuses "the basic mysteries of Christian faith" and is "totally contrary to real ecumenism."[50]

In contrast, a number of theologians not only promote syncretism as an ethical and theological position, they also acknowledge it as an anthropological and historical process. The debate about syncretism came to the forefront in interreligious dialogue in 1991, when Chung gave a speech at the Canberra assembly of the World Council of Churches.[51] For Chung, even the pluralist model is

> too academic, Western, and male. It is too academic because it treats the different religions as neatly arranged entities in clearly marked categories labelled Buddhism, Christianity, Shamanism, Confucianism, and the like. But this form of pluralism, in which the separate categories are distinct and do not cross one another's boundaries, exists only in academia. When I look at the popular religiosity of Asian women, the religions do not exist in that neat way under these name tags. There is a messy and fluid process of cross-permeation among the different religions. . . . I think this neatly separated pluralism is for male-centred institutional religions, because maintaining purity of doctrine has been the centre of their concern. But when I look at everyday life based women's cosmic spirituality in Asia, it is clear that what matters is not doctrinal purity, but what is liberating, what is healing, what is life-giving. Therefore the word "pluralism" as used in academia cannot really describe Asian women's religiosity.[52]

Chung, Ela, Emmanuel Martey, and others thus indicate the degree to which syncretism is a reality of postcolonial life.[53] Chung tells the story of a Korean woman who uses shaman rituals to obtain justice when her child is accidentally killed by a public official, to demonstrate that whatever religious leaders say or do, Koreans will continue to blend shamanism, Confucianism, Buddhism, and Christianity in their everyday lives.[54] In this view, syncretism simply exists (and has always existed).

Moreover, Jeffrey Carlson extends the notion of syncretism from postcolonial identity to the very essence of all religious identity. Carlson juxtaposes statements by Anselme T. Sanon, an African Catholic bishop, Raimon Pannikar, a self-proclaimed "multi-religious self" (Christian, Hindu, and Buddhist), and the anthropologist James Clifford to argue not only that all religion is, "inevitably, a form of syncretism," but also that

> the phenomenon of religious interpenetration . . . is at the very heart of personal and communal religious identity. To have a religious identity is, inevitably, to be a "syncretic self," the product of a process of selective appropriation, internalizing elements drawn from vastly varied pools of possibility.[55]

Thus we cannot escape syncretism, either at the level of individual religious identity or as an inevitable social and historical process. Moreover, while religious syncretism is certainly not static, it develops in historical and ideational contexts that can be identified.

To understand the implications of syncretist thinking, we should be aware of both the distinction and the linkages between syncretism as an ethical and theological position and syncretism as a historical process.[56] Some anthropologists, for example, question the utility of syncretism as both an analytical concept and a solution to religious violence. If all religion is ultimately syncretic, we must then also see the Crusades, the Inquisition, and the Reformation, among other instances of religious violence, as syncretic processes that have resulted in highly exclusivist practices.[57] This approach also provides important insight into so-called Islamic fundamentalism. As Olivier Roy points out, the central paradox here is that "the return to the Text is made possible only by the restoration of a *new* tradition."[58] What is called fundamentalism, in other words, opposes tradition instead of embracing it in a new stage of the continual syncretic process.

Theologians such as Chung and Carlson have attempted to address these reservations by going beyond the historical recognition of syncretic processes in constituting religious belief. Both argue in favor of understanding syncretism as a fact of religious life. Yet, at the same time, Chung is attempting to legitimize a conscious ethical and theological position that she calls "survival liberation-centered syncretism."[59] Carlson, similarly, sees value not only in recognizing syncretism historically, but in promoting syncretic understanding as a means of "responding creatively to violence in this 'death age.'"[60] Understanding syncretism, for Carlson, breaks down the violence of self/Other categorizations. "When identity is inevitably syncretic, under whose banner should we fight? And who are they, our enemies?"[61] For these theologians, reflexivity and self-awareness in syncretic ethics can lead to a) liberation from oppressive theologies and b) the collapse of reified notions of alterity in favor of "religious deterritorialization," such that there is no concrete Other against whom we can engage in exclusivist reaction.[62] Their understandings do not assume that syncretism alone resolves problems of inequality and violence, rather they argue that the historical fact of syncretism can be used to harness a self-conscious (and potentially self-critical) type of ethics.

Conclusions and Further Questions

What are the implications of these debates in religious thought for world politics? International theorists such as Jean Bethke Elshtain, Nicholas Rengger, Michael Loriaux, Richard Falk, and William Connolly have begun to break down the Enlightenment barriers to the study of religion by discussing seriously the theological ethics of Augustine, Luther, and others, reevaluating theological conceptualizations of justice and reconciliation, and calling into question the modernist neglect of religious belief.[63] Nevertheless, as most contributors to this volume point out, the analysis of religious attitudes, ethics, and praxis by students of world politics more generally has been lacking. Even much of contemporary "critical" International Relations remains dominated by Enlightenment worldviews that cast religious belief, thought, and action in overly essentialist terms. These worldviews, as Scott Thomas and Vendulka Kubálková also argue, present religion as either dogma or irrational emotion (or both), and thereby inhibit our understanding of its implications in world politics.

Theological and religious thinking, however, can help to reframe debates on the role of culture in international politics in productive ways. This article has analyzed several specific theological views on multiculturalism in world politics, including religious pluralism, apologetics, and syncretism. Each of these perspectives, while differing significantly from the others, challenges the exclusivist views of religion that dominate popular understandings as well as persisting assumptions of International Relations. Each perspective also—like others before them—mirrors historical developments as well as trends in political philosophy.

Theological pluralism, for instance, has many resonances with liberalism, yet probes more deeply into the meaning of alternative systems of belief in ways that ultimately challenge liberalism's Enlightenment presuppositions. Apologetics, on the other hand, is one of many possible dialogical processes that are designed to overcome the problems associated with alterity, though it seeks to do so through a robust defense of belief and identity. Syncretist religious ethics, like much deconstructionist philosophy, points to the contingency and multiplicity of identity. Taking these approaches seriously may well resonate with aspects of the English School, and, I believe, certainly resonates with constructivist ontology. But more than asserting that the study of religion must be connected to any particular approach to International Relations, I argue that what is important is thinking through the implications of the theological conceptions outlined above. These encourage students of international politics to understand religion as evolving rather than reified. They also point to the necessity of thinking through the implications of religious and theological perspectives on culture as a means of enriching our understanding of the ethical possibilities apparent in world politics.

The student of international politics, conversely, should not ignore her traditional preoccupation with the problem of power in assessing the value of theological ethics. Highlighting power similarities and differentials, including whether religious practices reinforce or challenge dominant economic and political structures of power, is a contribution that students of politics can and should make to the study of religion. The recognition of power asymmetries is certainly not absent from religious debate: witness, for example, the very existence of something called liberation theology. The debate about the value and legitimacy of syncretism has also taken place largely in a context in which postcolonial religious thinkers are challenging well-organized and well-funded sites of traditional religious power.[64] Students of international politics can thus contribute to the study of religion by detailing, for example, the way in which it is difficult for either apologetical discourse or pluralist ethics to be enacted in situations exempt from unequal power differentials. Yet to oversimplify any of these trends in religious thought or reduce their possibility to that of power differentials would also be a mistake. Such a path would impose a teleology, rather than open our analyses to the contingency and ethical possibilities that these debates make apparent.

Students of international politics should look at the intersection between ethics and praxis in analyzing religious contributions to debates about multiculturalism, rather than understanding belief merely as dogma. In order to accomplish this, we need to explore further the connections between religious and philosophical conceptions of identity and multiculturalism. This definitely requires an interpretive stance, one that privileges not only the study of "society" and "rules," but also (and especially) their interaction with the varieties and inter-minglings of religious identities that are produced by both individuals and groups. Moreover, we need to incorporate both the relations of power prevalent in the world and the opportunities opened by differing religious stances when analyzing the possibilities of religious ethics. It is thus critical to reincorporate religious understandings of identity, dogma, and praxis into debates about the composition and possibilities of multiculturalism and political community in world politics.

Notes

I thank David Gitomer, Michael Loriaux, Bill Maurer, and Elora Shehabuddin for saving me from a number of potential errors and misconceptions across fields. I also thank two anonymous reviewers for their very helpful comments. Any remaining errors, of course, are mine.

1. Quoted in David Campbell, *National Deconstruction: Violence, Identity, and Justice in Bosnia* (Minneapolis: University of Minnesota Press, 1998), 1.

2. Jeffrey Goldberg, "The Education of a Holy Warrior," *New York Times Magazine,* 25 June 2000, 36.

3. Barbara Kingsolver, *The Poisonwood Bible* (New York: Harper-Collins, 1998), 26.

4. Orientalism, according to Edward Said's seminal work, is a Western academic tradition, a style of thought, and a discourse "by which European culture was able to manage—and even produce—the Orient politically, sociologically, militarily, ideologically, scientifically, and imaginatively during the post-Enlightenment period." See *Orientalism* (New York: Vintage Books, 1979), 3f. See also Fred R. Dallmayr, *Beyond Orientalism* (Notre Dame, IN: Notre Dame University Press, 1996) and Richard King, *Orientalism and Religion, Postcolonial Theory, India, and 'The Mystic East'* (London: Routledge, 1999).

5. This is of course an oversimplification of Marx's arguments about alienation. See, for example, Daniel Pals, *Seven Theories of Religion* (Oxford: Oxford University Press, 1996), 137–38.

6. Said, *Orientalism,* 61.

7. Tzvetan Todorov, *The Conquest of America: The Question of the Other* (New York: HarperCollins, 1992), 249.

8. Todorov thus questions the capacity of "perspectivalists," who assume the necessary plurality of truth, to commit to religious belief, a debatable position that this article treats later. See *The Conquest of America,* 189–90.

9. Charles Taylor with K. Anthony Appiah, Jürgen Habermas, Steven C. Rockefeller, Michael Walzer, and Susan Wolf, *Multiculturalism:*

Examining the Politics of Recognition, ed. Amy Gutman (Princeton, NJ: Princeton University Press, 1994).

10. Ibid. For sophisticated treatments of the debate in IR, see Nicholas Rengger, *Political Theory, Modernity, and Postmodernity: Beyond Enlightenment and Critique* (Oxford: Blackwell, 1995) and Chris Brown, *International Relations Theory: New Normative Approaches* (New York: Harvester Wheatsheaf, 1992).

11. William E. Connolly, "Pluralism, Multiculturalism, and the Nation-State: Rethinking the Connections," *Journal of Political Ideologies* 1, no. 1 (1996): 61. See also Campbell, *National Deconstruction,* 161.

12. Campbell, *National Deconstruction,* esp. chap. 6.

13. K. Anthony Appiah, "Identity, Authenticity, Survival: Multicultural Societies and Social Reproductions," in *Multiculturalism: Examining the Politics of Recognition,* 150.

14. Most students of religion who use these distinctions focus on the first three. See, for example, Harvard Indologist and theologian Diana Eck's *Encountering God: A Spiritual Journey from Bozeman to Banaras* (Boston: Beacon Press, 1994). Syncretism is much more contested as a legitimate category, especially among Christian theologians. Korean liberation theologian Chung Hyun-Kyung calls for a "survival liberation-centered syncretism." See, for example, *Struggle to Be the Sun Again, Introducing Asian Women's Theology* (Maryknoll, NY: Orbis Books, 1994).

15. Campbell, *National Deconstruction,* 213.

16. Tone Bringa quoted in ibid., 213.

17. Ibid., 208.

18. Goldberg, "The Education of a Holy Warrior," 34.

19. Ibid.

20. For example, Goldberg takes the instructors' distinction between *dar-al-Islam* (the Islamic world, or zone of peace) and *dar-al-harb* (the rest of the world) as a sinister and simplistic justification for ongoing military campaigns against the West. Yet Sohail Hashmi points out that this type of rigid bifurcation misreads recent Muslim thinking and takes no account of the multiple interpretations within Islamic theology. See Goldberg, "The Education of a Holy Warrior," 64, and Sohail H. Hashmi, "Interpreting the Islamic Ethics of War and Peace," in *The Ethics of War and Peace: Religious and Secular Perspectives,* ed. Terry Nardin (Princeton, NJ: Princeton University Press, 1996), 158–59.

21. Goldberg, "The Education of a Holy Warrior," 70. This is of course a reference to the argument made infamous by Samuel Huntington, "Clash of Civilizations?" *Foreign Affairs* 72, no. 3 (1993): 22–47. John Esposito asserts that such attitudes are an example of transference of the fear of communism during the Cold War to the fear of Islam today. See *The Islamic Threat, Myth or Reality?* 3d ed. (Oxford: Oxford University Press, 1999), 218.

22. African Traditional Religion (ATR) is a composite name for the "host" religions of Africa (non-Islamic and non-Christian). ATR, "Christianity, and Islam all vigorously claim the allegiance of Africans, while African Traditional Religion continues to be a major source of meaning and receives formal acknowledgment as a living religion." See Mercy Amba Oduyoye, *Daughters of Anowa: African Women and Patriarchy* (Maryknoll, NY: Orbis Books, 1995), 110, and Emmanuel Martey, *African Theology: Inculturation and Liberation* (Maryknoll, NY: Orbis Books, 1993), 39.

23. Chung sees these categories as applying primarily to "the encounter between Christianity and other religions and cultures of the world." See *The Wisdom of Mothers Knows No Boundaries,* Women's Perspectives: Gospel and Cultures, pamphlet 14 (Geneva: World Council of Churches Publications, 1996), 30. Here I apply it more broadly, following the popularization of the typology in interreligious dialogue.

24. See, for instance, Todorov, *The Conquest of America* and Théo Tschuy, *Ethnic Conflict and Religion* (Geneva: World Council of Churches Publications, 1997).

25. Goldberg, "The Education of a Holy Warrior," 34. However, this view is contested. For example, we might see the evidence that many Muslims from Central Asia study in Pakistani and Egyptian madrasas as a definite security threat to the West, as does Goldberg, but another view might understand it as symptomatic of dispersed communities or diasporic practices. See, for example, Pnina Werbner, "The Place Which Is Diaspora: Citizenship, Religion and Gender in the Making of Chaordic Transnationalism," *Journal of Ethnic and Migration Studies,* vol. 28, no. 1: 119–133 (January 2002).

26. Kingsolver, *The Poisonwood Bible.*

27. See *Guidelines on Dialogue with People of Living Faiths and Ideologies* (Geneva: World Council of Churches Publications, 1993), 22.

28. S. Wesley Ariarajah, *Gospel and Culture: An Ongoing Discussion within the Ecumenical Movement* (Geneva: World Council of Churches Publications, 1998), 7.

29. Ariarajah, *Gospel and Culture,* 4–7, 14–15.

30. Quoted in Raghavan Iyer, ed., *The Essential Writings of Mahatma Gandhi* (Delhi: Oxford University Press, 1990), 149. See also Mohandas Karamchand Gandhi, "Extracts from My Experiments with Truth," in *Christianity Through Non-Christian Eyes,* ed. Paul J. Griffiths (Maryknoll, NY: Orbis Books, 1996).

31. In the postwar years, the World Council of Churches (WCC) attempted to "define the right attitude of the [Christian] church to other religious traditions," initiating a study on "The Word of God and Men of Other Faiths." From this study came the idea that the WCC should "develop the concept of 'dialogue' as the primary mode of relating to people of other faith traditions." See *Guidelines on Dialogue,* v.

32. *Guidelines on Dialogue,* 12.

33. Chung, *The Wisdom of Mothers Knows No Boundaries,* 30.

34. David Gitomer, "Tell Me One Thing, Krishna: A Personal Reflection on Catholic Faith and Religious Pluralism," in *As Leaven for the World: Catholic Reflections on Faith, Vocation, and the Intellectual Life,* ed. Thomas Landy (Franklin, WI: Sheed and Ward, 2001).

35. Ibid.

36. *Guidelines on Dialogue,* 13.

37. Ibid., 11.

38. Emerito Nacpil, quoted in Ariarajah, *Gospel and Culture,* 20.

39. Griffiths states that his conception of apologetics "is directed against an underlying scholarly orthodoxy on the goals and functions of inter-religious dialogue. This orthodoxy suggests that understanding is the only legitimate goal; that judgement and criticism of religious beliefs or practices other than those of one's own community is always inappropriate; and that an active defense of the truth of those beliefs and practices to which one's community appears committed is always to be shunned." See *An Apology for Apologetics: A Study in the Logic of Interreligious Dialogue* (Maryknoll, NY: Orbis Books, 1991), xi.

40. Ibid., 49.

41. Apologetics should be an occasional, not systematic, practice of religious spokespersons and occur only when doctrines are challenged from the outside; it should not threaten violence, it should not be part of a "program of military, economic, or cultural imperialism," and it should not be based on an "assumption of ethnic or cultural superiority." See ibid., 78.

42. Ibid., 79.

43. Ibid., 62.

44. Ibid., xi.

45. Scholars of religion as well as anthropologists debate the degree to which this fact disrupts the Orientalist argument of Said. For an excellent treatment of this issue, see Richard King, *Orientalism and Religion.*

46. Jean-Marc Ela, *African Cry* (Maryknoll, NY: Orbis Books, 1986). The book was originally published as *Le Cri de l'Homme Africain* (Paris: Librarie-Editions L'Harmattan, 1980).

47. Emmanuel Martey, in *African Theology: Inculturation and Liberation,* argues that both function symbiotically.

48. *Guidelines on Dialogue,* 14.

49. Ibid., 14–15.

50. Quoted in Jeffrey Carlson, "Crossan's Jesus and Christian Identity," in *Jesus and Faith: A Conversation on the Work of John Dominic Crossan,* eds. Jeffrey Carlson and Robert A. Ludwig (Maryknoll, NY: Orbis Books, 1994), 35–36. The Catholic Church's recent statements on the superiority of Catholicism would also seem to harm such "real ecumenism," however.

51. Ariarajah, *Gospel and Culture*, x-xi, 47–50.
52. Chung, *The Wisdom of Mothers Knows No Boundaries*, 30–31.
53. It is also a reality of life in a world in which migration levels are continually on the rise. For example, the ethnic composition of the population of Orange County, California, has shifted tremendously in the past two decades, and the student body of the University of California–Irvine reflects this shift. See "Higher Education in Orange County," *Orange County Profiles* (Fullerton, CA: Center for Demographic Research, CSU, 1998). A number of students in my international relations course testified to the hybridity of their own religious identities, stemming from both the colonial experiences of their parents (primarily in Asia) and the experience of migration to the United States: One was a Muslim educated in Catholic schools, another vacillated between Buddhism and Christianity, another's family was "born again" but retained shamanist practices, etc.
54. Chung, *The Wisdom of Mothers Knows No Boundaries*, 28–29.
55. Carlson, "Crossan's Jesus and Christian Identity," 38.
56. Both should be distinguished from the debate in anthropology about syncretism as a type of biogenetic necessity. Neither the notion that religious identity is inevitably a product of the historical interpenetration of identities nor the ethical stance that legitimizes culling what are deemed "positive" religious and cultural beliefs and practices necessarily imply any biological understanding of hybridity. On this debate in anthropology, see William Maurer, *Recharting the Caribbean* (Ann Arbor: University of Michigan Press, 1997), 10–11, and Robert Young, *Colonial Desire: Hybridity in Theory, Culture, and Race* (London: Routledge, 1995).
57. Other anthropologists criticize concepts of hybridity and syncretism for presupposing an underlying, "essential" version of religion. For an excellent overview of this debate, see Charles Stewart, "Syncretism and Its Synonyms: Reflections on Cultural Mixture," *Diacritics* 29, no. 3 (1999): 40–62.
58. Olivier Roy, "Le réseau des madrasas," *Le Monde*, 7 May, 2002.
59. Chung, *The Wisdom of Mothers Knows No Boundaries*, 33.
60. Carlson, "Crossan's Jesus and Christian Identity," 42.
61. Ibid.
62. Chung, *Struggle to Be the Sun Again* and Carlson, 42.
63. See Jean Bethke Elshtain, *Meditations on Modern Political Thought* (New York: Praeger, 1986); Jean Bethke Elshtain, *Augustine and the Limits of Politics* (Notre Dame, IN: University of Notre Dame Press, 1995); Michael Loriaux, "The Realists and Saint Augustine: Skepticism, Psychology, and Moral Action in International Relations Thought," *International Studies Quarterly* 36, no. 4 (1992): 401–20; Richard Falk, *Explorations at the Edge of Time* (Philadelphia: Temple University Press, 1992); William E. Connolly, *Why I Am Not a Secularist* (Minneapolis: University of Minnesota Press, 1999); and

William E. Connolly, *The Augustinian Imperative: A Reflection on the Politics of Morality* (Newberry Park, CA: Sage, 1993).

64. See, for example, Talal Asad, *Geneologies of Religion: Discipline and Reasons of Power in Christianity and Islam* (Baltimore, MD: The Johns Hopkins University Press, 1993) and Asad, "Modern Power and the Reconfiguration of Religious Traditions," *Stanford Humanities Review* [http://www.stanford.edu/group/SHR/5-1/text/asad.html] (2 December 2000).

CHAPTER 3

TOWARD AN INTERNATIONAL POLITICAL THEOLOGY

Vendulka Kubálková

Enlightenment publicists and philosophers wielded none of the torture instruments of the Catholic inquisitions, nor did they burn dissenters under some Protestant dispensation. But when it came to religion in all its aspects, they strangled free inquiry just as effectively by the commanding force of the fashion they imposed.[1]

—*Edward Luttwak*

C an International Relations (IR) as a discipline contribute to the study of the worldwide resurgence of religion? This is not an idle question, because the international context within which this resurgence is taking place is the primary domain of IR expertise.

I answer this question in the affirmative. In this paper I outline the foundation of what I call International Political Theology (IPT). Its acronym, IPT, quite consciously rhymes with IPE (International Political Economy), the earlier subfield of IR, at first also difficult to imagine or conceive. IPE was intended at the time of its conception to respond to the neglect of economic factors in the IR discipline. IPT similarly seeks to correct another systematic omission in IR: the neglect of the role of religions, culture, ideas, or ideologies in "social scientific" accounts of world affairs.[2]

The parallel with the earlier creation of IPE is very apposite. In the case of IPE it was the fact that suddenly, to paraphrase Robert Gilpin's famous dictum, it was not possible to separate the pursuit of power (as studied in the discipline of IR) and the pursuit of wealth (left out of the IR discipline to the students of economics). Similarly now, as Mark Juergensmeyer put it,

> What appeared to be an anomaly when the Islamic revolution in Iran challenged the supremacy of Western culture and its secular politics in 1979 has become a major theme in international politics in the 1990s. The new world order that is replacing the bipolar powers of the old Cold War is characterized not only by the rise of new economic forces, a crumbling of old empires, and the discrediting of communism, but also by the resurgence of parochial identities based on ethnic and religious allegiances.[3]

I use the term "theology" in the name of the framework deliberately to shock and also to indicate the need to bring to an end what Luttwak has called

> a learned repugnance to contend intellectually with all that is religion ... [based on the] mistaken Enlightenment prediction that the progress of knowledge and the influence of religion were mutually exclusive.[4]

My use of the term "theology" does not go as far as political theologians' claim that political theorizing should have its ultimate ground in religious revelations, although their position is compatible with my framework. Nonetheless I have no qualms about using the term. Theology was once synonymous with philosophy and science. Following the understanding of sociologists of religion, I take *theos* not in its common secular meaning as erroneous beliefs in supernatural extraterrestrial existence, but I take "theology" and *theos* to refer to the systematic study of discourses and the relations among them concerning world affairs that search for—or claim to have found—a response, transcendental or secular, to the human need for meaning. My purpose is to find a way of bringing the study of religion and IR together—possibly for the first time—in a manner that would minimize their distortion and facilitate their understanding. IPT can accommodate in one framework the pioneering but so far fragmented micro and macro attempts to come to grips with the significance of religion in IR.[5]

I vividly recall the late Susan Strange's exhortation that IPE must be constructed from first principles rather than concepts fit together from its apparently constituent disciplines. I would like to take that exhortation to heart. Within positivist frameworks, however, the "first principles" approach simply cannot be applied without emasculating the essence of religion. Thus for IPT I have had to draw the blueprint using a nonpositivist ontology of the rule-oriented constructivist framework first introduced by Nicholas Onuf in 1989.[6] The constructivism that I use in this paper, however, ought not to be confused with the positivist-friendly forms of constructivism, frequently referred to as soft constructivism, co-opted by the US IR mainstream as one of its two or three main theoretical approaches.[7] As Steve Smith puts it, "the radical possibilities promised by social constructivism" have been "hijacked by a mainstream," and the dominant, now increasingly popular form of constructivism of Alexander Wendt, Peter Katzenstein, etc., have been assigned "an unthreatening role of an adjunct explanation for those things that the positivist mainstream finds difficult to explain."[8]

The framework I use is different. It eschews the constraints placed on IR theorizing by positivism and "materialism" as well as by the treatment of the state as a unitary and the main actor in IR (of all these, the mainstream, or soft, constructivists reject only materialism but share positivism and state-centrism). To positivists, religion stands in sharp contrast to reason, and is not to be taken seriously. Religion is either a "private affair of individuals," a domestic issue of states, or it is liminal; in any event, it eludes the territorial boundaries characteristic of state-centric IR studies. The mainstream or, soft, constructivists are prepared to consider ideas, including religious ideas, and changing identities and state interests but subordinate them to the rational choice theory.[9] Within these positivist, materialist, and state-centric constraints, the mainstream by definition cannot theorize religion in IR. Conversely, rule-oriented constructivism is not positivist; it regards IR as a very important slice of social reality without being state-centric, or to the exclusion of all else. Rule-oriented constructivism corrects the materialist cast of IR without lapsing into the opposite extreme, "idealism," as do some mainstream constructivists (e.g., Wendt, who claims to have substituted structural realism with structural idealism).[10]

Table 3.1 indicates the different "levels" at which religions have become more visible. The levels refer to different segments into which sociopolitical reality has been carved out by Western (modern) academia, to be stored and cultivated in different departments, situated on different floors, and in different buildings of the Western social science edifice. In the contemporary world, there is apparently an increasing visibility of religion on all of these levels, and their connectivity becomes ever more important: from the greater religiosity and spirituality of individuals (in the "private" domain, which is excluded by social scientists altogether) to a greater role in the "domestic" setting and to the international, indeed transnational/global context. Without the possibility of moving between the different levels for an account of their interrelated relevance, large pieces of the puzzle will be missing. Rule-oriented constructivism can easily move amongst these levels.

I divide this chapter into four sections. First, by way of introduction, I discuss a rather unlikely topic, the "third debate" in IR and its repercussions for the study of religion. Second, I discuss the basic ontological characteristics of religion. Third, I outline rule-oriented constructivism and the place of religions and religion within this framework. Fourth, I conclude with a sketch of some issues that the framework enables us to address in developing IPT.

This paper is a pilot of a book of the same name. It is important to stress that I have written it with IR students in mind, not sociologists of religion, anthropologists, or historians of culture, although I will try to show how the framework that I propose makes their work accessible to IR students. The limited space does not permit me to do more than lay out the IPT framework. The study of religion in IR, in my view, has to start by finding an analytical space for it, on equal footing with secular discourses, beliefs, ideologies, and positivist theories. The main purpose of this article is to identify this analytical space.

The "Third Debate" and Religion: The Postmodernist John the Baptist

History, it seems, has repeated itself once again. To paraphrase Herbert Marcuse's famous words: that which was supposed to be subsequent has become coexistent. That which was supposed to transpire in orderly stages got somehow stuck coexisting together, as absurdly as night coexisting with day. Now it seems, we have another unlikely threesome stuck together: premodern, modern, and postmodern, or rather, their contemporary spokespersons confronting IR scholarship. Ironically, the "third debate" inadvertently primed the modern IR scholars for an encounter with world religions, the premodern. The postmodernist scholar stands in for John the Baptist, as a Christian theologian might say.

There has been, of course, nothing very religious about either of the main protagonists of the third debate. This involved, on one side, the positivist camp, and on the other, anyone to whom the "post" label

Table 3.1   Religions in Social Relations

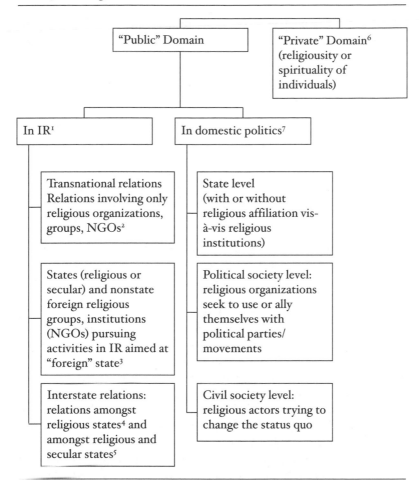

"Public" Domain	"Private" Domain[6] (religiosity or spirituality of individuals)

In IR[1]	In domestic politics[7]
Transnational relations Relations involving only religious organizations, groups, NGOs[2]	State level (with or without religious affiliation vis-à-vis religious institutions)
States (religious or secular) and nonstate foreign religious groups, institutions (NGOs) pursuing activities in IR aimed at "foreign" state[3]	Political society level: religious organizations seek to use or ally themselves with political parties/ movements
Interstate relations: relations amongst religious states[4] and amongst religious and secular states[5]	Civil society level: religious actors trying to change the status quo

Notes: [1]Recently began to be studied; for example, Rudolph and Piscatori, *Transnational Religion.*
[2]For example, Catholicism; Latin American Catholicism and Protestantism; liberation Catholics of the left and Evangelicals of the right in Latin America; Vatican Council II; Latin American Episcopal Conference (CELAM); Catholic World Youth Congresses; relations of religions and religious groups in, for instance, Lebanon, Egypt, Iran, Afghanistan; cooperation or emulation.
[3]For example, West African Sufis as Muslim missionaries in Africa; Western involvement with post-Communist churches, European and American philanthropic organizations and German episcopate in East Central Europe.
[4]For example, Iran, Lebanon, Iraq, Saudi Arabia; pan-Arabist powers versus their opponents in the Middle East and Western involvement.
[5]For example, U.S. versus Iran; the West in the Middle East.
[6]Enhanced, for example, by the Vatican II shift from *libertas ecclasiae* to *libertas personae.*
[7]Traditionally studied in sociology/political science.

might stick. The protagonists in the third debate—the modern secular IR scholars and their postmodernist critics—reject/ignore religion. As James Kurth has observed:

> The post-modernist perspective can include "spiritual-experiences," but only those without religious (in the original sense of "binding") constraints. The New-Age movement can be interpreted as the ideal-typical-post-modernist spiritual expression. Post-modernists are also drawn to superficial, Americanized versions of certain Eastern religions, especially "lite" Buddhism and Hinduism. They are also drawn to an Americanized version of nature-worship, a sort of neo-paganism. For the most part, however, post-modernism is largely hyper-secularism, and it joins modernism in predicting, and eagerly anticipating, the disappearance of traditional religions.[11]

The "post" critics of the mainstream have succeeded in unsettling their mainstream colleagues by their seemingly strange and outlandish ways. We ought not to forget, however, the scientific rigor to which the IR discipline in the United Sstates is still committed and which from the vantage point of the UK and Europe may not be as obvious as to those of us working in the United Sstates. The IR mainstream insists on the strict "use of evidence to adjudicate between truth claims,"[12] and assigns theories that are not "testable" to the "margin of the field" because it is "impossible to evaluate their research program."[13] The postmodernist discourse of course has never met the positivist standard and certainly in this regard has been closer to some premodern ideas. We tend to forget just how brief the modern period in the history of ideas has been. Until only two hundred years ago or so, religions provided the dominant mode of thought, and thus many ideas even today have their roots in religion.

Be that as it may, IR scholars who followed the meandering path of the third debate have prepared for the emergence of religions as a subject of study by familiarizing themselves with certain concepts that postmodernist and religious discourse share. This is largely unacknowledged by postmodernist scholars. As far as I am aware, only some postmodernist feminists openly acknowledge the debt they owe to the religious traditions on which they draw.[14] Let me mention some examples of what issues have been raised through the postmodernist discourse, not always realizing that it also plays an important part in the construction of religion.

The entire shift of attention to the "inside," the "insider's perspective," to feeling and "emotional identification" that we recognize in some postmodernist writings, has religious antecedents. Here we un-

doubtedly trace the influences of romanticism: the movement originating in the late eighteenth century as a revolt against modernity's rationalism and based on medieval emotionalism. In philosophy and in
art, romanticism focuses on the irrational and the nonrational, and on
feeling rather than thought. For example, originally intended to make
believers feel the pain of Jesus, emotionalism charged the concept and
command of love (*agape*) with emotional force. This has served in turn
as a source of the emotional force used by many secular ideologies, for
example, nationalism. The stress on identity, the insider's perspective,
and the inside/outside distinction, prominent in the work of many
postmodernist writers, has always been central to religious thought
and practice.

Phenomenology, another source of inspiration for postmodernist
scholars, also owes much to religious influences, particularly in regard
to the shift from the focus on outward appearances to the attention to
consciousness, the experience of the body, intuition, perspective, and
engagement requiring empathy, along with careful linguistic textual
and historical studies. One might even say that phenomenologists listen to the inner "voices" coming from deep within. This idea derives
from the preoccupation of religions with inner meaning. Religion and
art are prime examples of human attempts to find meaning and value
in life. A concern for "emancipation," drawing on the engagement of
the Frankfurt School with the work of Sigmund Freud, also resides in
large measure in the mind, in knowing and understanding the human
predicament as a precondition for, if not the realization of, emancipation itself.

Hermeneutics, named after the Greek god of communication, Her-
mes, adds interpreting and reflecting as approaches to knowledge.
Hermeneutics, not surprisingly, originated in schools of theology
where its methods were developed for the interpretation of sacred
texts. At the hands of scholars like Paul Ricoeur, hermeneutics were
extended to the search for the sacred in "texts," the sense of which was
allegedly lost through the modernist notion of the human being as the
center of the universe. Entering a plurality of "worlds," Ricoeur argued, helps people to become decentered. Ricoeur's reliance on
metaphor—the weaving together of fragments of identity stressed by
some feminists—parallels religious practices.

Ricoeur's student Jacques Derrida used his teacher's concept of
play to show that words interact so that meaning is never fixed. Like
theologians, postmodernists "tell stories," rejecting the modernist ob-
session with "theory" and its endless strictly modernist pursuit. Derrida aims at destroying and deconstructing modernist secularized

texts, which he terms "logocentric," thereby suggesting that the words and ideas of such texts always point to an external reality. It is often overlooked that the goal of Derrida's deconstruction was to create a space for attention also to sacred texts. Derrida believed that after the deconstruction of the foundations of Western secular philosophy, other cultures and religions would be considered more relevant by Westerners.[15]

Finally, the third debate also addressed the problem of "incommensurability," the notion that theoretical approaches refer to different realities, an even more intractable problem of the antifoundationalist view that there is no reality, but only different interpretations of a text in the readers' minds. The consequence of Francois Lyotard's famous antifoundationalist "incredulity toward metanarratives" is the belief that there are no foundations, outside any individual theory, that could serve as a neutral arbiter between competing theoretical accounts.[16] Postmodernism—like religion—questions the notion of reality presented by positivist IR texts.

It is possible, of course, to be a romantic/phenomenologist/ hermeneuticist without being religious. One can live without meditation, prayer, or any of the disciplines designed for the research of the self and its sense of cosmic connection. To many, the limits that modern rationalism imposes on our modes of knowledge are entirely acceptable. The many attempts to compensate for these limits and to fill in this void are not. The religious concern for the soul, as the next section will argue, runs a lot deeper, and neither modernity nor the postmodernists have managed to supplant it.

The Ontology of Religions

I start with the discussion of ontology for two reasons. First, the utility of rule-oriented constructivism as the basis of IPT rests on its ontological nature. The constructivist framework is conceived so broadly that it can accommodate otherwise mutually exclusive ontological claims, as for example, those of religion and positivist social science. Second, I make a distinction between religion and religions. An inattention to the ontology of religion produced the confusion of religion as an alternative way of looking at the world on one hand, and religions as materially existing institutions organized for the pursuit of "religion" on the other.

The meaning of "religion" has been, for analytical purposes, lost. Religions, reduced to institutions, have become as easy to deal with as any other nonstate sociopolitical institutions. In the international context, religions have either been treated as one amongst many epistemic communities, or as nongovernmental or transnational organizations.[17] Religions have then been found to fall into one of two categories: either good or bad. They have been categorized either as elements of transnational civil society,[18] as elements defining larger, international, or transnational entities such as civilizations,[19] or, if their adherents engage in violence, as terrorist groups outside international law. Social scientists—certainly in American IR—have treated religious organizations as acting in accordance with rational choice theory. This simplification has resulted in a profound misunderstanding of the strength of passion that may imbue religious organizations and the various ways in which this passion may compensate for a lack of material capability, the latter being another pillar of American IR thought. This has produced some surprises when on occasion the religious organizations act "irrationally" or "nonrationally" and with a force at odds with their material strength, thus confounding positivist expectations. To correct this simplification, I make the distinction between "religion" and "religions," the former as a precondition for the understanding of the latter and the latter nonreducible to the former.

It is infeasible to discuss religion in IR without appreciating that the difference in religious and secular thought is ontological, that is, in what in each of them "counts for real."[20] All spiritual communities, all religions, Western and Eastern, share a distinction between ordinary and transcendental reality. This difference in ontology leads to epistemological and methodological differences between religious and secular ways of looking at the world. Attempting to fit religious experience into a positivist framework can only emasculate it, caricature it, distort its meaning, and underestimate its strength. A serious consideration of the role of religion in IR must start with the exploration of the ontological foundation of religious discourse.

According to most religious thought, the structure of the ordinary world, with its assumptions of separate and distinct cause and effect, the spatial arrangement of objects, and the linearity of time, does not exhaust reality. Most religions share the idea that the world as revealed to the temporal senses is only one item in a hierarchy of being. Religious thinkers argue that secular humanists see only a small part of the picture when they view nature as impersonal and as lacking a cosmic design capable of explaining and justifying human experience. Humans, in this view, are a unique link between the material world and the larger cosmos with its powerful forces that shape and structure reality. Human experience is seen as only one dimension of a multidimensional reality that is ordered by design rather than chance. This larger reality is greater than the limited reality of human experience, but is impervious to ordinary sensory perception. This external world and the ordinary world of sense and thought, most religions insist, are intertwined.[21]

All major religions also share a strikingly similar view of transcendental reality; sociologists of religion argue that creating or constructing gods is one of the human universals, a practice going back at least 14,000 years to the ancient world of the Middle East.[22] Theologians, of course, deny that God (or the gods) are human constructions. They might accept that the human being is *homo sapiens* but they would contend that he or she is also *homo religiosus,* a species in need of finding a system of beliefs essential to the self-definition of the believer, what we now call "identity."[23] All religions are organized on the basis of beliefs that are fundamental not only to reality, but even more importantly, to human identity.

The Western "faith" in secularism and anthropocentrism is unprecedented in human existence. Liberal secularism, scholars agree, is not something that comes easily and naturally to us and has to be consciously taught and promoted. This tension is illustrated in the continuous efforts to substitute nontheistic and secular beliefs for religion. Forms of paganism, nationalism, and other ideologies have played societal roles comparable to that of religions, at least in terms of their outward manifestations and the strength of their beliefs. Particularly after its demise, Soviet Marxism-Leninism is recognized as a secular religion; humanism has been described as a religion without God, and liberalism as Christianity without God.

The reality named "God," however, is different from other kinds of *theos.* Theologians agree that the reality of God surpasses human comprehension. God, philosophers have argued, is the uncaused cause, the "not effect of a cause." As such, God is not "out there," waiting to be discovered or observed by the processes of rational thought and scientific observation. Most religions, and certainly the Jewish, Muslim, and Christian, agree that it is impossible to describe the transcendent reality of God in normal conceptual language. (There is, by the way, an ironic parallel with the postmodernist dislike of modern logocentric meta-narratives.) For religions, of course, the transcendental meta-reality does exist, though it cannot be expressed in either ordinary or scholarly language, let alone subjected to social scientific "tests." The meaning ascribed to the reality of God is fixed nonetheless by social conventions and can be expressed in everyday language. This rendition is imperfect and requires reflection, interpretation, illumination, repetition, metaphor, and ritualization. Thus Christianity,

Islam, and Judaism derive *divine* meaning from stories (sacred texts), which are constantly read and reread and subjected to exegesis.

The ongoing representation of what eludes representation is required to provide the believer with a map of reality. The map orients the individual and fixes his or her identity in ontological terms. The identity of the believers can be lost only with the loss of faith. Many psychoanalysts and psychologists agree that modernity's malaise and the loss of identity that attends it come from its secular nature and the absence of any substitute for religion. According to Erik Erikson, who popularized the term "identity crisis," for most people "having identity" is an important part of healthy life, and "losing identity" is a signal of the onset of serious psychological, psychiatric, and general health problems.[24] Religious belief and the identity it provides binds the believer to action, to the making of sacrifices, even to the willingness to sacrifice one's life for the sake of belief. Believers who fail in this may well feel extreme remorse.

Postmodernist antifoundationalism cannot be reconciled with the foundationalist claims of the positivists. Similarly, there is no method of resolving the conflict between the transcendental and the secular, on ontological or epistemological grounds. There is much more at stake here than disputes among communities that have different and mutually exclusive visions of the good life. Both ontologies insist on using the term "rational," but both define rationality by controlling the criteria of evidence and rules of inference assigned to its observations and concepts. Postmodernist and modernist scholars reject the possibility that there might be evidence of divine intent and the suggestion that spiritual events or spiritual beings such as angels might be real. Religious believers view this *prima facie* rejection as secular irrationality.

In the believer's view, the origins of religious experience are beyond the realm of human choice, let alone the "rational choice" around which most social science discourse revolves. The freedom of conscience that is given such prominence in liberal thought means in religious discourse the exact opposite. At the most fundamental levels of a believer's existence, it means following the dictates (not choices) of conscience, for conscience has no choice but to follow belief.[25] Historical narrative, myth, moral discourse, blessing, cursing, confessing, adoring, metaphor, symbol, analogy, parable loom large in religious discourse, as it accommodates both a transcendent reality (not confined to sensory experience) and the secular, the "divine realm of positivist social science." There is nothing in the positivist bag of tricks to match this achievement, not that positivists have ever tried or would ever consider it worth trying. The failure to negotiate the problems of incommensurability successfully is not an affliction only of positivists. As Fred Frohock has argued:

> Liberalism . . . is not a suitable political philosophy to resolve or even manage disagreements over the meaning of human experience at the levels sometimes found in the spiritual-secular disputes.[26]

Thus I now turn to rule-oriented constructivism in search of a framework that can resolve this incommensurability for social science and IR.

From the Social Science "Turn" to the Linguistic "Turn" to Constructivism

The incommensurability of the positivist and religious understandings of the world is indeed profound. In search of a way to conceptualize *meaning,* we have to reach beyond those modern ontologies and epistemologies that have deprived us, in the name of the pursuit of social science, of intellectual access to a large part of human experience. To understand meaning, we have to understand human action and language and reason and rationality anew. We, scholars of social theory and IR, have to retrace the path we have taken. We have to go back at least to the point at which modern social science took a wrong turn.

Following the path of modern knowledge and particularly taking the turn of positivist epistemology, we reach a point where we are unable to reveal some of the most fundamental features of human existence. The understanding of speech, intersubjectivity, and action cannot be grasped through the mechanical separation of subject and object, agent and structure, free will and determinism. A U-turn is required; we need to abandon the narrow semantic understanding of language as a mirror of reality, whose sole purpose is to reflect accurately and record not only things but also *actions.* Meaning cannot be found in mirror reflections alone.

The alternative path is a long one. It takes us through some distinguished intellectual territory. There we find Aristotle and the recognition of man as a political animal endowed with *speech,* rather than just the *voice* that animals possess. Speech enables people to share meanings and to discuss their judgments on what is good and bad, just or unjust. Along this other path we find we must revisit the concept of praxis as well, and the unity of theory and practice as Marx described it. Then we are on the way to an understanding of the world of human beings as not given or natural, but as "created" through their actions.

We find that this path leads beside and arguably beyond empiricism, naturalism, and structuralism; beside and arguably beyond the utilitarian, motivational account of action; beside and arguably beyond the imputation-based model of antecedent causes and consequent effects. We find an equally distinguished scholarly heritage that appreciates the "passions," and how they may, and often do, override self-interest and self-preservation. We discover that the explanation of an action depends on the context in which the action takes place, and that this long and distinguished alternative path culminates in the linguistic "turn."

Rule-Oriented Constructivism and Religion

There are obviously different ways to construct IPT. Different stops can be made along the alternative path I have just sketched. In my construction, I rely on the work of Nicholas Onuf. He is an American IR/social theorist who addresses the American IR/social theory scholarship he knows most intimately. His constructivist framework has the kind and degree of rigor without which, in North America, nobody gets a hearing. Onuf's framework is secular but it inadvertently creates a large space for the appreciation of religious experience too. Although it is called "rule-oriented," it is in fact an anthropology of society, showing how rules influence the nonlinguistic aspects of human existence as well.

Rule-oriented constructivism claims the ability to provide a framework for all social theory because its ontology anatomizes the real social world at its most basic level. It articulates human universals, like the ability to use language and—radically important for my present discussion—the ability to reason. Rule-oriented constructivism's ontology is the common thread in the ever-changing range of social activities in which people engage, shaping the world and in turn being shaped by it. Rule-oriented constructivism points to words, speech acts, and rules as the key ontological elements of human interaction and of the human view of the world. With words, people obliterate the divide between "is" statements and "ought" statements so dear to the positivists. With words, people move effortlessly back and forth across this divide. Rule-oriented constructivism is a "way of studying social relations," a "system of concepts and propositions." It states that a tripartite typology of rules permeates the life of society. As Onuf explains:

> People make sense of their situation through conjecture and ceremony (assertive rules), confront their adversaries by using techniques

of destruction (directives), and provide for their needs by hunting and
gathering (commissive rules).[27]

Not only do speech acts and rules take assertive, directive, and commissive forms, but nonlinguistic aspects of society based on this or
that type of rules display distinct characteristics.

This is where I come to the key thesis of my paper. As I will show,
religions are a possible manifestation of assertive rules that we have
tended to dismiss as nonmodern, primitive, and nonrational, if not irrational. The positivist preoccupation with analytic-deductive methods has become the only way many of us, certainly the rational choice
theorists in the United States, think about the way we think. Only the
rational-instrumental pattern of thought, of speaking, can then be regarded as "rational."[28] Most people on this planet, however, by these
standards of Western culture, do not think at all if thinking means only
the rational-instrumental pattern of thought.

In the following sections, I will try to show how much even in Western society we depend on linguistic and nonlinguistic forms derived
from these prescientific assertive rules. I will also try to show that,
given a choice amongst assertive rules, the ones with a strong emotional association might win even if "rational choice" would dictate
otherwise. Here, there is ample space for appreciating the role of emotions generated by religion as a source of one of the most powerful
human passions. It is within a social framework conceived along these
lines that it is possible to theorize religion and IR side by side, the passion alongside the rational-instrumental reasoning. I divide the rest of
this section into two parts in order to locate, first, *religions* and then
religion within this constructivist framework.

Constructivism and Religions
as Social Constructions

It should not be too difficult to accept the argument that religions as
institutions have been socially constructed, although to a design that
believers would claim has been revealed. There is a growing body of literature addressing the organization of churches and religions, their
various relations to state and society and to each other. Often the discussion of religion and IR does not advance beyond seeing religions as
yet another form of organizations—national, if they coincide with the
state boundaries; international, if several states are implicated;
transnational, if their coincidence with states is difficult to find or explicitly rejected.

Constructivism clarifies these distinctions whilst going beyond this fairly narrowly cast concern for religion in IR. The social arrangement consistent with religion (based on assertive rules) has been that of informal networks and associations, stressing the status of priests and granting them significant prestige. It is this form that most religions take if developing spontaneously "from below."[29] The politicization of religion, however, has introduced "alien" elements of wealth and power compatible with directive or commissive rules. The intrusion of these factors usually meets with fierce opposition, from within the religion or from outside, as borne out by the entire historical experience of the Reformation or of Protestantism versus Catholicism since the time of the Reformation, in general or in specific parts of the world, notably in Latin America.[30] There is also a considerable literature concentrating on the prestige of religious figures and their ability to facilitate or mediate international conflict.[31]

Constructivism draws our attention to a danger of sliding into state-centrism, either by connecting religions and states too closely or by seeing civilizations as jigsaw puzzles composed of states of the same religious cast.[32] Similarly, there is the opposite danger of seeing religions and states as totally separate. For example, Juergensmeyer simplifies the issue when he argues that for understanding the world today it is necessary to see two interacting and competing frameworks of social order: secular nationalism (allied with the nation-state) and religion (allied with large ethnic communities).[33] There is no way of a priori generalizing, and only a careful examination of rules and their interplay will reveal the nature of these relations.

Much of the contemporary writing on religion in IR falls somewhere into this category. It is, however, the next topic that holds the key to overcoming the divide that separates faith and reason and that places religions into their IR context.

Constructivism, Human Mind, and Religion

By "religion," in constructivist terms, I understand:

1. a system of rules (mainly instruction rules) and related practices, which act to
2. explain the meaning of existence, including identity, ideas about self, and one's position in the world,
3. thus motivating and guiding the behavior of those who accept the validity of these rules on faith and who internalize them fully.

Unlike some interpretations of religion, my definition deliberately omits any direct reference to a divine being, although its existence can be postulated without contradicting the definition. Nor do I include such elements as a specific type of organization developed by religion, viz., its symbols and rituals, for all of these are subsumed in the "related practices" and can be handled within the constructivist framework, as social institutions. I also omit a reference to a divine being so as not to exclude secular discourses and ideologies, which can display all the overt indicators of religion, including emotional efficacy. Religion and its organizations have, after all, perfected a number of features that different ideologies or nationalisms have successfully copied.

I have already referred to consciousness as recognized rules and practices that have been acted upon in the past and have become internalized. This definition is consistent with Adda Bozeman's view of culture and civilization as encompassing those values, norms, institutions, and modes of thinking to which successive generations in a given society have attached primary importance.[34] Religions are the key parts of cultures, and even modernity and its postmodernist critics (as I tried to show) have firm roots in Christianity.

My definition of religion as a central component in most cultures and civilizations is based on two human universals identified by constructivism: language and reason. Religion consists of specific types of rules and is accepted on faith, and this acceptance, I will argue, represents a form of reasoning. The first aspect, that religions are systems of rules, is not difficult to accept. The argument that faith is a form of reasoning is more problematic. If it can be sustained, however, the juxtaposition of faith and reason introduced by modernity and leading to the rejection of religions in the social scientific enterprise does not hold.

Religions as Rules

Let me first explore what types of rules can be found in religions. Religions are made up mainly of assertive speech acts and instruction rules. While commandments might seem to be commands (directive rules), on closer inspection it is probably better to call them declarations (which Onuf takes to be a species of assertive speech acts). Nevertheless, it is usually possible to identify directive rules and commitment rules backing up the declarations and instruction rules, which give a religion its general character, although religious rules carry their own special "back up." To a believer, religious sanctions are derived from the divine authority, and the essence of religion is generally faith. Asserted truths, the codification in ordinary language of that which "passeth all understanding," are accepted on faith and backed up often by powerful emotions.[35] One's identity, one's understanding of the world, one's main values, are typically received in assertive rules articulated by human agents, albeit based on revelation, and, as already mentioned, when internalized they constitute the core of consciousness and culture.

Rules provide guidance but by themselves do not determine human behavior. It is at this point, in regard to the relationship between rules and reason, that the relevance of this discussion to religion will become apparent.

People use reason or judgment to decide whether to accept or reject rules and what course of action to take. Religion is no exception. Judgment arises from knowledge about the context of the rules involved in a situation and about the consequences of following or violating them. Forms of judgment are closely linked to the process of reasoning, and speech acts can be seen as instances of applied reasoning, since using rules is equal to exercising judgment. Let me first explore assertive rules in relation to religion and to modernity before I proceed to the discussion of the form of reasoning associated with them.

As forms of applied reasoning, assertive rules give rise to the most basic of all rules in the immediate demand they make on the hearer. Assertive and instruction rules state a belief coupled to the speaker's wish or intention that the hearer accept this belief. Children learn to appreciate this kind of rule first, before they are mature enough to respond to directives and then to take on the responsibilities of choice and mutuality offered in promises and commitment rules. Assertive rules require no more than a passive acceptance of certain information, including information about values. Education typically takes this form. Assertive rules assume that the hearer does not know, or could not know, and obviously ought to know. They elevate the agent, priest, or professor, by granting him or her a special status and standing and an enormous aura of respect. Assertive rules may be addressed to one person at a time, but the way they are styled often suggests a collective for an audience, for entire categories of hearers are uniformly in need of instruction. Religions take the form of assertive rules. Religions foster a concept of a collective amongst others by limiting our needs and wants.

In contrast, modernity's main currency are commitment rules. The contract is the model form of such rules, which are built around the individual. This is a characteristic feature of the West and of modernity.

Commitment rules are the domain of liberalism, characteristically based on the specification of individual rights and responsibilities. Western culture, liberalism, capitalism, individualism, modernity, and international relations are of a mainly commissive nature. True enough, commitment rules exist in mixes with directive rules and instruction rules to provide sanctions, enforcement, and so on, and the right balance within these mixes is of concern to the guardians of liberalism, individualism, democracy, or capitalism, or indeed of international relations.

Bozeman was not using constructivist terms but was clearly consistent with them when she argued that the unprecedented success of the universalization of the states-system invented in medieval Central Europe, the readiness with which many empires voluntarily dismantled to become its parts, was due to the commissive, nondirective, and nonassertive nature of the rules of the international system, as promised in the famous formula *cuius regio, eius religio,* that is, leave each state's central beliefs and values intact.[36] With the rules and practice of diplomacy that originated in the West came the vocabulary of political symbols, also composed in the West. Societies transforming into states adopted the idea of rules, institutions, and practices of governance of the "community of states."[37] With this acceptance, many states began to practice the standards of Western intellectual and material achievement and the values thereof, a process culminating not in the elimination of indigenous religions and cultures but, on the contrary, in the resurgence of religious beliefs across the world.

The predominantly assertive nature of religions goes some way to explaining their neglect in social science. We have got accustomed to viewing the assertive-based religions as archaic and ancient, if not an extinct form of social activity. Political systems based on assertive rules and hegemony, their characteristic condition of rule, have been regarded as premodern, impervious to change, and antagonistic to Western values.

In fact, Onuf describes religions as forms of hegemony (to which assertive rules give rise as a form of rule) in the language of Antonio Gramsci, who, however, used the term "hegemony" in a different context altogether. Hegemony in this understanding appears to be the rule of values rather than rule by people. Hegemony refers to the promulgation and manipulation of principles and instructions by which superordinate actors monopolize meaning, which is then passively absorbed by subordinate actors. These activities constitute a stable arrangement of rule because the ruled are rendered incapable of comprehending their subordinate role. They cannot formulate alternative programs of action because they are inculcated with the self-serving ideology of the rulers, who monopolize the production and dissemination of statements through which meaning is constituted.[38]

The issue here is that assertive rules are by no means an exclusive domain of premodern and antiquated forms of social relations. Critics of the West used the term "hegemony" in reference not to religious practices but almost exclusively to the Western form of rule regardless of its stated nature (in liberal doctrine) as based on commissive rules. It is fair to say that the central values and beliefs of any society, of whatever nature, are packaged in the form of assertive statements that are not conducive to questioning. The reason I am stressing this point is that in our preoccupation with rationality—used by some authors as synonymous with modern or Western—we have played down the hegemonic function of our own central values and beliefs.[39]

"Acceptance on Faith" and Passions

All of us engaged in social sciences use the term "hypothesis," not always appreciating its connection to assertive speech acts. *Hypothesis* is a dignified way of referring to intuition, conjecture, belief, guess, dogma, or speculation, which is, or is not, then subjected to further "real rational" treatment, based on the rules of "falsification" or "verification." Generally speaking, three sorts of consequences of abduction are possible, all of them normative.

The first sort points to religion. Conjecture takes on tremendous normative force through incantation and ritualization. Believers are discouraged, indeed prohibited, from subjecting their faith to the rational inquiry appropriate for "this world." Faith, however, exhibits the distinct form of reasoning characteristic of religion. This is the nonlinear form of reasoning I have previously described: It draws on consciousness and eludes the methods of deductive or inductive reasoning and their rules of inference and evidence. The religious experience is built on a noninferential mode of cognition analogous to sense or feeling. The unknown is crucial in interpreting the experience. Rhetorical devices, similes, metaphors, intuition (to all of which I have already referred) need to be used. Belief here precedes reasoning and controls it, unlike secular discourse, where beliefs are introduced but allegedly remain subordinated to reasoning.

The second sort of social consequences stemming from adductive reasoning has nothing to do with religion and points to science. All of us formulate hypotheses, guesses, or conjectures, which we then proceed to verify (or falsify) either by inductive or deductive reasoning according to positivist rules. Research based on induction takes the form of either "hunting and gathering" for clues—from the parts to wholes—or, more typically for positivists, attacking the problem based on a deductive form of reasoning, from wholes to the parts.

The social consequences of the third sort might lead to the establishment of a secular religion. Marxism followed this path, and so does modernist culture more generally. Conjectures are lifted out of context, advertised as scientific truths, and disseminated through the mass media. No less than religious beliefs, secular notions of individualism, liberalism, consumerism, and all the rest are repeated *ad nauseam,* presented in Hollywoodesque stories, public spectacles, and strict codes of behavior. In academia also, many social scientists firmly believe in their scientific objectivity, yet a great deal of what gets written and said is based on a set of shared myths. Books are written about books, articles about articles, and articles about books. Theorists write about writing, theorize about theories, and create heroes whom they honor in rituals.

The upshot of my argument is that constructivism is open to consideration of adductive reasoning and acceptance on faith alongside rational-instrumental reasoning. It can engage with discourses based on faith as with those based on narrowly defined reason without facing problems of incommensurability. Thus it will not be taken by surprise when advances in cognitive science will one of these days challenge once and for all the dogma of the rational choice theory and turn its simplistic structure into a more complex edifice that reproduces itself in social structures of every sort and at every level. Even before such a "paradigm shift" is forced upon us by discoveries somewhere in the natural sciences, constructivism has no difficulty accommodating individual emotions influencing choices as an integral part of the human process of reasoning.[40] Constructivism, in other words, can show how the human level involving feelings and emotions relates to the state level in a complicated process of accommodating religious thinking and feeling as forms of reasoning and as important aspects of how we construct our world.

Conclusion: The Paths to IPT

The framework that I have outlined in this paper is by no means the only way to develop an international political theology. IPT has been developing spontaneously from many angles and directions. Many specialists on religions follow the path of religion into the international arena, and IR scholars realize the need for serious adjustments in their discipline to accommodate the "intrusions" of religious factors.

Many writers, irrespective of their disciplinary denomination, have reached constructivist conclusions, albeit without adopting its terminology. Bozeman, the international cultural historian, as well as IR theorists such as Herrit Gong, Martin Wight, and even Hedley Bull spoke constructivism before it became "codified." Constructivism is often simply common sense. Constructivism is a way of thinking, just as much as positivism is, and as I have argued elsewhere, it takes some getting used to.[41] Eventually, one need not go through all the technicalities every time one uses constructivism, any more than one needs to discuss in detail Auguste Comte, the Vienna Circle, Robert Keohane, or other intellectual fathers of positivist belief as a preface to any positivist-based research.

Rule-oriented constructivism has many other advantages over positivism. The positivist goal of theoretical parsimony has eliminated far too much from the IR discipline and made our job much too easy. Constructivism is perhaps more realistic in revealing the multitude of social relations (whether we call them contexts, social arrangements, civilizations, cultures, or games) and their tremendous complexity. Constructivists insist that international relations should be conceptualized as a social construction on many interacting levels. None of these levels should be shut out a priori by a theoretical framework. This challenges the exclusivity of the state-centric focus still prevalent in IR studies. Having stressed the enormous complexity that constructivism draws to our attention, in contrast to the more parsimonious IR frameworks, it is important to note that despite its complexity, constructivism can support detailed, empirical case studies.[42]

IPT emphasizes research from an insider's perspective, such as comes natural to constructivism but that needs to be much greater than that afforded by Western and particularly U.S. parochialism (a view, as the term aptly conveys, through the perspective of one's own parish). Once we dispense with the a priori imputation of rational choice to actors, it is mandatory to establish the social context within which they act. Religion is often at the core of the social arrangement or structure within which actors operate. It is within this framework that we find out what is, or is not, defined as "rational" in any given situation. This makes it mandatory for students of IR to devise new curricula that integrate the study of religion(s), rather than "color in" religions as "bad" or "good" based upon a priori, out of context evaluations. In other words, we should use the existing scholarship and integrate the discourses of religion and IR, analyzing both as rule based within a framework such as I have proposed.

This method eliminates many simplifications, most notably in regard to the idea underpinning modernization theories, opposition to which is allegedly (found in many accounts) the root cause of the contemporary resurgence of religion.

The modernization thesis indeed does not stand up under constructivist scrutiny. Anticipating constructivism as well as IPT, Bozeman pointed out that ideas or rules do not travel well and are never received and accepted without modifications. Such ideas become either rejected or at best accepted in a syncretic form, but never in the pristine form of its place of origin. This refutes once and for all the typically North American notion on which modernization theories have been based, which despite policy failures and periodic refutation seems always ready to resurface in new forms. It also casts doubt on the notion that opposition to modernization somehow drives the resurgence of religion. The opposite can in fact be argued, namely that religions can play a pivotal role in the modernization of their societies, idiosyncratic though these modernization processes might be.

Bozeman links the entire proclivity of the West to modernize others and universalize its values to religious influences. She ties this modernization impulse to Christianity, to its missionary zeal and a feeling of shame and guilt not present in most other religions. This persistent Western tendency is manifest in the concern with other parts of the world and the drive to "modernize" and "develop" them. However, each corner of the planet, she argues, continues to maintain its own traditions of life and thought, which often predate by thousands of years the Western social arrangements. Cultures, comprised of rules and practices, are society's primary structuring ideas; they undergird political society and symbolize its continuity in time. Political institutions, state or nonstate, are all grounded in culture.

To a constructivist, the processes variously described as globalization or modernization are changes of the identity of the agent, of his or her agency, and of the social structure, all of which are based on and accessible through the understanding of changes in rules. Rules have to be implemented or supported by other rules, and thus these changes create responses inside societies, affecting people as individuals. The reconfiguration of authority in a world experiencing distinct material shifts seems to have been unsettling across the world.

The most noticeable response has come from those parts of the world where the influx of new rules has been simultaneous with material changes that seem to undermine/threaten the very existence of these communities. There are individuals in different parts of the world and across all social classes who respond to the new rules with disenchantment, disappointment, and fear, particularly if modernity's promises are not upheld. A feeling of loss of identity often follows. Thus these individuals may respond readily to anybody defending the familiar certainties. Utilitarian, material gratification is not always the outcome, as promised by the rational choice theory. Nor do the failures of the rational choice predictions spare any part of the world. For example, as recently noted in 2000, the "happiness index," even in the United States, was at an all-time low, despite almost ten years of booming economy and its widespread material benefits across the social spectrum.[43]

In the Third World, as Jeff Haynes has argued, it is mainly secular states that act as agents of modernization, and assume an increasingly broad role in the domestic arena.[44] Often due to a lack of understanding, and not by design, they unnecessarily encroach, or appear to encroach, on the "private domain." The changes wrought by the implementation of directive rules tend to disturb individual certainties and identities. In other words, the noble ideas of democracy, capitalism, and the "user friendly" commissive rules in the form of which all of this arrives require directive rules for their implementation that override the local assertive rules. Despite some material benefits that these processes may bring and particularly as modernity's promise of far-reaching material improvements has not been fulfilled, the legitimacy of the state—the agent making the new rules that implement, for example, IMF or World Bank guidelines—is weakened. The political legitimacy of the state, that is, the acceptance by the populace of its actions as good and morally right, is undermined, creating space for opposition forces to become new agents challenging the status quo and creating political instability.

Postmodernist writing correctly echoes the worldwide distrust for the Enlightenment systems of hegemonically disseminated assertive rules, secular ideologies, and worldviews that claim universal applicability and promise progress based on reason and man's ability to control his own destiny. These grand schemes have brought social and economic disruption, or disruption of such social institutions as the family. These processes coincide with the communication revolution and the influx of new ideas, that is, a range of choices of assertive rules, such as those referring to unrestricted rights, including the right to practice religion. This opens further the scope of action for opposition forces.

Religious forces are put into a position to pursue a public role—often performed with a vengeance—and become agents in social construction, both in the domestic as well as in the international sphere.

The understanding of these religious forces ought to reveal that by virtue of their social role they are incompatible only with other religions advocating competing claims. Based on assertive rules, they are eminently compatible with other assertive systems of rules, such as nationalism. They are in fact broadly compatible with directive rules of any political organization and thus eminently suitable for political exploitation.

The IR discipline may tune in only at the point when a civil war implicates foreign states, when international conflict occurs, or when the involvement of an international organization is required. Mainstream constructivists as well tune in only at the point when the international level comes to the fore and they must acknowledge that, to paraphrase the soft constructivists, states might have accepted some ideas that led to a change of their identities and consequently of their interests, and hence also of their intersubjective (interstate) agreements.[45] The mainstream constructivists, however, would subordinate these processes to the logic of instrumental rationality.[46] That this change has its root in religion would be purely coincidental. Religion per se would remain outside scrutiny of the U.S. mainstream, or soft constructivist.

Whether we argue that the greater visibility of religion is a consequence of or a last-ditch defense against modernity, or indeed a potential ally of modernity, there is yet another dimension of religion that remains totally outside IR's concerns because it does not fit into IR's state-centric perspective.[47] This is the historically documented, never-ending human search for meaning that reaches "beyond the restricted empirical existence of the here and now" and/or the often desperate and apparently irrational clinging to the means of such a search.[48] This search may set aside utilitarian gratification and elect the path whose authority is based on the beliefs and practices of generations of one's ancestors. Within this context, surely a turning to religion at a time of turmoil that appears to threaten one's very existence is perfectly rational.

I conclude with my initial thought. If liberalism and capitalism and the early stages of what we now call globalization required that IR scholarship correct its course by incorporating economics into its concerns, then yet another corrective may now be in order. What economists were to the first expansion of IR, sociologists, sociologists of religion, cultural historians, and anthropologists are to the present broadening. IR needs to draw on their expertise. Returning again to Gilpin's famous dictum about IPE to the effect that IR is about power and wealth, I add that IR in the contemporary world with its ever-increasing global stakes is not only about power and wealth but perhaps even more so about values and the meaning of the very human existence. Hence IPT.

Notes

A number of colleagues and friends helped me tremendously with this work-in-progress project. I would like to thank Ralph Pettman and Joe Potts for editing my English prose, to Nick Onuf for going over my rendition of his framework, to Henry Hamman for urging me to write on this subject in the first place, to Fred Frohock for the gift of his marvelous little book, which influenced me very much. However, I have written this essay for the Reverend Canon Henry N. F. Minich, to whom I would like to dedicate it.

1. Edward Luttwak, "The Missing Dimension," in *Religion, The Missing Dimension of Statecraft,* eds. Douglas Johnston and Cynthia Sampson (New York: Oxford University Press, 1994), 8.
2. This extension is by no means new. For example E. H. Carr made a distinction among categories of political power in the international sphere: "military power, economic power, and power over opinion," stressing the importance of not neglecting the latter. See E. H. Carr, *The Twenty Years Crisis* (London: Macmillan, 1962), 108. See also Vendulka Kubálková and A. A. Cruickshank, *Marxism and International Relations* (Oxford: Oxford University Press, 1989), 262, and Vendulka Kubálková, Nicholas Onuf, and Paul Kowert, eds., *International Relations in a Constructed World* (Armonk, NY: M. E. Sharpe, 1998), 37.
3. Mark Juergensmeyer, *The New Cold War: Religious Nationalism Confronts the Secular State* (Berkeley and Los Angeles: University of California Press, 1993), 1–2.
4. Luttwak, "The Missing Dimension," 9–10.
5. See, for example, Adda B. Bozeman, *Politics and Culture in International History* (Princeton, NJ: Princeton University Press, 1960); Gerrit W. Gong, *The Standard of "Civilization" in International Society* (Oxford: Clarendon Press, 1984); Susanne Hoeber Rudolph and James Piscatori, eds., *Transnational Religion and Fading States* (Boulder, CO: Westview Press, 1997); Johnston and Sampson, *Religion, The Missing Dimension;* Daniel Philpott, "The Religious Roots of Modern International Relations," *World Politics* 52, no. 2 (2000): 206–45; Jeff Haynes, *Religion in the Third World* (Boulder, CO: Lynne Reinner, 1994); Jeff Haynes, *Religion in Global Politics* (London: Longman, 1998); and Mark Juergensmeyer, *Terror in the Mind of God: The Global Rise of Religious Violence* (Berkeley and Los Angeles: University of California Press, 2000).
6. Nicholas Greenwood Onuf, *World of Our Making: Rules and Rule in Social Theory and International Relations* (Columbia: University of South Carolina Press, 1989).

7. Stephen Walt, "International Relations: One World, Many Theories," *Foreign Policy*, no. 110 (1988): 29–46, and Peter Katzenstein, Robert Keohane, and Stephen Krasner, "International Organization and the Study of World Politics," *International Organization* 52, no. 3 (1998): 645–85.

8. Steve Smith, "Foreign Policy Is What States Make of It: Social Construction and International Relations Theory," in *Foreign Policy in a Constructed World*, ed. Vendulka Kubálková (Armonk, NY: M. E. Sharpe, 2001),

9. Philpot, "The Religious Roots of Modern International Relations."

10. Alexander Wendt, "Identity and Structural Change in International Politics," in *The Return of Culture and Identity in IR Theory*, eds. Yosef Lapid and Friedrich Kratochwil (Boulder, CO: Lynne Rienner, 1996), 47. See also Alexander Wendt, *Social Theory of International Politics* (Cambridge: Cambridge University Press, 1999), 32.

11. James Kurth, "Religion and Globalization," The 1998 Templeton Lecture on Religion and World Affairs, Foreign Policy Research Institute, May 1999.

12. Katzenstein et al., "International Organization," 678.

13. Robert Keohane, *International Institutions and State Power: Essays in International Relations Theory* (Boulder, CO: Westview Press, 1989), 173–74.

14. Arvind Sharma and Katherine Young, eds., *Feminism and World Religions* (Albany: State University of New York Press, 1999).

15. Ibid., 11.

16. François Lyotard, *The Postmodern Condition: A Report on Knowledge* (Manchester, UK: Manchester University Press, 1986), xxiv.

17. Susanne Hoeber Rudolph, "Introduction: Religion, States and Transnational Civil Society," in *Transnational Religion and Fading States*, 2.

18. Ibid.

19. Samuel P. Huntington et al., *The Clash of Civilizations: The Debate* (New York: Council on Foreign Relations, 1993).

20. Fred M. Frohock, *Healing Powers: Alternative Medicine, Spiritual Communities, and the State* (Chicago: The University of Chicago Press, 1995), 47.

21. Ibid.

22. Karen Armstrong, *A History of God: The 4,000-Year Quest of Judaism, Christianity and Islam* (New York: Ballantine Books, 1993), 4.

23. Ibid., xix.

24. Erik H. Erikson, *Life History and the Historical Moment* (New York: Norton, 1975).

25. Frohock, *Healing Powers*, 163.

26. Ibid., ix.

27. Onuf, *World of Our Making*.

28. Ibid., 102.

29. Rudolph and Piscatori, *Transnational Religion and Fading States.*
30. Daniel H. Levine and David Stoll, "Bridging the Gap Between Empowerment and Power in Latin America," in *Transnational Religion and Fading States,* and Edward A. Lynch, "Reform and Religion in Latin America," *Orbis* 42, no. 3 (1998): 263–81.
31. See, for instance, Johnston and Sampson, *Religion, The Missing Dimension.*
32. Huntington et al., *The Clash of Civilizations.*
33. Juergensmeyer, *Terror in the Mind of God,* 30.
34. Bozeman, *Politics and Culture in International History.*
35. The Blessing in Rite I, *The Book of Common Prayer,* 339, used in the Anglican masses every Sunday. It is a paraphrase of Philippians 4:7. See also Peter 1:2.
36. Bozeman, *Politics and Culture in International History.*
37. Gong, *The Standard of Civilization.*
38. Onuf, *A World of Our Making,* 209–10.
39. Ralph Pettman, *Commonsense Constructivism* (Armonk, NY: M. E. Sharpe, 2000).
40. The recent neuroscientist literature, the "neurobiology of human rationality," includes Francis Crick, *The Astonishing Hypothesis: The Scientific Search for the Soul* (New York: Charles Scribner's Sons, 1994); Antonio R. Damasio, *Descartes' Error: Emotion, Reason, and the Human Brain* (New York: Putnam Books, 1994); and Antonio R. Damasio, *The Feeling of What Happens: Body and Emotion in the Making of Consciousness* (New York: Harcourt Brace and Company, 1999).
41. Vendulka Kubálková, ed., *Foreign Policy in a Constructed World* (Armonk, NY: M. E. Sharpe, 2001), esp. chap. 3.
42. Kubálková et al., *International Relations in a Constructed World* and Kubálková, *Foreign Policy in a Constructed World.*
43. Alexander Stille, "A Happiness Index with a Long Reach: Beyond G.N.P. to Subtler Measures," *New York Times,* 20 May 2000, A17, A19.
44. Haynes, *Religion in the Third World* and *Religion in Global Politics.*
45. Peter J. Katzenstein, "Introduction: Alternative Perspectives on National Security," in *The Culture of National Security: Norms and Identity in World Politics,* ed. Peter J. Katzenstein (New York: Columbia University Press, 1996).
46. Ibid., 27.
47. Peter van der Veer, "Political Religion in the Twenty-First Century," in *International Order and the Future of World Politics,* eds. T. V. Paul and John A. Hall (Cambridge: Cambridge University Press, 1999).
48. Haynes, *Religion in Global Politics,* 214.

Part II

War, Security, and Religion

Chapter 4

Does Religion Make a Difference?

Theoretical Approaches to the Impact of Faith on Political Conflict

Andreas Hasenclever and Volker Rittberger

A s observed by many scholars, a renaissance of religious traditions is taking place virtually all over the globe.[1] Contrary to
once widespread expectations that religion would gradually
disappear as a political force in modernizing societies, religious communities have been getting stronger in many nations over the last two
decades or so. Their leaders put forward grievances about discrimination, raise claims as to how state and society should be organized, and
mobilize the faithful into action. Social institutions such as schools,
charities, and hospitals are run in the name of their respective religious
denominations. In many Muslim countries, there are calls for the introduction of the *sharia* as public law. In India, Hindu nationalists attempt
to establish their creed as the state privileged religion. In the United
States, the "Christian Right" tries to capture the state for the dissemination and implementation of the eternal truth as they understand it.

Often the political resurgence of religious communities is accompanied by violent clashes in and between nations—take, for example, the bloody conflicts in Algeria, Bosnia, East Timor, Kashmir, Nigeria, Palestine, and Sri Lanka, among others. Scholars differ significantly in their interpretations of this correlation depending on their theoretical point of view. *Primordialists* argue that differences in religious traditions should be viewed as one of the most important independent variables to explain violent interactions in and between nations. Collective actors at the national as well as the international level tend to form alliances around common cosmologies, and tensions arise and escalate primarily between alliances with different cosmologies. *Instrumentalists* admit that conflicts may be aggravated by divergent religious creeds, but they insist that they are rarely if ever caused by them. From their point of view, the correlation of violent clashes with the resurgence of old religions is not surprising, but neither is it necessary. Riots and wars would have occurred in any case as a consequence of political and socioeconomic inequalities in and between nations. By contrast, *moderate constructivists*[2] argue that in many situations it is only the juxtaposition of true believers and sinister pagans that enables political entrepreneurs to mobilize their constituencies into violent action. Acts of violence require legitimation, and religion and religious leaders can provide such legitimation. But then they may also deny it. Religious leaders can refuse to bless the weapons, and then violence may not occur even if significant socioeconomic and political inequalities exist in or between societies.

In the next section, we will briefly discuss primordialism, instrumentalism, and moderate constructivism as rival perspectives on the impact of faith on the course of conflicts. Subsequently, in the third section, we will introduce an elite-based model of strategic choice. This model distinguishes between *conflict* defined by the issues in contention and *conflict behavior,* ranging from peaceful accommodation to aggressive self-help. In the fourth section, we will argue that although differences in religious creeds are hardly ever a genuine source of violent clashes, under certain conditions they have the potential to escalate conflict behavior. In the fifth section, we will proceed to examine three types of strategies that are expected to help control or reduce the violence-promoting impact of religious creeds on the course of confrontations: (1) strategies of deterrence and repressive denial that aim at increasing the costs of violent resistance and uprisings; (2) strategies of socioeconomic development and democratization that are designed to overcome the underlying modernization crisis; and (3) a dialogue strategy that seeks to delegitimize the use of violence for the advancement of religious or other interests.

In this context, we will refer, *inter alia,* to the ideas of Hans Küng, which are currently much debated in Germany and elsewhere.[3] Küng proposes that strategies be devised to initiate a dialogue—or to reinforce the ongoing dialogues—among the world's major religions in order to achieve and strengthen an interreligious world ethic. As stated in the preamble of the UNESCO Charter, Küng's strategy emphasizes that "since wars begin in the minds of men, it is in the minds of men that the defenses of peace must be constructed."[4] It is important, therefore, to strengthen people's principled disapproval of violence. The principled disapproval of violence may derive from intra- and interreligious dialogues but also from other sources. In general, it is expected to broaden the space for cooperative forms of conflict management during social and economic crises, thus preventing political conflicts from escalating into violent clashes.

Three Theoretical Perspectives on the Impact of Faith on Political Conflict

As already mentioned, we distinguish three theoretical perspectives on the role of religions in political conflicts: primordialism, instrumentalism, and moderate constructivism. The primordialist perspective is adopted by Samuel Huntington, Gilles Kepel, Jeffrey Seul, and Bassam Tibi among others.[5] They argue that the embeddedness of nations in civilizations will be the most important determinant of world politics in the twenty-first century. The pivotal characteristic of each civilization, in turn, is the religion or cosmology on which it is based. Hence, we have Buddhist, Christian, Confucian, Hindu, Islamic, Judaistic, and Taoist civilizations. In the Cold War era, the superpowers were able to suppress the conflict-generating force of divergent creeds. More generally, the global competition between East and West, together with a highly skewed distribution of military capabilities in the international system, strongly reduced the impact of particular cultural characteristics on foreign policy behavior. Now that the Cold War is over, primordialists expect the dawn of a new world order in which cultural similarities and differences will become highly salient for international behavior and interactions.

In this view, cultural similarities and dissimilarities produce converging and diverging state interests, respectively. States with similar religious traditions and cosmologies will form alliances directed against those with whom they have little in common in cultural and religious terms. Violence will be largely confined to interactions that take place *between* civilizations. At the same time, states with similar religious traditions and cosmologies will work hard to accommodate their disputes in order to strengthen their joint power position vis-à-vis other civilizations.

According to the primordialist perspective, the reorganization of world politics will be accompanied by civil unrest and international wars. Domestically, non-Western civilizations will purge themselves of the remnants of the Cold War era. Religious militants face and take up the task of either ousting Westernized political elites from power or converting their members into zealous believers, who recant secularism and devote themselves to building political institutions that protect and promote the religious traditions of their nations. In multireligious societies such as Bosnia, Indonesia, Malaysia, Nigeria, or Sudan, primordialists expect a fierce struggle for power between communities with irreconcilable understandings of the sacred. In the end, either these societies will fall apart or one community will gain dominance and suppress the others. Internationally, civil unrest in multireligious societies might tempt third parties to intervene on behalf of their brethren. This, in turn, may lead to a horizontal escalation of the conflict and provoke war between states of different civilizations.

A second group of scholars, whom we label instrumentalists, reject the view that differences in religious traditions and cosmologies are genuine *causes of political conflict.*[6] Instrumentalists do not deny the current renaissance of religious movements. They argue, however, that in most cases this is the result of growing economic, social, and political inequalities in and between nations. Therefore, when we observe

Table 4.1 **Three Approaches to Analyzing the Impact of Faith on Political Conflict**

	Primordialist	*Instrumentalist*	*Moderate Constructivist*
Basic conflict	Cultural	Socioeconomic	Socioeconomic
Causal status of religion	Independent variable	Spurious correlation	Intervening variable
Expectations	Culturally based, realignments and wars of religions	Socioeconomic. Cleavages and civil wars	Socioeconomic. Cleavages, political conflicts, and contingent militancy and violence

the faithful turning into warriors, we should not attribute this change to any particular dogmatic dispute, but should understand it as a consequence of the unequal distribution of power and wealth between the parties. At the international level, instrumentalists do not expect any major departure from the traditional patterns of state practice. In the new century, as it was in the old, politics between states will be determined by power and material interest, not by culture or religion.[7] A number of observations are adduced to support this view. Two of them are particularly important:

(a) Domestically, the politicization of religious traditions and the radicalization of religious communities are especially likely in times of economic decay, social disintegration, or state collapse.[8] Desperate people subject to poverty, marginalization, or physical threats turn to their religious traditions in search of an alternative political order that satisfies their need for welfare, recognition, and security. In this context, religious communities operate primarily as refuges of solidarity, sources of cultural reaffirmation, and safe havens. Power-seeking political elites then try, often successfully, to exploit this renewed interest in the sacred for their own aggrandizement.[9] As they recast political adversaries as foes of faith, they acquire the support of those whose faith has become their last resort. What is significant, however, is that the mobilization of religious communities in most cases *follows* the economic and social decline of its members. There are only very few cases of violent clashes between prospering and respected communities. By contrast, such clashes become highly likely when religious groups suffer economic and political deprivation. As Ted Robert Gurr notes in regard to ethnopolitical conflicts:

> The origins and dynamics of ethnopolitical conflict are highly complex. Theories that emphasize the supposedly crucial role of a single factor, such as historical animosities or religious differences, should be avoided. Such factors usually become significant because they are invoked by contemporary ethnopolitical leaders seeking to mobilize support among threatened and disadvantaged peoples, not because religious or historical differences generate a primordial urge to conflict.[10]

Instrumentalists tend to portray the ability of political entrepreneurs to instrumentalize old myths and sacred traditions for their own aggrandizement as virtually unlimited. According to Anthony D. Smith, there are countless cultural, ethnic, and religious markers floating in each nation that can be called upon by self-interested leaders for the purpose of forming group identities and mobilizing their members into collective action.[11] Evidently, inventing combat-capable communities requires some preexisting raw materials such as common myths, common language, and common religious traditions. But these raw materials exist in abundance. To put it differently: If serious political and economic cleavages exist in a nation, it should be easy for political entrepreneurs to give meaning to these cleavages in terms of cultural, ethnic, or religious discrimination. The observed relationship between religion and violence then amounts to a *spurious* correlation, and there is not much point in exploring the political consequences of the revival of religion any further.

(b) At the international level, instrumentalists are unable to discover a coherent trend toward new alliances along religiously or culturally defined fault lines. By contrast, the constellation of power and material interest still goes a long way toward explaining international interactions. This is especially true in the security area. For example, when the military potential of a regional state such as Iraq increased, neighboring countries began to look for external support, disregarding both their common religious ties with the ascending power and the incompatible understandings of the sacred shaping the civilization of the potential ally.[12] What seems to count in the final analysis is the balance of forces that should be reestablished.

Additionally, they argue, even in the recent past there have been simply too many wars fought in religiously homogeneous areas to give much credit to the primordialist expectations.[13] Take, for example, the violent clashes between clans in Somalia, the genocide in Rwanda, or the First Gulf War. What these conflicts, together with many other civil wars, have in common is the fierce competition between domestic elites who are ready to do almost anything to keep or get political power. In response to these findings, Joseph Nye argues that we are not witnessing the formation of a new, coherent world order, but a process of fragmentation and regionalization. This process does not follow the logic of Huntington's "clash of civilizations" but is fueled by a "narcissism of small differences."[14] Similarly, Daniel Patrick Moynihan notes: "Ethnic conflict does not require great differences; small will do."[15] Put differently, comparatively minor divergences in the understanding of the sacred, as exist for example between Sunnis and Shiites or between Catholics and Protestants, become highly significant in the escalation of international as well as domestic conflicts, while the many and supposedly more significant commonalities of the engaged parties are pushed into the background.

The empirical evidence thus does not support the primordialist hypothesis regarding the *autonomous conflict-generating power* of religious differences. Belief in divine truth seemingly attains greater political significance only in times of economic, social, or political unrest. Additionally, the mobilization of religious communities depends on the contingent interests of power-conscious elites. At the international level, there is still no evidence for a stable pattern consisting of alliance formation *within* civilizations and security competition *between* them. Instrumentalists recognize, however, an *impact of religious convictions on conflict behavior.* Political entrepreneurs time and again invoke the sacred to mobilize their constituency into violent action. But in the contemporary instrumentalists' understanding, the causal pathway is unambiguous: The politicization of religions leads to the escalation of given disputes and never to their de-escalation.

In this chapter, we wish to present and defend a third position located somewhere between primordialism and instrumentalism. Its representatives can be called moderate constructivists.[16] Moderate constructivists regard social conflicts as embedded in cognitive structures such as ideology, nationalism, ethnicity, or religion. These structures, which consist of "shared understandings, expectations, and social knowledge," provide actors with value-laden conceptions of the self and others and consequently affect their strategic choices.[17] For instance, cognitive structures help to identify friends and foes independently of any given dispute, and, following moderate constructivists' reasoning, this distinction often makes a crucial difference for the management of otherwise similar conflicts.

There are two major zones of agreement between moderate constructivists and instrumentalists. In both schools of thought, power and interests play a crucial role in *explaining* politics. Even though often overlooked by their critics, this is no less true for moderate constructivists than for instrumentalists.[18] Indeed, the former never denied the importance of egoistic motives and material factors in human and social life. As Alexander Wendt has recently noted:

> The fact that relations of production and destruction consist of shared ideas does not change the fact that they confront actors as objective social facts with real, objective "material" effects. Inequality and exploitation exist, even if they are constituted by ideas.[19]

What is peculiar to the moderate constructivists' position is that power and interests are embedded in cognitive structures that give meaning to them. But we should never conflate the constitutive effects of intersubjective understandings with the causal effects of existing "relations of production and destruction," to use Wendt's term.[20]

Hence, moderate constructivists are not uncomfortable with the instrumentalist thesis that most contemporary conflicts are conflicts about power and wealth and not about religion.[21]

The second zone of agreement is the importance attached to political leaders.[22] Both schools of thought acknowledge that wars do not occur spontaneously. The Carnegie Commission on Preventing Deadly Conflict, which comprised scholars of both theoretical denominations, has put it as follows:

> Mass violence results when leaders see it as the only way to achieve their political objectives, and they are able to mobilize groups to carry out their strategy. Without determined leaders, groups may riot but they do not start systematic, sustained campaigns of violence to achieve their goals; and without mobilized groups, leaders are unable to organize a fight.[23]

Similarly, Laustsen and Wæver remind us that religion understood both as a mental construct and as a social practice is never in itself a party to a conflict: "It is not religion as such that acts. The movement is driven by strategic action in a political context by some leaders, and the action program is formulated at the interface of politics and religion."[24]

According to instrumentalists and moderate constructivists, political leaders thus play a crucial role in the outbreak of armed conflicts. When leaders think that armed combat is in their interest, they will start to muster mass support for their plans and try to invoke the religious traditions of their societies in order to legitimize their choices.

It is here, however, that moderate constructivists part company with the instrumentalists. While the latter suggest that, ultimately, determined leaders can manipulate religious traditions at will and that the justification of violence is at best a rhetorical but not a substantial problem, moderate constructivists insist that religious traditions are intersubjective structures that have a life of their own. They depend on social practices and discourses, which, as Wendt argues, "are inseparable from the reasons and self-understandings that agents bring to their actions."[25] Therefore, the rhetorical power of political entrepreneurs is far from unlimited. They have to convince the rank and file of their interpretation of a given situation, and these interpretations are in principle always vulnerable to countervailing arguments that may undermine not only the validity of these interpretations but the authority of those who advance them. When, for instance, political leaders contend that a given war is for the sake of God and therefore justified, others can stand up and dispute this claim by showing that their reading of the holy texts does not support the rightness of violent action in the conflict concerned (or in any conflict). In the final analysis, it is then up to the audience to decide whose arguments they trust more.

Moderate constructivists, therefore, propose to view religion as an intervening variable, i.e., as a causal factor intervening between a given conflict and the choice of conflict behavior. In this way, the impact of religious traditions on conflict behavior is deeply ambiguous: They can make violence more likely, insofar as a reading of holy texts prevails that justifies armed combat; on the other hand, they can make violence less likely, insofar as a reading of holy texts prevails that delegitimizes the use of violence in a given situation or even generally. From here it is only a small step to the moderate constructivist recommendation to devise dialogue strategies that strengthen people's prudential or principled disapproval of violence.

Before we outline a conflict model based on these moderate constructivist insights, two further preliminary remarks are appropriate: (1) There is little systematic research on the impact of religious faith on the course of conflicts. Nor is there much systematic research on adequate strategies for dealing peacefully with conflicts that include a religious dimension. This chapter should therefore be understood primarily as a theoretical contribution to the ongoing debate about the impact of religious faith on the course of conflicts. It seeks to lay the foundations for further research in this field of inquiry without trying to anticipate the results of this research. (2) The background of our analysis is peace and conflict research. That is, we are interested in the identification of conditions for peaceful conflict management and settlement. In other words, we are concerned with the prevention of violence, or, when it occurs, with its early termination in such a way that the goals and means of peacemaking remain mutually commensurate.

Four Determinants of the Strategic Choices Made by Political Entrepreneurs

Under the conditions of scarcity and value pluralism, conflicts among groups are a universal feature of social life. They cannot be avoided but must be taken as a corollary of human nature. What is subject to variation, however, is the way in which conflicts are dealt with. The parties involved can refrain from using violence or they can choose to fight for their cause; if they decide to turn to violence, they still have many options, ranging from selected breaches of the peace to all-out war. If and how violence is applied, in turn, depends on a multitude of factors.[26] These factors include, *inter alia,* the nature of the conflict, the intensity of the differences, the relative feasibility of equifinal strategies, the characteristics of the involved parties, their historical experiences with each other, their general attitude toward violent modes of conflict management, and the broader social environment of the parties, that is, the national and transnational contexts in which the conflict is embedded. To keep this extraordinary causal complexity manageable, theoretical simplifications are necessary and justified. This model proposes to focus on the strategic choices of elites in social conflicts.[27] The rationale for this analytical reduction has been nicely spelled out by Michael Brown:

> Although mass-level factors are clearly important underlying conditions that make some places more predisposed to violence than others, and although neighboring states routinely meddle in the internal affairs of others, the decisions and actions of domestic elites often determine whether political disputes veer toward war or peace.[28]

Elites are conceptualized as rational actors who calculate the cost and benefits of alternative strategies in order to maximize their utilities. They are generally interested in keeping or improving their privileged positions vis-à-vis both their own rank and file and other groups. In social conflicts, they do not seek only to prevail but also to make as few costly concessions as possible. They are neither naturally predisposed to, nor do they rule out, the use of violence to make adversaries comply with their demands. They know, however, that violence is a risky policy instrument. Using it in the pursuit of a group's goals is likely to produce hostile reactions by the targeted actors. The confrontation may last longer than originally expected, and the result may be the disintegration of one's own group. Moreover, armed combat usually involves significant opportunity costs. To be effective, it requires considerable organizational and material resources that could be used for other purposes.

From the elites' perspective, the expediency of violent strategies therefore is in part determined by their prospects of success. Controlling for the strength of the adversary, the prospects of success, in turn, are a function of at least two master variables: (1) the mobilization of the rank and file and (2) the support that the group's goals *and* strategies enjoy within the broader society.

For the prospects of success of a violent strategy to be good, the rank and file should be prepared to invest time and resources in collective action and to sustain periods of even intense confrontation. If elites doubt that the group members will follow their lead, they will think twice before openly advocating or even provoking armed combat. As a result, we can adopt the following rule of thumb: The higher the mobilization of the rank and file in a given conflict, the more likely, *ceteris paribus,* are the group's elites to choose violent strategies. Moreover, the adversaries in a social conflict never act in isolation, and violence is always prone to antagonize bystanders. Third parties are tempted to join the victimized side, and this may ultimately lead to a group's defeat. Therefore, we should expect the elites' choices to be affected by the degree of support they can muster for their cause and their strategies in the broader society. This implies that the prospects of success decrease to the extent to which their goals, and the means by which they attempt to achieve them, are rejected by important social groups. Such a decrease of societal support, in turn, has repercussions on the degree to which the rank and file are likely to be mobilized: The risk that involvement will not pay increases, and the readiness of the group's members to invest time and resources in a conflict strategy involving violence decreases correspondingly.

In summary (table 4.2), the probability that elites will choose violent strategies to pursue their goals varies with both the mobilization of the group's members and the support provided by the wider societal environment. In the following, we will distinguish three determinants that are widely held to influence the mobilization of a group's members. Subsequently, we will turn to the probability of societal support for elites that pursue violent strategies in social conflicts. These considerations will form the analytical framework for further reflections on the impact of religious faith on the course of conflicts.

The Degree of Mobilization Depends on the Nature of the Conflict

Among scholars the distinction between conflicts about interests and conflicts about values is commonplace.[29] Conflicts about interests deal with the distribution of goods or social positions that are in short supply but unambiguously desired by competing groups. The central challenge for conflict management therefore is scarcity and not the intersubjective frame of reference that helps actors distinguish valuable and invaluable goods, legitimate and illegitimate claims, and appropriate and inappropriate actions. In conflicts about values, however, actors disagree precisely about this frame of reference. They contest each other's moral orientation and the corresponding understanding of what

Table 4.2   Determinants of Elites' Strategic Choices

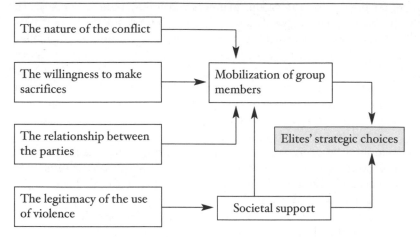

is a just and fair social order. The competition for governmental positions, for instance, can be regarded as a conflict about interests. By contrast, a conflict about a state's constitution falls into the category of conflicts about values. Whereas the first case deals with the distribution of scarce positions, in the second case the most general principles of state organization and state action are at stake. Conflicts about values therefore go to the heart of a political community. They shake the fundamentals of a given social order and they can bring about far-reaching social change.

It is not surprising that, as a rule, conflicts about values are more prone to violence than conflicts about interests.[30] This is the case for at least three reasons: First, individuals identify with the values of their group or community. If the latter are at stake, this is perceived as an existential threat. As a result, the readiness of a group's members to mobilize more resources for the defense of these values and also to use violence, if necessary, increases *ceteris paribus.* Second, the use of violence in conflicts about values is regarded as morally justified. It is the defense of what a group recognizes as right or wrong, as just or unjust, and of what makes up its identity. The adversary thus appears not just as somebody who attempts to pursue his or her interests at the disadvantage of one's own group, but as an outlaw who violates fundamental norms of social conduct. In so doing he or she forfeits his or her right to fair and nonviolent treatment. Finally, the readiness to use violence in conflicts about values is reinforced by the belief that compromises are impossible, and that a defeat would be tantamount to a total reversal of one's beliefs. Therefore, the logic of such conflicts is one of all or nothing.

The Degree of Mobilization Depends on the Self-sacrificing Attitudes of the Group's Members

The second determinant that affects the mobilization of a group's members is their individual willingness to make sacrifices. The more committed they are to invest time and resources, the more practicable will be, *ceteris paribus,* the implementation of violent strategies by the group's leaders. As already mentioned, the use of violence is expensive and risky. The group members and their sympathizers in the wider societal environment must reckon with repressions and counteroffensives on the part of their adversary. Therefore, when making the decision to use violence, elites must be sure that the rank and file are prepared to pay a high price for achieving their aims. A lack of willingness to make sacrifices among the group's members leads the elites to the conclusion that the use of violent strategies is not advisable. Even if core values are at stake, therefore, the probability decreases that elites will resort to such strategies to pursue their goals.[31]

The Degree of Mobilization Depends on the Relationship between the Conflict Parties

The willingness to use violence in a conflict is higher the less cooperative strategies of attaining the group's goals appear to be available. This depends on the relationship between the adversaries. Cooperative strategies for conflict management presuppose a certain degree of trust. Each party must be convinced that it will not be harmed or double-crossed when making concessions to, or cooperating with, the other. If this minimum of trust is lacking, chances are high that each party will choose noncooperative, that is, self-help strategies for conflict management. Such strategies aim at achieving one's goals without taking the other's preferences into consideration. Therefore, they tend to lead quickly to an escalation of conflict behavior in the direction of violent self-help.[32] Jacob Bercovitch and Richard Jackson, for instance, report some statistical evidence that interstate conflicts have a high likelihood of escalating into war if the parties to the dispute have a long history of antagonistic competition. Conversely, "few states that are friendly . . . end up in armed conflict with each other."[33]

The Degree of Societal Support Depends on the Public Justification for the Use of Violence

In our model, the elites' strategic choices depend not only on the mobilization of the rank and file but also on the real or anticipated reaction of the wider societal environment. This is because the prospects of success in a given dispute are in part determined by the behavior of those who are not directly involved in the focal conflict.[34] Leaders must balance the expected effects of violent measures on the targeted group with their justifiability to a wider audience. Otherwise, they risk strengthening the adversary by antagonizing bystanders and alienating allies. Therefore, we expect elites to take care of the legitimacy of violence in a particular situation, when considering its application. At a minimum, they will devote time and energy to framing a conflict in terms that lend credibility to their claim that violence is unavoidable. Conversely, when violent strategies cannot be justified, the danger is high that external support will be redistributed at the expense of the militant conflict party. Consequently, the militant party's chances of achieving its goals decrease. As a side effect, this will also have negative repercussions on the mobilization of the group members and sympathizers and thus again diminishes its prospects of prevailing in a given confrontation.

Religious Faith and Conflict Escalation

Thus far we have argued that the decision of political elites for the use of force is conditional on both the mobilization of their constituencies and the support of important third parties. If the group members are not prepared for armed combat and if the wider societal environment considers the use of force illegitimate, political leaders are unlikely to fall back on this policy instrument. The risk of being destroyed by state authorities or otherwise being punished would simply appear too great. In a second step, we now dynamize the strategic choices of established as well as oppositional elites. Rather than simply reacting to environmental constraints, they try to manipulate them to their own advantage. If, for instance, political entrepreneurs think that the use of force in a particular political setting can further their interest, they will try to raise the willingness of the rank and file to endorse and support a more belligerent approach. Additionally, they will try to persuade the wider audience that their strategic choices are consistent with commonly accepted moral standards. In this context, the exploitation of religious differences may prove particularly convenient. Conversely, if political elites fail to mobilize their constituency and to legitimize the use of force before a broader audience, according to our model, they will *ceteris paribus* abstain from escalating a given conflict.

Upgrading One's Own Claims and Downgrading the Claims of the Adversary

The interpretation of social conflicts as religious confrontations leads to their transformation and radicalization. Identifying the claims of one party with the commands of God or the cosmic order gives them an uncontestable superiority over competing claims, which now appear to be blasphemic, having no moral justification at all.[35] At the extreme, satanic traits are ascribed to the adversary. For example, during the civil war in former Yugoslavia, the fate of the Serbian president and of his followers was identified with that of Jesus, whereas the Bosnian Muslims were compared to Judas, the traitor, being not in a position to ever be forgiven. In such conflicts, no means seem to be illegitimate, and the adversary has no right to mercy because it has excluded itself from the God-wanted Order. One's own cause, by contrast, is sacred and its fulfilment serves true peace. This will be achieved when the adversary is annihilated and the true believers are again able to live in agreement with their faith.

Increase of Willingness to Make Sacrifices

Since Cicero's *De Natura Deorum,* perfect unselfishness in service to the divine is considered a trait of the true believer. As Scott Appleby observes, by locating the believers in a sacred cosmos that rewards martyrdom, faith sets free impressing forces.[36] Those who are seized by the divine give everything and fear nothing even if they have to pay the price of grief or death for their loyalty. Religiously motivated suicide commandos such as those of Hamas or Al Qaeda show how strong such convictions can be: Committing such deeds, they believe, will make them enter paradise as martyrs. By idealizing suffering in this world and promising rewards in another, faith enhances the margin of action that political elites enjoy. They know they can demand and expect great sacrifices from the group's members even over a long period of time.[37]

Loss of Trust

In a holy war, the parties are likely to mistrust each other deeply: One cannot expect sincerity from representatives of evil. Rather, they can be expected to use any concession for their own self-aggrandizement. The adversary is seen as a fanatic, who will attempt to achieve his goals by any means. In other words, the parties are locked in a zero-sum game. Both are convinced that the other side will relentlessly seize every advantage for its own struggle for supremacy. Each party therefore tries to make use of every option to improve its standing in the conflict. In so doing, the conception of the other as an enemy is reinforced and the prospects for a peaceful mode of conflict management become dim. Expectations and actual behavior are reproduced in such a way as to become a self-fulfilling prophecy. A vicious circle of antagonism and, eventually, violence results from which it is difficult to escape.[38]

Access to Religious Institutions

Finally, by skilfully employing sacred symbols to justify their strategic choices, political entrepreneurs may gain access to, and use the resources of, religious institutions. As Barry Rubin observes, in many societies these institutions are the only functioning social organizations except for the state.[39] To win over the hearts and minds of the clergy (or parts of it) may prove crucial for extremist groups in their attempt to gain support beyond their small cadre of followers. This may be particularly easy when religious authorities have long-standing grievances against the state or are otherwise dissatisfied with the political status quo. Recent findings of Jonathan Fox point in this direction:

> When grievances over religious discrimination are high, religious institutions appear to facilitate mobilization for protest. The presence of religious institutions also tends to promote mobilization for rebellion when political discrimination and grievances of autonomy are at high levels.[40]

Three Strategies of Conflict De-escalation

Thus far we have argued that political leaders time and again instrumentalize the sacred for their own aggrandizement. This is not to say that they find it always convenient to bolster their cause with religious arguments and symbols. There may be circumstances in which ethnic or ideological sermons are more suited for the mobilization of the rank and file and the justification of violent strategies. Moreover, we should not exclude a priori the appropriateness and authenticity of religious arguments that denounce repressive rule and call the faithful to armed resistance.

Most world religions acknowledge situations in which the recourse to violence is considered legitimate. In order to identify such situations, they have elaborated extensive normative frameworks such as the theory of just war in Christianity. The apartheid system in South Africa, for instance, created a situation in which numerous scholars and practitioners alike advanced good reasons to show that armed resistance to this particular situation of racial discrimination was justified by the Christian tradition.[41] Similarly, in the 1970s and 1980s prominent proponents of liberation theology such as Ernesto Cardinal, Gustavo Gutiérrez, and Juan Luis Segundo argued that the poor in Latin America, at least under certain conditions, have a right to violent rebellion.[42] If there are no alternative means for changing an unjust political and economic system that produces massive suffering and early death among its population, violent action by and for the poor should be understood as counterviolence and, consequently, as a legitimate instrument for achieving overdue social change. As William Jones, a representative of black liberation theology, has put it:

> The violence of the oppressed, the group for which liberation theology speaks, is a response to a prior, "original" violence that created and maintains the oppression that liberation theology attacks. Hence the moral rationale of *counter*-violence, of *self*-defense and of *just* war.[43]

Therefore, when we observe the faithful turning into warriors, this must not be necessarily the result of elite manipulation.

For the purpose of this chapter, however, we concentrate on the discussion of counterstrategies that are designed to contain or reduce any conflict-escalating power of religious traditions.[44] As indicated in table 4.3, we assume that the invocation of the sacred by one party as against the other often makes a crucial difference for the course of political conflicts. Here, we rely on an insight, formulated by Appleby, Juergensmeyer, and Rapoport among others, that political confrontations escalate comparatively fast and are fought with particular ferocity when differences of religious faiths get involved.[45] Or, to put it differently, the invocation of the sacred matters for the way that (otherwise similar) conflicts are dealt with. The likelihood that the adversaries will not use force to make their claims prevail is *ceteris paribus* higher in conflicts that are not framed in religious terms by political leaders.

This said, we once again stress that *differences* in religious creed are rarely, if ever, genuine causes of violent clashes within and between nations. Moreover, we subscribe to the instrumentalist thesis that in most cases parochial self-interest lurks behind religious rhetoric. Political entrepreneurs competing for power are eager to exploit a given socioeconomic crisis or political discrimination for their own aggrandizement. This conjecture is corroborated by the finding that religious communities usually live in peace—understood as the absence of civil unrest or war—as long as the society as a whole prospers.[46] The success of political entrepreneurs who instrumentalize the sacred for their own purposes thus turns on a highly unequal distribution of wealth and power in a given society.

To be sure, what is taken to be an unequal, or more precisely an *unfair,* distribution of power and wealth in most societies does not exist independently of religious traditions and their authoritative interpretation by respected custodians of the sacred.[47] Proponents of liberation theology, for instance, remind us that poverty and oppression in Latin America, at least until the historic meeting of the Latin American bishops at Medellin, Colombia, in 1968, were presented in the official teachings of the Roman Catholic Church as part of the natural order and therefore ultimately grounded in the will of God.[48] Consequently, liberation theology spent much time and energy on arguing and preaching the opposite. Accordingly, all Christians, including the poor, have a sacred obligation to engage for a better society and to

Table 4.3   Three Strategies of Conflict De-escalation

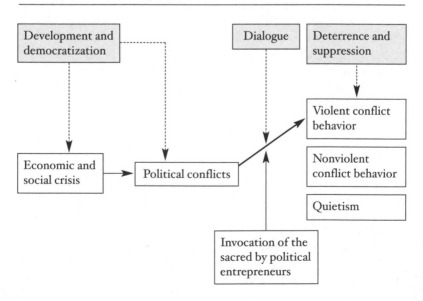

correct the grave and life-destroying concentration of power and wealth in the hands of small elites in Latin America and elsewhere. To put it in more general terms, inequality and injustice within and between nations never come as brute facts, but rather perception and evaluation of inequality and injustice depend on intersubjectively shared interpretations of common experiences.

In the following, however, we bracket this intersubjective constitution of inequality and injustice. We start with the—in our view plausible—observation that in most cases and in most places of the world the renaissance of religious traditions and the emergence of new religious movements follow grave socioeconomic and political crises.[49] Of this the stunning success of liberation theology in the 1960s and 1970s is no exception. As Gutiérrez notes, in the 1950s the growth potential of the Latin American economies was considered exceptionally high by politicians and economists alike.[50] The social climate on the continent was optimistic, and the citizens were generally expected to participate in the coming boom. It was not until the 1960s that these hopes were fundamentally disappointed at least for the vast majority of the poor. Their lot did not improve, but deteriorated. It was exactly under these conditions that liberation theology experienced its take-off and successfully denounced the established political and economic order as "institutionalized violence" and incompatible with the gospel of Jesus.[51]

When approaching the relationship between the discernible allocation of power and wealth within and between states and the corresponding legitimatory discourses, we prefer to represent this relationship in terms of stationary equilibria. That is, historical patterns of rule within and between nations tend to be accompanied by supporting patterns of ideological, religious, or moral justification. However, when the concentration of power and wealth in and between nations significantly exceed intersubjectively accepted margins of inequality, when the gap between the rich and the poor becomes wider, when the number of the poor rises and the poor are further marginalized, the established justifications for any uneven distribution of material and nonmaterial goods come under stress. At this point in time, new ideas tend to emerge and old traditions to be reinterpreted. And it is exactly in such an atmosphere of social crisis that political entrepreneurs may invoke the sacred to further their own ambitions and even to mobilize their constituencies into violent action.

In the remainder of the chapter, we will discuss three different types of (counter)-strategies that are expected to help control, and if possible to reduce, the violence-promoting impact of religious faith on political conflicts: (1) strategies of deterrence and repressive denial, which are designed to increase the costs of violent uprisings; (2) strategies of socioeconomic development and democratization that are designed to manage the modernization crisis; and (3) the dialogue strategy aiming at delegitimizing the use of violence in conflicts. In the final part of this section, we will briefly discuss two conditions for a successful implementation of the dialogue strategy.

Strategies of Deterrence and Repressive Denial

Strategies of deterrence and repressive denial form part of a larger tradition of statesmanship known as realpolitik, or power politics.[52] This tradition focuses on managing conflict behavior with a view to upholding the political status quo by suppressing demands for change. Whatever his or her motivation, an adversary shall be made to realize that he or she cannot succeed in a confrontation at acceptable cost. In our context, this means that the flames of religious hatred are to be extinguished by the icy water of force. The invocation of the sacred in political conflicts is to be balanced by the demonstration and, if necessary, the employment of profane coercion. Political entrepreneurs reaching for power, as well as revisionist nations, should be made aware either that they cannot succeed or that the price to be paid for victory is excessively high. Similarly, the rank and file as well as the wider societal environment are to be intimidated up to a point where even highly mobilized activists and supporters renounce the use of force, which they no longer expect to help them achieve their goals.

A look at the behavior of many incumbent national elites in countries threatened by or subject to civil strife, as for example in Algeria, Egypt, Iraq, or Syria, reveals that they often fall back on strategies of deterrence and repressive denial for the purpose of holding down militant opposition and pacifying the wider society.[53] Due to the protracted development crisis that affects many developing countries, the distributive margins of governments have become so narrow that the legitimacy of these national elites has eroded. Only well-paid troops, "praetorian guards," seem to be able to forestall or suppress rebellions. They eliminate militant activists (and sometimes even bystanders) and threaten parts of the population with mass arrests and the destruction of their livelihood if they do not refrain from supporting the militant opposition. These massive threats raise the costs of supporting rebellious groups. They are designed to outweigh the potential mobilization effects of the counterelites' appeals to the sacred and the religiously motivated willingness to make sacrifices. Strategies of intimidation and suppression therefore aim at building up coercive superiority, which guarantees the psychophysical control of society. Open resistance is turned into an act of desperation and entails very high risks.

In order to make strategies of deterrence and repressive denial work in multiethnic and multireligious societies that suffer a collapse of state authority, Chaim Kaufmann recommends the geographical disentanglement of populations with divergent ethnic ties and religious creeds.[54] He argues that intermingled settlement patterns create enduring incentives for armed combat once the taboo on using violence is broken.[55] From a strategic point of view, geographically dispersed people are practically indefensible. They are extremely vulnerable to deadly raids, which in turn provoke counterattacks that fuel a never-ending circle of violence. To avoid such an outcome, Kaufmann proposes the establishment of homogeneous regions with secure access to the outer world. These regions are designed to strengthen the defensive over the offensive, thereby reducing the incentives for aggressive behavior by denying easy success. As Kaufmann puts it:

> The safest pattern [in torn countries] is a well-defined demographic front that separates nearly homogeneous regions. Such a front can be defended by organized military forces, so populations are not at risk unless defenses are breached.[56]

If the strategy of separation is not followed, Kaufmann predicts that violent conflicts in multireligious societies will result in spontaneous refugee flows and possibly in ethnic cleansing.[57] The social costs of population movements before escalation are certainly high, but the price paid in human lives if religious and ethnic groups are still demographically intermixed when hostilities arise will be dramatically higher.

Similarly, Samuel Huntington advises the major powers in the new world order to abstain from intervention into the internal affairs of alien civilizations.[58] The relations between civilizations should be governed by a policy of mutual respect bolstered by the ability of each major power to deny others any important military success. The leading actors of each civilization should come to an agreement as to how to divide the world into spheres of influence and should then engage in the traditional balancing behavior that renders the system stable. As in the Cold War era, only such a stable balance of power is supposed to forestall the horrors of World War III that would now take the form of a deadly struggle for religious hegemony.

Strategies designed to intimidate and suppress militant opposition groups are highly dubious as a means of maintaining or restoring a peaceful social order. Admittedly, there may be situations in which the use of force against organized militant activists by legitimate state actors is justifiable on moral and legal grounds. This presupposes, however, that these militant activists have already challenged the state's monopoly of force and are openly and willfully violating the rules of civilized conflict behavior, for instance by suicide attacks on civilian population. Additionally, any state's forceful counteraction must continue to respect fundamental human rights and humanitarian rules. Unfortunately, in many parts of the world these conditions are not honored by state actors.

Furthermore, the success of deterrence and repressive denial—if a violent suppression can be said to be a success at all—remains uncertain. As Almond, Sivan, and Appleby observe, even extreme coercion against fundamentalist movements by state authorities in Syria was insufficient "to rout out these movements in their entirety. Any relaxation finds them rising once again to the surface."[59] Gurr and Harff as well as Kaufmann find the same pattern in Iraq.[60] The brutal action of Iraqi troops in the course of the Al-Anfal campaign—when populations of entire villages were killed by the use of poison gas—did not break the Kurdish will for autonomy or independence permanently. Similarly, the unyielding policy of the Algerian government toward the Islamic Salvation Front has until now remained largely unsuccessful.[61] On the contrary, the Algerian government's action sparked a spiral of violence and counterviolence. As in many other civil wars, scholars fear that the civil war in Algeria will be fought until the conflict parties are completely exhausted.

Finally, if it is true (as its proponents argue) that any effective operation of strategies of deterrence and repressive denial presupposes the geographical separation of hitherto intermingled populations with divergent ethnic ties or religious creeds, then this amounts to a virtually insurmountable barrier for these strategies to be successfully applied. As Michael E. Brown and Chantal de Jonge Oudraat laconically note: "Ethnic geography and demographic patterns . . . are factors that are not particularly manipulable."[62] Kaufmann's and Huntington's diagnoses may be sound, but their remedy clearly seems both impracticable and ethically problematic.

Strategies of Socioeconomic Development and Democratization

As already noted, it is a central tenet of instrumentalist scholars that the current political renaissance of religion is a consequence of a worldwide economic and developmental crisis. Thus, they conclude that the best way to reduce the attraction of religious communities for desperate people and to check their conflict-escalating potential is to overcome the underlying socioeconomic crisis. As a consequence, the likelihood of religious convictions being used for the mobilization of the rank and file will diminish. The number of people who are content will increase while militant groups lose their support in society. The majority of people will reject violence as a legitimate means in political conflicts and will turn to moderate religious and political leaders. In short, as the distributional conflicts in a society become less severe, the violent forms of protest will lose much of their appeal.

To illustrate this causal mechanism, Michael E. Brown points to the Middle East in the 1970s and the beginning of the 1980s, "when high oil prices and high levels of foreign aid from the United States and the Soviet Union gave governments more largesse to spread around. Potential opposition forces were pacified and, in essence, bought off."[63] Similarly Almond, Sivan, and Appleby observe that "a substantial economic improvement, as in Tunisia in the late 1980s and early 1990s, results in sympathizers [of fundamentalist movements] dropping out in droves."[64]

From this perspective, it is obvious that domestic as well as foreign policymakers interested in peace should foster economic growth with fair distribution in order to improve the economic and social situation of the most disadvantaged in societies affected by economic decline or even collapse. Senghaas maintains, for example, that the current crisis in many developing countries can be defused by imitating the success story of OECD (Organization for Economic Co-operation and Development) states.[65] For this purpose, development aid should be used to stimulate good governance, the establishment of well-functioning markets, and the education of the people. In the medium and long term, prosperity will be the result. Even more importantly, economic growth will cause gradual pluralization and democratization of developing societies. This is supposed to further reduce the political salience of religious faith.[66] As in Europe in the nineteenth and twentieth centuries, secularization processes should then gain momentum, referring questions of faith to the private sphere of individuals. As a result, religious differences will not, or will only at the margins, translate into political differences.

The central problem of implementing economic development and democratization strategies is that they presuppose a viable state.[67] Senghaas, for instance, argues that the positive experiences in Europe and East Asia would have been unthinkable without the state as a modernizing force.[68] In many developing countries as well as in numerous regions of the former Soviet Union, however, the state cannot operate as "crisis manager" because it is itself part of the current crisis.[69] Additionally, in these parts of the world, religious institutions are often the only functioning social organizations that can muster the loyalty of people and that can serve as reliable networks of political communication.[70] The expectation that economic and social conflicts can be defused by virtue of economic development and democratization is therefore in many cases deceptive. It remains to be seen, then, how the instrumentalization of religious faith by power-seeking elites can be kept in check.

Dialogue Strategy

The dialogue strategy seeks to delegitimize the use of force in political conflicts. It is designed to enhance the inner resistance of people to engage in, or to support, armed combat. In contrast to the two other strategies discussed so far, which operate primarily on external incentives for action, the dialogue strategy relies on convincing arguments that motivate people from within. They should renounce the use of violence for principled reasons as inappropriate and unjust. The proponents of the dialogue strategy thus engage in the proverbial struggle for the hearts and minds of the people. And it is exactly here where Appleby and Küng see an opportunity for the world's great religious communities and their leaders to promote principles and instruments of peaceful conflict management within and between the societies in which their members live.

Notwithstanding their own preferences for peaceful modes of conflict management, Appleby and Küng take the religious motivation of those who follow the call to arms by self-appointed guardians of faith seriously. Both authors are convinced, however, that the rank and file of militant movements, as well as their sympathizers in the wider societal environment, are more often than not misguided in their religious zeal and that they erroneously attribute spiritual origins to profane power struggles. As Appleby has put it, inclination of ordinary believers toward the use of force in particular conflicts is more often than not the consequence of a sort of "religious illiteracy."[71] Therefore, established religious authorities dispose of considerable intellectual and organizational resources to counterbalance the mobilizing rhetoric of political entrepreneurs or threatened state officials.

Among scholars working in the field of religious studies it is generally accepted that the great world religions encompass a multitude of sources and traditions.[72] These sources and traditions have emerged in particular historical constellations and reflect the spirit of their times. Consequently, religious communities in general and religious authorities in particular are challenged to apply the received *depositum fidei* to new social and political circumstances. In this never-ending process of rereading and rearranging the canon of respected traditions, gaps between "professed" belief and "operative" belief are unavoidable. Some traditions gain importance in a given historical situation while others are pushed into the collective subconscious of a religious community. In this context, the interpretation of sacred scriptures and doctrines by militant leaders calling for armed combat against the unfaithful is just one interpretation amongst others. Moreover, it is most often a rather marginal one within their own communities. Aside from those texts that might be used to legitimate violence, to demand sacrifices in the case of war, and to condemn persons of a different religious creed, in all great religions one finds a wealth of sources teaching the incompatibility of faith and violence, and demanding sacrifices for peace and respect for persons of different religious creeds.[73] According to Appleby, this civilizing dimension of the sacred should not be underestimated in its peace-building potential and it will probably gain in importance over the next decades:

> Within each of [the] great traditions, notwithstanding their profound substantive differences, one can trace a moral trajectory challenging adherents to greater acts of compassion, forgiveness, and reconciliation. The competing voices of revenge and retaliation that continue to claim the status of authentic religious expression are gradually rendered as "demonic."[74]

According to the proponents of the dialogue strategy, religious authorities all over the world increasingly recognize the duty to protect the sacred traditions of their communities against those who try to instrumentalize them for their own aggrandizement. In this regard, they can take a number of initiatives that address the four determinants of elites' strategic choices, as developed in preceding sections.

(1) First of all, established religious authorities are in a position to denounce the framing of a given conflict as a dispute of faith.[75] As we have repeatedly stressed, differences in the understanding of the sacred are only in very few cases the real causes of violent confrontations. Moreover, all great world religions subject the legitimation of the use of force against individuals and groups to strict criteria that are rarely met by any of the antagonists. By opposing the inflammatory

rhetoric of political entrepreneurs or threatened officials, religious authorities can therefore significantly reduce the mobilization of the rank and file of, as well as the social support for, a militant movement with a propensity toward violence.

Additionally, Küng and Kuschel remind us that the great world religions share a common set of moral values and norms that are designed to protect the individual and the community against violence and the material exploitation by powerful actors.[76] Küng refers to this "zone of overlapping consensus" in interdogmatic affairs as an emerging global ethic.[77] Its core is formed by the golden rule and four commandments: (i) the obligation to a culture of nonviolence and deep respect for life; (ii) the obligation to a culture of solidarity and a fair economic order; (iii) the obligation to a culture of tolerance and a life in truthfulness; and (iv) the obligation to a culture of equality and partnership between man and woman.

Together, these rules affirm *inter alia* "a conviction of the fundamental unity of the human family, and the equality and dignity of all human beings" and "a sense of sacredness of the individual person and his or her conscience," as was already stated in 1970 by the first World Conference on Religion and Peace in Kyoto.[78] If taken seriously and preached by established religious authorities, any attempt to dehumanize the antagonists in a conflict would therefore find its limits in the global ethic that makes the great world religions natural allies in their quest for the peaceful settlement of political conflicts. In fact, it can be expected that the emphasis of shared moral fundamentals by established religious authorities of divergent creeds will make a crucial difference in the propensity of antagonistic elites to propagate violence as a means of conflict resolution. As Rubin, Pruitt, and Kim argue, one of the most important sources of preventing the escalation of conflicts are social bonds formed by common group membership.[79] It is precisely in this direction that a global ethic works.

(2) Established religious authorities have the power to channel the willingness of the faithful to make sacrifices into peaceful actions designed to redress their grievances. Social movements that do not only strive for radical political reforms but also commit their followers to strict nonviolence arose time and again from the midst of the great world religions—take, for example, the Indian Congress movement for independence, the Cambodian Pilgrims of Truth, the Pashtun reform movement in northwestern Pakistan, the Civil Rights movement in the United States, and the Tibetan liberation movement.[80] The central figures of these movements, Mahatma Gandhi, the Buddhist primate of Cambodia Samdech Preah Maha Ghosananda, the "Muslim St.

Francis" Abdul Ghaffar Khan, Martin Luther King Jr., and the present Dalai Lama, never doubted that their political demands as well as their strict adherence to nonviolent strategies of protest resulted necessarily from their religious beliefs. The moderating influence of Christian churches was also helpful, if not decisive, for the rather peaceful end of apartheid in South Africa.[81] Their leaders—chief among them Desmond Tutu—managed to delegitimize the use of violence, stressing at the same time the Christian obligation for reconciliation.

Similarly, in the 1970s and 1980s prominent figures of the Roman Catholic hierarchy in Latin America firmly advocated nonviolent forms of protest against the abuse of power by military juntas in their respective countries.[82] Chief among them were the bishop of Recife, Dom Helder Camara; the archbishop of São Paulo, Dom Paulo Evaristo Arns; and the archbishop of El Salvador, Oscar Romero. Together with many other activists in Latin American countries, they publicized gross human rights violations by governmental forces; relentlessly protested against torture and demanded the release of political prisoners; assisted opposition groups, providing them with sanctuary and organizational resources; and supported prodemocratic movements in their countries. For their moral and political engagement, many bishops, priests, and nuns paid a high price. Oscar Romero, for instance, was assassinated in 1980 by a right-wing death squad shortly after he had publicly urged soldiers to disobey orders from superiors to kill civilians.

(3) As already mentioned, if preached emphatically by religious authorities, the moral common ground between the great world religions at least theoretically impedes the dehumanization of the opposing party and its members in a given dispute. Practically, however, political conflicts often escalate to a point where the antagonists have developed intense hostile feelings toward one another. In violent conflicts of this kind, negotiating a lasting settlement is rather complicated, to say the least. Trust has become a scarce good in the interactions of the involved parties. They are entrapped in circles of self-fulfilling prophecies that seemingly render any cessation of hostilities impossible before an all-out victory or defeat of one side or an imposed settlement by a third, hegemonic party. Under such conditions, religious leaders may use, and at least sometimes did use, their authority to mediate between the parties.[83] Due to their reputation as respected representatives of the sacred in the world, religious authorities are in a position to support the reestablishment of mutual trust between the adversaries in that they oblige all sides to honor fundamental religious values. They can reopen channels of communication, provide a

conference forum and help develop face-saving formulas for conflict settlement. Moreover, they are also in a position to monitor agreements and to issue credible evaluations of any progress made or of infractions that may have taken place. In so doing, they facilitate the cooperative management of conflicts even in extremely tense situations. Thus religious authorities can play a decisive role in avoiding that the spectrum of possible conflict behavior narrows down to that of using and perpetuating aggressive self-help.

(4) Finally, established religious authorities have the moral standing and the necessary resources not only for denouncing the rhetoric of political entrepreneurs and threatened state authorities, but also for giving voice to the poor and oppressed in societies suffering grave socioeconomic inequities and severe political and cultural discrimination. The common solidarity rule to side with the disadvantaged within and among nations was already formulated in 1970 during the first meeting of the World Conference on Religion and Peace in Kyoto. It was reaffirmed by the ecumenical Parliament of the World's Religions in September 1993 and was on the agenda of the Millennium World Peace Summit in August 2000. On the one hand, by adopting such a critical and reformist position vis-à-vis the political establishment, religious authorities avoid being instrumentalized by ruling elites who, in a number of countries, have a vital interest in using religious traditions to keep the desperate from uprising and to ensure quietism on the side of the poor and oppressed.[84] On the other hand, religious authorities enable the articulation of grievances, thus operating as a safety valve before dissatisfied people engage in, or sympathize with, violent actions. Yet it is the lack of functioning social and political institutions to channel protest and to respond to grievances that is what most scholars have identified as one of the most important sources contributing to the escalation of conflicts.[85] Conversely, reliable and effective channels for articulating grievances decrease the legitimation of violence.

Two Conditions for a Successful Implementation of the Dialogue Strategy

Despite sporadic success of religiously motivated peacemakers and despite considerable theoretical progress toward a normative unity within dogmatic plurality, the way to a common global ethic that really affects people and their behavior is still a long one. In our view, there are at least two major problems that impede the achievement of such an ethic and the implementation of social practices derived therefrom.

First, there is an often-discussed dilemma situation between the different religious communities: Before they can strengthen the resistance against violence in their own communities, they have to be sure that the other communities do the same. If this is not the case the peaceful would become the stupid, as often feared by conservative scholars.[86] Therefore, confidence-building measures between the religious communities are needed to avoid the occurrence of dilemma situations. Effective monitoring of each other's behavior minimizes the risk of cheating and of suffering relative losses. That is, any exploitation of the other's cooperation is discovered early and thus loses its attraction. In this context, it might be helpful that there are only very few states without a religious minority. The majority's treatment of their minorities might then be taken as an indicator of the great religions' readiness to cooperate with each other.

Thus, it is to be expected that the trust between the world's great religious communities will grow to the extent to which they act as advocates for persons of different religious creeds in their own areas of influence. In so doing, they would show that they are serious about the universal validity of the abovementioned minimum moral standards. A culture of mutual respect would then arise in the societies concerned. This would help to prevent the danger of demonizing one's adversary in social conflicts. In order to speed up the process of minority protection, religious communities could agree on the establishment of common nonstate courts of appeal for discriminated minorities, who would be free to bring forward their complaints to such courts. The latter would be endowed with the competence to decide about religious discrimination and to make their decisions public.

A second obstacle on the way to an interreligious recognition as peacemaker is the problem of guilt. All great religious communities were, or are, more or less entangled in violent political clashes. They explicitly took sides in such clashes or did not prevent their faith from being exploited for the legitimation of violence and for the mobilization for war. A fundamental reorientation in the way indicated above would therefore be equivalent to an admission of guilt. The established religious leaders, in particular, would find that hard to accept, for their most valued asset would be at stake: their credibility. They must fear that they will lose followers and cause damage to their mission as they understand it. The question as to what could lead them to recognize, and to comply with, a common world ethic therefore deserves further scrutiny.

It is to be expected that religious leaders—as every other social elite—will attempt to reevaluate their programs and change their behavior only when the damage caused by proceeding the same way as before is greater than that caused by a programmatic reorientation. If, in such a situation, they remain inflexibly tied to their status quo position, they run the risk of being replaced by more reform-minded members of the leadership group. Thus, an important impetus for laying greater emphasis on interreligious common ground will depend on whether or not intrareligious reform movements gain strength.

As Appleby, Esposito, Juergensmeyer, Little, and Voll among others observe, there are moderate critics of religious demagogy and intolerance in every world religion today.[87] These critics argue that peace is possible only with, and not against, persons of different religious creeds and that it contradicts the very essence of religion to push through one's own convictions with violent means. The reform movements within the different religions will gain the support of their respective faithful to the extent to which the programs of militant fundamentalists prove to be counterproductive or self-destructive. For it shall not be forgotten that the political renaissance of religions has arisen from the weaknesses of modernity. It was the disappointment at the unkept promises of modernizing elites with regard to an increase of welfare that has instilled new plausibility into old teachings and has lifted their representatives to new heights of reputation and power. This is why the latter will lose support to the extent to which they are regarded as part of the problem themselves, as being partly to blame for violence and grief. In other words, if religious faith is not able to bring about the promised future, it will face the same fate as the promises of secular modernity.[88]

In table 4.4 we summarize our discussion so far. We put a plus sign next to the dialogue strategy, for moderate constructivists are well aware that the propagation of peace-loving attitudes alone is no guarantee for a lasting peace. Dialogues must be supplemented, as far as possible, with economic and political development strategies and sometimes—as a last resort—with means of force. Nevertheless, the success of these strategies depends, in the final analysis, on the willingness of vast segments of the population to respect the rights of minorities and to reject violence as a means of conflict management. Additionally, this majority should be ready to support democratization and a system of broadly inclusive constitutional government.

Concluding Remarks

As Johnston and Cox remind us, the influence of religious communities on politics and policies—real as it is—must not be overestimated.[89] The sources of conflicts and the course of conflict processes

Table 4.4   Three Strategies to Cope with the Impact of Faith on Social Conflicts

	Deterrence and Suppression	*Development and Democratization*	*Dialogue (+)*
Focal Point	Conflict behavior	Socioeconomic conflict	Conflict attitudes
Countermeasure	Police and military force	Material welfare	Moral enlightenment
Goal	Making violence irrational	Making violence unnecessary	Making violence illegitimate
Causal Mechanism	Containment by physical force denies political success	Welfare lowers identification with religious communities	Exposing the political instrumentalization of religious traditions
	Containment by physical force counterbalances increased willingness to make sacrifices	Welfare decreases mobilization and public support for violent strategies	Emphasizing the intrinsic value of all human beings
		Participation increases the expected utility of nonviolent forms of social protest	Enabling cooperation by enhancing mutual trust and monitoring agreements

are usually highly complex. Religious factors often play only a subordinate role as a source of conflicts, but an important one in conflict processes. Therefore, religious visions of peace can take on a practical significance in dealing with confrontations short of violence, as the role of Christian churches in South Africa or Mahatma Gandhi's Indian independence movement have shown. Thus the question is not so much whether religious faith can influence the course of conflicts—this is without doubt—but rather when religious faith has an escalating or a de-escalating effect. The pertinent research undertaken in peace and conflict studies is just beginning. Nevertheless, we hope that the prospects for, and the limits of, the dialogue strategy will be thoroughly explored in future. It is not yet foreseeable that today's social and political crises can be defused with the help of economic growth and democratization alone. Neither is it desirable, nor is it to be expected, that social tensions are or will be controlled by a state's ruling elite using force against parts of its population. This is why we have to search for ways that keep open the space for strategies of peaceful accommodation if not reconciliation. Perhaps the dialogue strategy that counts on the delegitimation of violence and the popular resistance against it turns out to be a useful starting point in doing so.

Notes

Earlier versions of this chapter were presented at the 2000 annual meeting of the International Studies Association in Los Angeles and at the London School of Economics conference Religion and International Relations on 27 May 2000. The authors appreciate the many pertinent comments they received on these occasions. Especially, we want to thank Martin Beck, Jonathan Fox, Peter Mayer, Mark Neufeld, and two anonymous referees for their helpful critiques of earlier drafts.

1. For recent reviews of the burgeoning literature on this subject, see Jonathan Fox, "Religion as an Overlooked Element of International Relations," *International Studies Review* 3, no. 3 (2001): 53–74, and Anthony Gill, "Religion and Comparative Politics," *Annual Review of Political Science* 4 (2001): 117–38.

2. We hold this position to be moderate, because its proponents generally accept the causal impact of material factors such as power and wealth on political choices and the resulting interactions. These material factors, however, are embedded in cognitive structures of an intersubjective quality that gives meaning to them. For moderate constructivism in IR, see Emanuel Adler and Michael Barnett, "Security Communities in Theoretical Perspective," in *Security Communities,* eds. Emanuel Adler and Michael Barnett (Cambridge: Cambridge University Press, 1998), 12–13, and James Fearon and Alexander Wendt, "Rationalism v. Constructivism: A Skeptical View," in *Handbook of International Relations,* eds. Walter Carlsnaes, Thomas Risse, and Beth A. Simmons (London: Sage, 2002), 58–60.

3. See especially Hans Küng, *Projekt Weltethos,* 5th ed. (München: Piper, 1992); Hans Küng, *Global Responsibility: In Search of a New World Ethic* (New York: Crossroad, 1991); Hans Küng, *Weltethos für Weltpolitik und Weltwirtschaft* (München: Piper, 1997); Hans Küng and Karl Josef Kuschel, eds., *Erklärung zum Weltethos: Die Deklaration des Parlaments der Weltreligionen* (München: Piper, 1993).

4. UNESCO Charter, preamble [http://www.unesco.org/general/eng/about/constitution/pre.shtml] (10 December 2000).

5. See Samuel Huntington, "The Clash of Civilizations?" *Foreign Affairs* 72, no. 3 (1993), 22–49; Gilles Kepel, *The Revenge of God: The Resurgence of Islam, Christianity and Judaism in the Modern World* (Cambridge: Polity Press, 1994); and Bassam Tibi, *Krieg der Zivilisationen* (Hamburg: Hoffmann and Campe, 1995).

6. See among others Mark Juergensmeyer, *The New Cold War? Religious Nationalism Confronts the Secular State* (Berkeley and Los Angeles: University of California Press, 1993); Ted Robert Gurr, "Minorities, Nationalists, and Ethnopolitical Conflict," in *Managing Global Chaos: Sources of and Responses to International Conflict,* eds. Chester A. Crocker, Fen Osler Hampson, and Pamela Aall (Washington, D.C.: United States Institute of Peace Press, 1996); Thomas Meyer, *Identitätswahn: Die Politisierung des kulturellen Unterschieds* (Berlin: Aufbau, 1997); and Dieter Senghaas, *Zivilisierung wider Willen: Der Konflikt der Kulturen mit sich Selbst* (Frankfurt: Suhrkamp, 1998).

7. See Harald Müller, *Das Zusammenleben der Kulturen: Ein Gegenentwurf zu Huntington* (Frankfurt a.M.: Fischer, 1998) and Joseph Nye, „Conflicts after the Cold War" *The Washington Quarterly* 19, no. 1 (1995): 5–24.

8. See Mahmud A. Faksh, "The Prospects of Islamic Fundamentalism in the Post-Gulf War Period," *International Journal* 49, no. 2 (1994): 183–218; and Ibrahim A. Karawan, *The Islamist Impasse,* Adelphi Paper 314 (Oxford: Oxford University Press, 1997), 14–17.

9. See Michael E. Brown and Chantal de Jonge Oudraat, "International Conflict and International Action: An Overview," in *Nationalism and Ethnic Conflict: An International Security Reader,* eds. Michael Brown et al. (Cambridge, MA: Massachusetts Institute of Technology Press, 1997), 254–55, and Dieter Senghaas, "Schluß mit der Fundamentalismus-Debatte! Plädoyer für eine Reorientierung des Interkulturellen Dialogs," *Blätter für Deutsche und Internationale Politik* 40, no. 2 (1995): 187.

10. Gurr, "Minorities, Nationalists, and Ethnopolitical Conflict," 74. As Gurr explains in *People versus States: Minorities at Risk in the New Century* (Washington, D.C.: United States Institute of Peace Press, 2000), 3–13, his approach is confined to analyzing the behavior of ethnopolitical groups, which are to be distinguished from most of the religious movements at the core of the present chapter. These differences notwithstanding, we share the analytic importance that Gurr attaches to enduring political and economic discrimination on the one hand and to group leaders and their strategic choices on the other.

11. See Anthony D. Smith, "The Ethnic Sources of Nationalism," *Survival* 35, no. 1 (1993): 53.

12. See Müller, *Zusammenleben der Kulturen,* 44–46.

13. See, for instance, Errol A. Henderson and Richard Tucker, "Clear and Present Strangers: The Clash of Civilizations and International Conflict," *International Studies Quarterly* 45, no. 2 (2001): 317–38.

14. Nye, "Conflicts after the Cold War," 17.

15. Daniel Patrick Moynihan, *Pandaemonium: Ethnicity in International Politics* (Oxford: Oxford University Press, 1993), 15.

16. See among others Emanuel Adler, "Seizing the Middle Ground: Constructivism in World Politics," *European Journal of International*

Relations 3, no. 3 (1997): 319–63; Ted Hopf, "The Promise of Constructivism in International Relations Theory," *International Security* 23, no. 1 (1998): 171–200; and Alexander Wendt, *Social Theory and International Politics* (Cambridge: Cambridge University Press, 1999), 20–21.

17. Alexander Wendt, "Collective Identity Formation and the International State," *American Political Science Review* 88, no. 2 (1994): 389.

18. See, for instance, Adler, "Seizing the Middle Ground," 333, and Hopf, "Promise of Constructivism," 177.

19. Wendt, *Social Theory*, 95.

20. See also Adler, "Seizing the Middle Ground," 330.

21. See, for instance, Harvey Cox, "World Religions and Conflict Resolution," in *Religion, the Missing Dimension of Statecraft*, eds. Douglas Johnston and Cynthia Sampson (Oxford: Oxford University Press, 1994), 266; and Douglas Johnston, "Review of the Findings," in *Religion, the Missing Dimension*, 263.

22. See R. Scott Appleby, *The Ambivalence of the Sacred: Religion, Violence, and Reconciliation* (Lanham, MD: Rowman and Littlefield, 2000), 54–57, and Jack Snyder, "Nationalism and the Crisis of the Post-Soviet State," *Survival* 35, no. 1 (1995): 17–18.

23. Carnegie Commission on Preventing Deadly Conflict, *Preventing Deadly Conflict* (New York: Carnegie Corporation of New York, 1997), 30.

24. Carsten Bagge Laustsen and Ole Wæver, in this volume, 162.

25. Alexander Wendt, "The Agent-Structure Problem in International Relations Theory," *International Organization* 41, no. 3 (1987): 359.

26. See, among others, Jacob Bercovitch and Richard Jackson, *International Conflict: A Chronological Encyclopedia of Conflicts and Their Management 1945–1995* (Washington, D.C.: Congressional Quarterly, 1997), 21–22, and Louis Kriesberg, *Social Conflicts*, 2d ed. (New York: Prentice-Hall, 1982), 87–90.

27. In the literature, the significance of elites in social conflicts is not in dispute. See Gurr, *People versus States*, 78–79; Kriesberg, *Social Conflicts*, 87–90; and Jeffrey Z. Rubin, Dean G. Pruitt, and Sung Hee Kim, *Social Conflict: Escalation, Stalemate, and Settlement*, 2d ed. (New York: McGraw-Hill, 1994), 20 and 24.

28. Michael Brown, "The Causes of Internal Conflict: An Overview," in *Nationalism and Ethnic Conflict*, 17.

29. See, among others, Vilhelm Aubert, "Interessenkonflikt und Wertkonflikt: Zwei Typen des Konflikts und der Konfliktlösung," in *Konflikt und Konfliktstrategie: Ansätze zu einer Soziologischen Konflikttheorie*, ed. Walter Bühl (München: Nymphenburger Verlagshandlung, 1972), 180–84, and C. R. Mitchell, *The Structure of International Conflict* (London: Macmillan, 1981), 35.

30. See Kriesberg, *Social Conflicts*, 30–35; Mitchell, *Structure of International Conflict*, 87 and 94; and Rubin, Pruitt, and Kim, *Social Conflict*, 15 and 85.

31. The willingness to make sacrifices, in turn, depends on a number of factors. Kriesberg, *Social Conflicts*, 134, observes, for example, that young people are comparatively easy to mobilize for the use of risky strategies.

32. See Kriesberg, *Social Conflicts*, 186–89, and Rubin, Pruitt, and Kim, *Social Conflict*, 84–87.

33. Bercovitch and Jackson, *International Conflict*, 14.

34. See, for instance, Gurr, "Minorities, Nationalists, and Ethnopolitical Conflict," 69; Kriesberg, *Social Conflicts*, 147; and Mitchell, *Structure of International Conflict*, 134–35. For reasons of complexity reduction, we will consider in this chapter the national societal environment of the parties only. It should be noted, however, that there is research demonstrating that elites attach great significance to the support of international as well as transnational actors when contemplating strategies for conflict management. See among others David R. Davis and Will H. Moore, "Ethnicity Matters: Transnational Ethnic Alliances and Foreign Policy Behavior," *International Studies Quarterly* 41, no. 1 (1997): 171–84.

35. See Juergensmeyer, *New Cold War*, 22–23, and David Little, "Religious Militancy," in *Managing Global Chaos*, 82–83.

36. Appleby, *Ambivalence of the Sacred*, 91.

37. See Little, "Religious Militancy," 87, and Smith, "The Ethnic Sources of Nationalism," 57.

38. See Renée de Nevers, "Democratization and Ethnic Conflict," *Survival* 35, no. 2 (1993): 33.

39. See Barry Rubin, "Religion and International Affairs," in *Religion, the Missing Dimension*, 24.

40. Jonathan Fox, "Do Religious Institutions Support Violence or the Status Quo?" *Studies in Conflict and Terrorism* 22, no. 2 (1999): 131.

41. See, for instance, Austin M. Ahanotu, "Religion and the Problem of Power: South Africa," in *The Terrible Meek: Essays on Religion and Revolution*, ed. Lonnie D. Kliever (New York: Paragon House, 1987), 230–34, and Appleby, *Ambivalence of the Sacred*, 34–40.

42. See especially Clive Henry Afflick, *The History and Politics of Liberation Theology in Latin America and the Caribbean* (Ann Arbor, MI: University Microfilms International, 1989), 119–25; Gustavo Gutiérrez, *Theologie der Befreiung*, 8th ed. (Mainz: Kaiser, 1985), 103–104; William R. Jones, "The Legitimation of Counterviolence: Insights from Latin American Liberation Theology," in *The Terrible Meek*, 189–216.

43. Jones, "Legitimation of Counterviolence," 192.

44. Therefore, our account is unambiguously biased in favor of peaceful means of political change.

45. See Appleby, *Ambivalence of the Sacred*, 104; Juergensmeyer, *New Cold War*, 153; and David C. Rapoport, "Comparing Militant Fundamentalist Movements and Groups," in *Fundamentalisms and the*

State: Remaking Politics, Economies, and Militance, eds. Martin E. Marty and R. Scott Appleby (Chicago: University of Chicago Press, 1993), 446.

46. See Appleby, *Ambivalance of the Sacred,* 119. This finding makes perfect sense in a moderate constructivist framework as well.

47. We are grateful to one anonymous reviewer for challenging us to clarify our argumentation at this point.

48. Gutiérrez, *Theologie der Befreiung,* 61–62; and Jones, "Religious Legitimation of Counterviolence," 201–05.

49. For a brilliant overview, see Keddie, *The New Religious Politics.*

50. Gutiérrez, *Theologie der Befreiung,* 74–77.

51. The term "institutionalized violence" as well as the corresponding notions of "collective sin" and "preferential option for the poor" found their way into official church documents. See Afflick, *History and Politics of Liberation Theology,* 120–25, and Christiano German, *Politik und Kirche in Lateinamerika: Zur Rolle der Bischofskonferenzen im Demokratisierungsprozeß Brasiliens und Chiles* (Frankfurt: Vervuert, 1999), 96–100. What remained contested among Catholics in Latin America, however, was the appropriate method of political change.

52. See Jack Donnelly, "Twentieth-Century Realism," in *Traditions of International Ethics,* eds. Terry Nardin and David R. Mapel (Cambridge: Cambridge University Press, 1992), 85–93; and Mitchell, *Structure of International Conflict,* 263–65.

53. See among others Gabriel A. Almond, Emmanuel Sivan, and R. Scott Appleby, "Politics, Ethnicity, and Fundamentalism," in *Fundamentalism Comprehended,* 499–500; Gurr, *People versus States,* 127; and Juergensmeyer, *New Cold War,* 24.

54. See Chaim Kaufmann, "Possible and Impossible Solutions to Ethnic Wars," *International Security* 20, no. 4 (1996), 136–75.

55. Similar arguments concerning the violence-promoting effect of intermingled populations with divergent ethnic ties or religious convictions have been advanced by Barry R. Posen, "The Security Dilemma and Ethnic Conflict," *Survival* 35, no. 1 (1993): 27–47, and Stephen Van Evera, "Hypotheses on Nationalism and War," in *Nationalism and Ethnic Conflict,* 38–41.

56. Kaufmann, "Possible and Impossible Solutions," 149.

57. Ibid., 170–71.

58. Huntington, *The Clash of Civilizations,* 513–14.

59. Almond, Sivan, and Appleby, "Politics, Ethnicity, and Fundamentalism," 502.

60. Ted Robert Gurr and Barbara Harff, *Ethnic Conflict in World Politics* (Boulder, CO: Westview Press, 1994), 105, and Kaufmann, "Possible and Impossible Solutions," 151.

61. See Milton Viorst, "Algeria's Long Night," *Foreign Affairs* 76, no. 6 (1997): 86–99.

62. Brown and de Jonge Oudraat, "International Conflict and International Action," 252.
63. Brown, "The Causes of Internal Conflict," 22.
64. Almond, Sivan, and Appleby, "Politics, Ethnicity, and Fundamentalism," 500.
65. Senghaas, *Zivilisierung wider Willen,* 185–86.
66. See, for instance, Robert Bartley, "The Case for Optimism: The West Should Believe in Itself," *Foreign Affairs* 72, no. 4 (1993): 15–18, and Senghaas, "Schluß mit der Fundamentalismus-Debatte!" 187–90.
67. See especially Jose Campos and Hilton L. Root, *The Key to the Asian Miracle: Making Shared Growth Credible* (Washington, D.C.: The Brookings Institution, 1996).
68. Senghaas, *Zivilisierung wider Willen,* 186.
69. See especially Robert Jackson, *Quasi-States: Sovereignty, International Relations, and the Third World* (Cambridge: Cambridge University Press, 1990) and Jack Snyder, "Nationalism and the Crisis of the Post-Soviet State," *Survival* 35, no. 1 (1993): 7.
70. Rubin, "Religion and International Affairs," 24.
71. Appleby, *Ambivalence of the Sacred,* 69. It is worth noting that Laustsen and Wæver in this volume reach similar conclusions from a post-structuralist interpretation of religion in conflicts. In a nutshell, they call for the "de-securitization" of faith, which means "respecting religion as it is," and not using it as an ideology. Consequently, religious discourses, if taken literally, oppose any brute instrumentalization by either party to a conflict.
72. See among others Appleby, *Ambivalence of the Sacred,* 30–34; Cox, "World Religions and Conflict Resolution," 267, and William Vendley and David Little, "Implications for Religious Communities: Buddhism, Islam, Hinduism, Christianity," in *Religion, the Missing Dimension,* 309–12.
73. This is also and especially true for Islam, which is often suspected by the Western public of promoting a ruthless urge for violent confrontations between Muslims and non-Muslims. Islam, however, is internally as multifaceted as are all other world religions; see, for instance, the brilliant chapter by John L. Esposito and John O. Voll in this volume.
74. Appleby, *Ambivalence of the Sacred,* 31.
75. See Appleby, *Ambivalence of the Sacred,* 72–80, and Küng, *Projekt Weltethos,* 86. A similar point is made by Scott M. Thomas in this volume.
76. See Küng and Kuschel, *Erklärung zum Weltethos,* 9–11. This common set of moral values and norms was articulated at the first meeting of the World Conference on Religion and Peace in Kyoto in 1970 and reaffirmed in a slightly different form by the Parliament of the World's Religions, which met in Chicago in 1993. On 27 August 2000, finally, a Millennium World Peace Summit opened at the United Nations in New York. The four-day meeting brought together an unprecedented

number of about 1000 spiritual leaders from 100 countries and dozens of faith groups. See Jane Lapeman, "World Religious Leaders Hold First Summit," *Christian Science Monitor,* 28 August 2000, A1; and Colum Lynch, "U.N. Summit Hears Plea For Religious Tolerance," *Washington Post,* 30 August 2000, A16.

77. Küng, *Weltethos für Weltpolitik und Weltwirtschaft,* 154.

78. Vendley and Little, "Implications for Religious Communities," in *Religion, the Missing Dimension,* 314.

79. Rubin, Pruitt, and Kim, *Social Conflict,* 127–28.

80. For the Congress movement, see Cox, "World Religions and Conflict Resolution," 270. For the Cambodia Pilgrims of Truth, see Appleby, *Ambivalence of the Sacred,* 123. For the Pashtun reform movement, see Robert C. Johansen, "Radical Islam and Nonviolence: A Case Study of Religious Empowerment and Constraint Among Pashtuns," *Journal of Peace Research* 34, no. 1 (1997): 53–71. For the Tibetan liberation movement, see Ashil Kolas, "Tibetan Nationalism: The Politics of Religion," *Journal of Peace Research* 33, no. 1 (1996): 51–66.

81. See Douglas Johnston, "The Churches and Apartheid in South Africa," in *Religion, the Missing Dimension,* 177–207.

82. See German, *Politik und Kirche in Lateinamerika,* 412–20.

83. See, for instance, the case studies in *Religion, the Missing Dimension,* esp. fn. 71. Another example are the services provided by religious NGOs such as the Buddhist Peace Fellowship, Mennonite Central Committee, the Muslim Peace Fellowship, Oz veShalom–Netivot Shalom, the Roman Catholic Community of Sant'Egidio, Thich Nhat Hanh's Tiep Hien, the World Conference on Religion and Peace, among many others. See Appleby, *Ambivalence of the Sacred,* 121–65.

84. Religions would thus function as the "opiate of the people." It is noteworthy that this side of religious traditions, which, for instance, deeply disturbed Karl Marx and Friedrich Engels, is ignored by most instrumentalist scholars. Proponents of liberation theology, by contrast, take seriously the role of religion as opiate of the people. See German, *Politik und Kirche in Lateinamerika,* 71–75, 84–87; Gutiérrez, *Theologie der Befreiung,* 61–62; and Jones, "Religious Legitimation of Counterviolence," 201–05. In a similar vein, Senghaas, *Zivilisierung wider Willen,* 175–84, denounces the instrumentalization of so-called "Asian values" by ruling autocracies in East and Southeast Asia.

85. See Brown and de Jonge Oudraat, "International Conflict and International Action," 253; Rubin, Pruitt, and Kim, *Social Conflict,* 133; and Van Evera, "Hypotheses on Nationalism and War," 53–54.

86. See, for instance, Kaufmann, "Possible and Impossible Solutions," 147, and Posen, "Security Dilemma and Ethnic Conflict," 27–34.

87. Appleby, *Ambivalence of the Sacred,* 140–43; Esposito and Voll, "Islam and the West," in this volume, 465–70; Juergensmeyer, *New Cold War,* 195; and Little, "Religious Militancy," 83–86.

88. This has also been confirmed by studies looking at recent developments in Arab countries. See especially Faksh, "The Prospects of Islamic Fundamentalism," 215, and Karawan, *The Islamist Impasse,* 31. The fundamentalist motto "Islam is the solution" has lost much of its power by virtue of the disappointing performances of the Iranian and Sudanese governments. See Gilles Kepel, *Jihad: the Trail of Political Islam* (Cambridge, MA: Harvard University Press, 2002).

89. See Johnston, "Review of the Findings," 263, and Cox, "World Religions and Conflict Resolution," 266.

Chapter 5

In Defense of Religion

Sacred Referent Objects for Securitization

Carsten Bagge Laustsen and Ole Wæver

It is a widely shared assumption that since the end of the Cold War, conflicts and wars are less driven by political-ideological systems. Also they are not much caused by economic motives or even the classical ones of territory and power as an aim in themselves. The roots of conflicts are increasingly related to culture and identity, be it the widespread labeling of conflicts as "ethnic" or the macro-interpretation of global politics in terms of a "clash of civilizations."[1] To Samuel Huntington, civilizations are ultimately defined to a large extent by religions.[2] Furthermore, he argues, one of the trends of the post–Cold War period is a "revitalization of religion throughout much of the world," which reinforces cultural difference.[3] Since the 1970s, the hope or fear of a "withering away of religion" started to be defied—not because of a lack of modernization, but because one of the unexpected side effects of modernization was a "revenge of God," an "unsecularization of the world."[4]

In the area of international security, this has most keenly been felt in the form of an alleged threat from "fundamentalism."[5] This has meant primarily Islamic fundamentalism, but the increasing influence of evangelic fundamentalism on U.S. foreign policy is a cause of worry to others.[6] Even observers critical of the rhetoric of (and research on) fundamentalism, like Peter L. Berger, state with great emphasis that "[t]hose who neglect religion in their analyses of contemporary affairs do so at great peril."[7]

The discipline of International Relations (IR) is disturbed by this for general and specific reasons. It shares with other modern social sciences the general predisposition for secularization, assuming that the world of tradition gives way to modernity, superstition and religion to science and rationality.[8] More specifically, the "founding act" of much IR thinking, the peace of Westphalia, is widely seen as the end of an era in which international relations and wars had been about religion. Kal Holsti, for instance, states about the period 1815–1914: "The secularization of international politics, begun in 1648 and virtually completed by the conclusion of the War of the Spanish Succession, continued without change."[9]

We are not going to assess the validity of the claim about a shift toward religiously driven conflicts. Instead we will explore the dynamics characteristic of security action on behalf of religion. How does securitization of religiously constituted referent objects happen? Even the "why" question can to some extent be answered, because by exploring the structure of discourse constitutive of threats to religious objects, we can show what makes this form of securitization particularly attractive and under what conditions. Based on the investigation of security action on explicitly religious objects, we take our insights to a broader field of security practice, which is commonly seen as "only political," but which actually contains important religious dimensions. Finally, this exploration of religion and securitization has wider implications for IR theory and security studies, which are explored in the third main section of the article.

In doing this, we will have recourse to the theory of securitization (the Copenhagen School), which explores the processes by which "something" (a referent object) is deemed threatened and security action taken in its defense. A central idea of securitization theory is that the character of the referent object makes a difference. Making the security speech act in the name of "the state" is different from doing it on behalf of "the nation," not to speak of "the whales" or "the liberal international economic order." Survival means something different to different referent objects, and an appeal to a defense of something triggers different dynamics dependent on the constitution of the referent object. In the sphere of religion, the first task is therefore to characterize the nature of religious beliefs and of objects constituted by a religious discourse. This implies an excursion into the writings of Søren Kierkegaard and Georges Bataille. On this basis, the first step of the analysis is to explore the logic of securitization of objects that are clearly of a religious nature, and the article here mainly uses illustrations from the fundamentalism question. This part of the analysis seeks to understand primarily *why* it is often particularly tempting to securitize religion, *how* it is done (the characteristic modalities of securitization in this sphere), and the question of *what* it does (what chain reactions are usually activated, for example the role of sacrifices, myths, rituals).

The second step of the analysis is to notice how what is taken to be specific to religion is actually present in many political ideologies. Thus, much securitization that at first would be seen as belonging to the sphere of politics is better understood if the mechanisms characteristic of the religious sphere are taken into account. This part of the argumentation draws on the writings of Slavoj Žižek, and pushes the analysis into its third step: the meta-theoretical implications of religion for securitization theory (and by inference much of IR theory).

If religion is not to be distilled as a special atavistic anomaly but seen as integrated into most politics, and with poststructuralist philosophy in recent years veering into ruminations on the necessity of self-reflection in relation to the religious dimension of the Western philosophical tradition, religion is rehabilitated as a dimension of (primarily poststructuralist) IR theory. Although the article starts out quite narrowly looking at what happens when you defend religious referent objects, its title takes on a more radical meaning when it ends up defending religion as an important dimension of theory and self-reflection in IR. This part of the article draws on—in addition to the poststructuralist philosophers—some of the older connections between religion and IR, notably among classical realists and the early English School.

The relationship between the three parts of the article is unconventional. In several respects, they build on each other, the way any cumulative analysis is expected to. However, there are also deliberate shifts of angle where the parts challenge each other. It might be seen like this: In the first part, religion is contained within the framework of securitization as one among several sectors. In the second part, religion and securitization are on par. And of great consequence, in the third part, religion becomes the overarching problematique from which also securitization—and thus the original framework—is interrogated.

Securitization and Religion

Securitization is one of the defining elements of the so-called Copenhagen School in security studies (other key elements are "sectors" and "regional security complexes").[10] Where security studies traditionally

operate in the same schema as the main agents of security policy—
talking about threats as objectively existing, trying to measure their se-
riousness and devise optimal counterstrategies—the theory of
securitization creates a second-order system observing the operations
of the main actors in the field of security studies. It studies how security issues are produced by actors who pose something (a referent object) as existentially threatened and therefore claim a right to use
extraordinary measures to defend it.

What is at stake in debates over security is the question of lifting
some issue above ordinary politics in order to assign it a special urgency and necessity. Therefore, security takes a specific rhetorical
form: Some referent object is posited as having a demand on survival
and as being existentially threatened; the threat has a swiftness and
drama high enough to make a point of no return credible—if not dealt
with in time, it will be too late—and therefore this issue can not be left
to ordinary practices. The actor that tries to define the situation like
this—the securitizing actor—thereby claims a right to use extraordinary measures, and the success of the securitizing move is ultimately
decided by the relevant audience in its decision to accept or not accept
this operation. Thus, security is neither objective (threats in themselves) nor subjective (a matter of perceptions), but intersubjective and
political: Who can securitize what and with what effects?

The process of securitization is a speech act. It is not interesting as
a sign referring to something more real: It is the utterance itself that is
the act. By saying the words, something is done (like giving a promise,
betting, naming a ship). By uttering "I apologize for my behavior" the
speaker *actually makes* an apology; he does not describe himself apolo-
gizing for his behavior. A sentence like "X is a security question" is not
a "constantive" but a "performative,"[11] and therefore, it does not have
truth conditions but felicity conditions. Security is a self-referential
practice. It is by labeling something a security issue that it becomes
one. Thus the exact definition and criteria of securitization is the intersubjective establishment of an existential threat with a saliency sufficient to have substantial political effects.

The approach as such does not push for a widening of the security agenda in the sense of securitizing as many questions as possible. Quite the contrary, the ideal of the securitization approach
is—*ceteris paribus*—de-securitization, that issues are not lifted
above normal politics with an urgency and "necessity" that often has
antidemocratic effects.

A major importance of the theory is to show the effects of securitization. When an issue is securitized, this has implications both "inter-

nally" (for instance by inhibiting debate and democracy) and "externally," by often stimulating conflict, security dilemmas, and escalation. However, different referent objects engender distinct dynamics. This is an element of the approach that is often underestimated. Because the theory has served to bring out "the securityness of security"—what it is that makes a security issue a security issue—there is a tendency to stress the commonality of security in different sectors and on different referent objects. However, it is important *what* the referent object is securitized *as*. An alleged threat to state sovereignty in the political sector has different implications than a threat to national identity in the societal sector.

To contribute to the avoidance of escalation and security dilemmas and possibly create constructive dynamics, the theory needs to be able to understand and to some extent predict patterns of securitization as shaped by the different kinds of referent objects and the different sectors. Understanding the nature of identity helps to find characteristic patterns in the societal sector.[12] Now the task is to do the same for religion. Therefore, the next section starts from the "what is religion?" question in order to get at the next step, to the question of what happens when religious objects are articulated in a security discourse.

Before this, we need in relation to the theory of securitization to clarify one theoretical issue, the question of sectors. So far religion has been dealt with in the Copenhagen School as part of the societal sector.[13] The most common identity-based communities in the societal sector are ethnonational—nations and "minorities"—but also those with regional identification, clans, extended family, and religions. The question is whether this does justice to religion or only covers religion *as community* and not religion *as religion*. Thus, it must be contemplated whether religion could or should be seen as a separate sector. In particular, we will focus on the instances of security discourse where the referent object is constructed in religious discourse, that is, the confluence of security and religious discourse.

Religion has previously been dealt with as societal, that is, as a form of identity-based community where "we Christians" is similar to "we Kurds." This captures religion in its function as source of community and identity—just as the political sector occasionally includes "world religions" when they are sufficiently well organized and "govern" people—but this does not do justice to the distinctly religious. Searching for the religious element in religion, we cannot rest satisfied with looking to religions as forms of communities or identities. Religious discourse does not defend identity or community, but the true faith, our possibility to worship the right gods the right way and—in some religions—thereby have a chance of salvation.

Defining Religion

Numerous approaches to the study of religion exist. Among them, theology and philosophy constitute a systematic way of investigating religion, and this approach will be our prime context of reference. One cannot understand a phenomenon without considering the way this very phenomenon is described by those confronting and practicing it. Amongst these religious men, we have chosen Kierkegaard's description of faith as our main approach to the study of religion. Kierkegaard's thinking is distinctly nineteenth- and twentieth-century Protestant, and yet the analytical distinctions can be used generally. Obviously, this privileges Christianity—and probably Protestantism— in our study. The impossibility of certainty about salvation is explicit, constitutive, and self-conscious here, and at best the general distinction between the immanent and the transcendent can be analyzed in other religions.

Once, in criticizing Kant's transcendental categories, Hegel ironically claimed that every time he asked for a piece of fruit at the greengrocers he got an apple, a pear, but never a piece of fruit. Like apples and pears, we have only Christianity, Islam, Hinduism, etc., never religion as such. Nevertheless, Hegel's argument was not that this prevents comparisons and the introduction of categories. The point is, however, that one has to accept that our way to the universal (religion as such) goes through the particular (Christianity).[14]

The common route out of the dilemma is often to subscribe to a methodological atheism in conducting a sociology of religion.[15] These sociological approaches nevertheless often ignore that which makes religion *religion*. This is most obvious in the functionalist school of reasoning, which dominated the sociology of religion for decades. Religion may, as Engels claimed, be opium for the people, but to have this calming effect it must exactly be religion. Describing religion by its functions or in a wider perspective as a product of social forces impoverishes religion.[16]

Thus it is difficult to find a sociological approach accepting the essence of religious discourse. However, we claim to have found one in Bataille's *Theory of Religion,* which in our view enables an understanding of the ways the distinction between transcendent and immanent is represented by man.[17] In our understanding, religious discourses share three fundamental traits. First, the principle of dis-

cursivation is faith; second, faith is coded through the distinction between transcendent and immanent; and third, religious dogmatics and
religious behavior can be seen as ways to bridge the distance between
the transcendental and the earthly realm through principles of mediation. Let us investigate these aspects of religious discourse in turn.

A Question of Faith

A defining aspect of a religious discourse is a claim to uniqueness and
intranslatability. This should be no surprise—the same could be said
about most other discourses. Hence, the relevant task is to investigate
the specific religious version of this claim. In a number of works,
Kierkegaard distinguishes between three main stages: the aesthetic,
the ethical, and the religious. We will discuss these three stages later,
and for now focus only on the idea that the movement between the
ethical and the religious stage has the character of a leap.[18] This idea is
of great heuristic value in describing faith. According to this idea, one
has to be within a religious discourse to accept the validity of it: One
cannot enter religious discourse through the work of reason and accordingly judge religious beliefs as true or false. The same goes for the
experience of religion: One cannot feel the magic of religion without
being religious.

Kierkegaard's understanding of religion is one of many reactions to
previous attempts to prove the existence of God. The one who is in
need of proof is not truly a believer, or more accurately does not have
faith. Kierkegaard's argument involves a short circuit between faith
and knowledge.[19] Faith must have the character of knowing. In believ-
ing, I am certain that God exists. On the other hand, the lack of assurance is absolutely necessary. Although I know that God exists, his
will remains only partly known. To cite the title of one of Kierkegaard's
most famous books: religion involves *fear and trembling*.[20] Without
fear and trembling we would just be puppets in a mechanical universe.
In this sense, the subject's freedom is made possible through the posi-
tioning of the distinction between the immanent and the transcendent. God withdraws to make human freedom and faith possible.

Kierkegaard's metaphor of the leap aims to describe the character
of faith. Faith is different from belief. Belief is informed by expectations. If a certain occurrence has happened several times, I expect it to
happen again. Or along the same path, faith is different from custom.
If my practice is just a continuation of my parents' practice, it cannot
qualify as religious practice. Whereas belief is founded on expectations, faith is founded in a groundless decision. It is my performative

declaration of faith or my participating in the wonder of religion that founds faith. Of course, one can have reasons for becoming a believer. Nevertheless, in following the miracle of faith these reasons are retroactively posited as superfluous. Arguing that faith is just learned is in some way being an atheist. Faith involves a subjective conversion of necessity (social or cultural forming) into faith (originating in a subjectivity). Faith needs through a subjective usurpation to be posited as my or our faith.

To address the character of faith further, let us investigate Kierkegaard's three main stages on the path of life, or three types of consciousness.[21] In the first stage, consciousness is described as *aesthetic*. This consciousness is characterized by the absence of fixed moral standards and by a desire to enjoy different emotional and sensuous experiences.[22] Kierkegaard's example is Don Juan, who sees freedom as the absence of any law.[23] In this sense the aesthetic consciousness strives for a bad (i.e., nonreligious) infinity. In contrast, Socrates, the tragic hero, works as an exemplar of an *ethical* consciousness. He accepts the moral law and renounces immediate impulses and desires. For Kierkegaard marriage is the perfect example of such a willingness to constrain sexual impulses and to accept *given* (i.e., external) obligations. The ethical consciousness is ready to give way in confrontation with the universal moral law. It is important to stress that the tragic hero is first and foremost a hero. In following the moral law, his or her consciousness can become pure. In contrast, man accepts in the *religious* stage that the moral law cannot be fulfilled, or in theological terms, that he is a sinner. He acknowledges that he is forever separated from God, and that the moral law can serve only as an approximation of the highest Good. It is this acceptance of sin and separation that serves as a foundation for faith. Being religious means to repeat the gesture of faith again and again. Abraham is the hero of faith. His readiness to sacrifice his beloved and only son Isaac—an act of madness confirming his faith in God—exemplifies the essence of faith.

The distinction between the ethical and the religious stage is helpful when distinguishing religion from morals and ethics. Whereas morality and ethics are given as taxonomies that can be known through reason, religion is given in abiding a Lord (or gods) whose will cannot be positively known. It requires an act of faith to bridge the distance between the human and the divine, a bridging that can be only temporary. Faith needs to be continuously affirmed. Hence, Kierkegaard describes religion as a suspension of the ethical.[24] The difference between the law given by man and the one given by God is crucial. In providing it with a more sociological formulation, we could claim, following Niklas Luhmann, that religion differs from other social systems in dealing with and accepting the *abyss* of faith. Religion interprets a contingency as transcendence; not just as unfulfilled opportunities, overload of information, risk, etc.[25]

For this reason, narratives about this abyss—about the giving of the word, the law, the book, and about God's withdrawal from the world after giving the law and hence his leaving his people with only faith and no proofs, etc., are often seen in religious discourse. Religious discourse differs from most other discourses by explicitly thematizing this act of constitution.

The fact that religion creates narratives about the constitutive abyss, or, in other words, about God(s), implies that it must involve a kind of *Letztbegründung*. Religious discourse somehow aims at stopping the threatening regress involved in all acts of constitution. Or perhaps better, and in less functionalist terms, it is defined by this kind of "transcendental justification." Giving a monotheist illustration of this claim, one could say that God measures up to that which cannot be reduced any further. Within religious discourse it is absurd to ask how and by whom God is constituted. God as creator is the *absolute* master. He is the one—the *only* one—who does not owe his being to others.

The Homogeneous and the Heterogeneous

Moving toward a sociological understanding of religion, we continue by investigating the ways the distinction between immanent and transcendent is represented by man. Or, differently phrased, we investigate how faith translates into identity. For logical reasons the otherworldly realm cannot be represented as such. If it could, it would not be transcendent. Facing an absent God, we are forced to make man-made images of him. Iconographical images are only one way of representing the divine. Religion involves a whole range of ways to approach the divine. We will mention some of these later, and presently show only how the distinction between the transcendent and the immanent is translated into a distinction between the sacred and the profane.

It is our claim that the distinction between transcendental and immanent is "translated" into a distinction between what Bataille labels the homogeneous and the heterogeneous sphere. Heterogeneous phenomena are those that cannot be assimilated into the normal part of social life. These hyperbolic aspects of social life have various faces. In

Bataille's text he mentions four domains of heterogeneity: (1) mana and tabu or more generally the holy and spiritual; (2) that which is discharged and rejected from the body: faeces, blood, and other evacuations; (3) that which provokes strong affective reactions; and (4) delirium, madness, violence, and excess.[26] Bataille's distinction can be seen as a distinction between *ordinary and extraordinary* activities, or, when the distinction is applied in the religious sector, as one between the *profane* and the *sacred.* To give a few obvious examples: A church is a house unlike other houses. Praying is not like working. The religious festival is not just a party, and the relic not just a bone.

To understand the full importance of the distinction between the homogeneous and the heterogeneous, we need to understand the grammar of Bataille's philosophical system. Bataille's philosophy is modeled according to a logic of a double negation. In brief, Bataille claims that being man is to negate what considered animalistic. Man is an animal in so far as he needs a law to constrain him. Bataille is inspired here by Sigmund Freud's and Jacques Lacan's writings on symbolic castration. Man is castrated in so far as the symbol (language, culture, writing, etc.) makes him speak. He cannot as an animal just follow instincts. Like Freud and Lacan, Bataille argues that the law is sustained through its transgression (negation). To give an example, the primordial negation of nature is confirmed through the anxiety arising in confrontation with our animal "past." Bataille, for example, mentions how the body and evacuations from the body give rise to anxiety.[27]

Bataille uses this logic to describe religion.[28] Again, animality is the point of departure. When one animal eats another of its own species, no transcendence is involved, only difference. The animal is pure immanence. The eater does not posit the eaten as an object.[29] "The animal is in the world like water in water."[30] It does not experience the split between subject and object. Man is denied this immanence. He is a consciousness longing for a self: a barred subject.

Religious activity is for Bataille given as attempts at reinstalling an immanent universe: a universe where man and God become one, just like the animal being "water in water." In Bataille's view, religion offers a way to overcome what bars the subject from its primordial (animalistic) being. Nevertheless, this new immediacy is possible only as a negation of a negation. It cannot be installed as it was: Man has lost his primordial being for good, and the striving for a new immediacy is thus always mediated by a primordial negation of nature. To give an example: In sacrificing parts of the harvest, man negates the product of his own negating activity (labor). The sacrifice is antithetical to production:[31] One sacrifices what is useful. Only through this second negation can man reach for God(s).

For Bataille, religion stands in opposition to morality. Morality belongs to the homogeneous sphere, while religion is defined by hyperbolic gestures transcending law and "thinghood" (the heterogeneous sphere). Morality is grounded in reason, while religion is grounded in hyperbolic gestures of faith. The divine order is beyond utility: It requires moments of madness and acts of useless expenditure.

The presentation in this section allows us to discuss the similarities between the ways Kierkegaard and Bataille approach religion. The first theorist is considered to be an honest and religious man, while Bataille was condemned for his pornographic writings. Reading them more closely, the similarities are however striking. Both understand religion as given by acts of hyperbolic madness—acts that destroy the sovereign self and make it tremble before the divine. An even more striking resemblance is noticed if Bataille's philosophical grammar, the logic of the negation of negation, is compared to Kierkegaard's theory of stages. Kierkegaard's *aesthetic* stage resembles Bataille's animality. Here, the self is consumed in the pursuit of enjoyment. The subject is a subject of an animalistic drive, and hence in this stage no constraints are experienced. The *ethical* stage equals Bataille's idea of the founding negation. The original negation is an act through which one distances oneself from the world and starts treating it as an object. The 'before', the cut is a fantasy in the sense that this founding gesture is exactly what makes man human. This primordial cut constitutes time, space, and manhood. Law is installed through a similar founding gesture. It cleaves the subject like a knife cutting.

In Kierkegaard's third stage, law is experienced as a law given by God. The religious consciousness acknowledges that purity cannot be measured according to compliance with the law. Man is a sinner who is left to approach God through acts of faith. However, they are forever separated. For both Kierkegaard and Bataille, the divine is approached in a negative way. Kierkegaard wrote about Abraham's sacrifice as an act of madness confirming his faith in God.[32] For Bataille religion negates morality in much the same way. For both, religion is hyperbolic, and hence, for both, sacrifice is the prototype of a religious experience.

Summing up, we have argued that religion has three main dimensions. It has faith as the guiding principle of discourse. This faith is possible only due to a distinction between immanent and transcendent, and this distinction is finally reinterpreted as a distinction between sacred and profane. Now, we will proceed and investigate what happens when the religious discourse and corresponding sacred objects enter the political realm. We are interested in a politics of an extreme kind: security politics.

Securitizing Religion

Previously, the Copenhagen School investigated the nature of a number of referent objects, most importantly states, nations, the environment, and firms, and found four corresponding criteria of survival: sovereignty, identity, sustainability, and avoiding bankruptcy. What is the candidate for religion? We claim that *faith* is the referent object, and that *being* is the criterion of survival. If the practice of faith is threatened, one's very identity as man (one's being) is endangered. Being is a kind of fundamental identity. In religion being is basically being before God, or, in a less monotheistic formulation, being before a transcendental realm. Man is naked confronting God or similar transcendent entities. Given identities (wealth, sex, employment) are of no primary importance. Religion deals with the constitution of being as such. Hence, one cannot be pragmatic on concerns challenging this being. This is not to say that identity is not important in religions—basically the distinction between the sacred and the profane is one of identity. Rather, it is to say that it is faith that makes a specific identity a religious one.

Faith addresses divinity. Through faith a distinction between the transcendent and the immanent realm is inserted; or inversely, this distinction makes faith possible. Nevertheless, divine transcendence needs to be represented by man. Hence, the distinction between immanence and transcendence is recoded as one between the profane and the sacred. Through this secondary coding a whole number of objects, persons, and practices are sacralized. These are endowed with divine power creating a magic aura around them. As spiritualized entities, they present themselves as extraordinary, glorified, intensified objects, persons, and practices. In general, sacred objects can be described as belonging to the heterogeneous realm. They are never just objects, persons, or practices. They are spirit manifested in matter.

These heterogeneous qualities are of great importance in securitizing sacred objects. The loss of a sacred object is often automatically seen as a loss, which destroys faith and annuls being. If sacred objects mediate between the transcendent and the earthly realm, losing these objects means losing contact with God. Hence, the act of referring to sacred objects as threatened typically means securitizing an issue (possibly implying immediate action by the state). Any challenge or threat is existential because the absolute and foundational character of the question of being makes compromise and concessions unimaginable. Religion easily becomes high politics. But still, never automatically; it takes political action to articulate a threat in the political realm.

It is crucial to remember that the securitization approach focuses on the processes through which issues are put on the political agenda with a claim for urgency in dealing with existential threats. Our main point is that religion is existential, and hence that threats against sacred objects are often seen as existential threats demanding immediate and effective action by the state or an entity endowed with similar power. Hence, it is always tempting to securitize sacred objects. In general, the possibility of success in making the security move on behalf of sacred objects is greater than when attempting to securitize most other objects. It is much harder for a firm arguing that its survival is at risk to succeed in making the security move, i.e., in demanding the same kind of action by the state as described above. Whether the security move succeeds depends crucially on the audience, often most importantly inhabitants of a state. For these inhabitants a threat to their being is often more urgent than questions concerning the survival of a specific firm. And, more importantly, a precondition for the availability of securitization is that a given referent object is intersubjectively understood to have an entitlement to survival, in contrast to a firm that should only survive if it competes efficiently. With being at stake, at least a certain audience (typically not a whole national population) will accept the necessity of survival of the referent object; whether they then accept the claim about an existential threat is a second empirical question.

Most religious conflicts in international politics are asymmetric. Often, secular states are attacked by religious groups. A threat from a religious group known for using terrorist methods is typically seen as a threat to the sovereignty of the state. In American foreign policy, threats from religious fundamentalism are considered to be of utmost importance. The new enemies are driven by faith, rather than power gains. Hence, threatening them is of no use, since they do not understand reason and knowledge. In the discourse on fundamentalist threats, it is often argued that the fundamentalists might not be many in numbers, but their faith makes them highly unpredictable and dangerous. They are seen as freed from any selfish calculation, and hence even ready to sacrifice themselves. This possibility (a religious attack on a secular state) can be seen as one of three main ways in which religion can be addressed within the realm of security politics:

1. A religious group is considered to be a threat to the survival of the state.
2. Faith is seen as threatened by whoever or whatever "nonreligious" actor or process (the state, technology, industrialism, modernism, etc.).
3. Faith is seen as threatened by another religious discourse or actor.

Religion is involved in all three situations, but different logics are involved. The first type of security policy can be against the spread of fundamentalism and the acts following it. Here, threats are seen as threats against the secular state. The enemy can be either without or within. The United States fear of Osama bin Laden is obviously a threat from without, while Islamism in Turkey exemplifies a threat from within. In Turkey some aspects of the actual practice of religion are seen as a threat to the *raison d'être* of the state. The struggle between secularism and religion is often seen as a struggle between modern and premodern conceptions of religion. It is a conflict between "fundamentalists" who do not accept the differentiation of church and state, and those who argue that religion belongs to the private realm.

Fundamentalism, especially, is often securitized. In fact, the very term "fundamentalism" often serves to securitize. Mark Juergensmeyer quotes a Tajiki communist leader justifying antidemocratic actions: "Islamic fundamentalism is a plague that spreads easily."[33] Juergensmeyer notes that "[m]uch has been written about the religious fear of secularism, but relatively little about the sometimes irrational hatred some secularists harbor against the potency of religion."[34] He cites a number of examples where "secular governments have taken abnormal liberties with the democratic process as a way of countering what they perceive to be a fundamentalist threat": Algeria, the Israeli eviction of Hamas supporters, India's 1992–93 ban on Hindu organizations.[35] Such measures are enabled by a theory that sees "fundamentalism" as a "known syndrome," which is dangerous and infectious. We "know" what fundamentalists are up to, and they have to be stopped in time. The rhetoric almost schematically follows the structure of security discourse.

The second possibility is to see the practice of faith as threatened. Israel is a well-known example of a securitization of faith. As the *raison d'être* of Turkey is secularism, for Israel it is Judaist faith. Other examples are Pakistan and Afghanistan. One of the official reasons given for the Serb action in Kosovo was the need to keep a whole range of churches in the hands of the Serbs.

Defense of sacred objects does not necessarily imply the use of a defensive strategy. The holy crusades can be seen as practices aimed at defending faith. Obviously, many discourses and motives are mixed in these actions. Nevertheless, we claim that religion is an important element. The holy crusades made sense as attempts to fulfill God's will. Religion has being (humanity) as reference, which often implies that the believer has been given an obligation to disseminate the word of God. Borders are thus no legitimate hindrance.

In the second category, we find the phenomenon that is usually called fundamentalism. The term is problematic because it serves to package a complex host of phenomena as fitting a specific ideal type that is ascribed a number of negative attributes. To avoid a long discussion over alternative labels we will take a look at "fundamentalism." We ask primarily what it is that is securitized by these movements around the world, and what can be said generally about the dynamics of conflicts involving fundamentalists. In the big fundamentalism project by the American Academy of Arts and Sciences, fundamentalism is seen

> neither as a "new religious movement" . . . nor as simply "traditional," "conservative," or "orthodox" expression of ancient and premodern religious faith and practice. Rather, fundamentalism is a hybrid of both kinds of religious modes. While fundamentalists claim to be upholding orthodoxy (right belief) or orthopraxis (right behavior), and to be defending and conserving religious traditions and traditional ways of life from erosion, they do so by crafting new methods, formulating new ideologies, and adopting the latest processes and organizational structures.[36]

This duality follows exactly from the focus in fundamentalism on *defense,* on being under pressure. The self-conception and discourse of fundamentalists cannot emphasize novelty as such because they are about defending the original and true form of a religion. But on the other hand, they often criticize fellow believers who are "not willing to craft innovative ways of fighting back against the forces of erosion. In other words, fundamentalists argue that to be 'merely' a conservative or a traditionalist in these threatening times is not enough."[37] The difference between religious "conservatives" and "fundamentalists" is a thorough securitization of the situation of (one's) religion. Reacting to a perceived erosion of traditional society and a marginalization of religion by secular modernity, fundamentalists are political activists engaged in a struggle over the proper place of religion in society and therefore the relationship between religion and politics. Rather than working for a particular theological position (i.e., about religious life as such), they fight for another ideology for the nation-state than that of the secular elite.[38]

Fundamentalist movements rise when "some members of traditional religious communities separate from fellow believers and redefine the sacred community in terms of its disciplined opposition to non-believers and 'lukewarm' believers alike."[39] The securitized nature of the challenge, the existential threat, allows the leaders to give all the separate "agenda items" a drama and urgency they would otherwise not have had:

> In many if not all cases, they were able to elevate their mission to a spiritual plane in which eschatological urgency informed even the most mundane world building tasks of the group. All of this unfolded in the name of defending and preserving a hallowed identity rooted in religious tradition but now under assault.[40]

Securitization is therefore almost explicitly part of their definition of fundamentalism.

Thus, when looking at the second type, we should remember that although it is about the defense of religion against politics (or other nonreligious threats), it is not religion as such that acts. The movement is driven by strategic action in a political context by some leaders, and the action program is formulated at the interface of politics and religion.

The third possibility is a clash between two religious discourses. Until recently it was argued that these conflicts characterized mainly the period before the peace of Westphalia. To give a more recent example, one could mention the status of Jerusalem, which for both Muslims and Jews is (and for Christians previously was) of utmost importance. Access to religious sites is of vital importance for all three groups and easily attains the character of high politics. Furthermore, the holy city is also considered to be the political capital for both Israelis and Palestinians. Another example is the conflict over the Ayodhya mosque in India. The militant Hindus claimed that the site of the mosque actually was a holy Hindu site and thus vital for the religious life of the Hindus. Accordingly, they tore the mosque down with their bare hands.

Probably, it is the third type that comes first to mind for most people if asked to think about religion and security or conflict. The crusades and holy wars function as the template for imagination. However, this type is most likely the least common of the three. Religion clashing with religion is not that common, whereas mutual securitization between fundamentalists and secularists is at play in many conflicts around the world. To label this "the new Cold War," as Juergensmeyer does in the book of the same title (subtitled *Religious Nationalism Confronts the Secular State*), is however, problematic.[41] These various "religious nationalists" are highly unlikely to (be able to) make common cause against the secular West. Religious nationalism confronting secular states is a widespread phenomenon, and a type of conflict that easily gets securitized with dramatic effects. It is therefore worth taking it seriously in all of its complexity, rather than reducing it to a simplistic monolith.

A final question at this stage is whether conflicts that make reference to religion are particularly violent. By now, we have shown why threats to religion are particularly prone to securitization and thus to a certain escalation, but religion is widely believed to play an increasing part in terrorism, political assassinations, and the most vicious wars, including civil wars.[42] Is there some special connection(s) of religion and violence in addition to religion securitization?

A first element of an answer comes from René Girard (and actually similar arguments in Kierkegaard),[43] according to whom an existential lack of being leads to mimetic desire, which produces an unstable society that solves its crises by the identification and killing of a scapegoat.[44] Much violence in relation to religion is thus symbolic and serves to uphold a community. However, as Juergensmeyer asks:

> Why and how are these symbolic presentations of violence occasionally linked to real acts of violence? Ordinarily they should prevent violent acts by allowing the urges to conquer and control to be channeled into the harmless dramas of ritual. Yet we know that the opposite is sometimes the case: the violence of religion can be savagely real.[45]

Juergensmeyer himself offers an additional layer of explanation: "Most religious acts are less like sacrifice than they are like war."[46] More specifically, religions often entertain an idea of a cosmic war, a great encounter between cosmic forces of ultimate good and evil, of divine truth and falsehood. The cases where religion offers moral sanction to violence, and especially to seemingly excessive and ferocious violence, are characteristically those where the personal, the social, and the cosmic levels are connected. At the personal level, there is a struggle between faith and lack of faith; on the social and political plane, concrete struggles take place that are finally connected to the cosmic struggle, and thus sacred legitimacy is extended to worldly causes: "[T]he sense of being situated in a religious cosmos leads naturally to images of warfare."[47] Juergensmeyer explains this by connecting religion to a language of ultimate order, which therefore needs to account for, and quell, disorder. The particular process that leads to violence thus has as one element the direct linkage of cosmic war and worldly struggles, and another crucial move is to interpret this struggle as literal war. Religiously motivated terrorists, for instance, have acted on the assumption that it was "a widely shared perception that the world was already violent: it was enmeshed in great struggles that gave their own violent actions moral meaning."[48]

In our framework, we can reinterpret and clarify Juergensmeyer's two crucial insights. They are both about a process of securitization in which the religious referent object loses some religious characteristics.

One element is a desire to overcome the separation of transcendent and immanent, of order and disorder, to achieve a final victory. The gap is no longer to be mediated, it is to be traversed. Religion is in this case impoverished by losing the constitutive distance between the human and the divine and the ensuing necessity of a leap across the abyss of faith. The human and divine are made continuous, and a paradoxical form of certainty replaces anxiety.

The other element, which also pushes religiosity to the background, is what might be called the Clausewitz effect. If it is characteristic, in Clausewitz's famous definition, that war is the continuation of politics by other means, war in another sense overrides politics: The logic of war (victory as the *Ziel* of war) replaces the logic of politics (the specific *Zweck* of the war). Because the *Ziel* is polarly defined (victory/defeat), it produces an extreme intensity whereby the only rational action is to follow the grammar of war, if need be by defying all limitations.[49] In our case, war is originally the continuation of religion by other means, but a similar reversal sets in and the logic of war replaces that of religion. In the words of the (later assassinated) extreme Jewish nationalist Rabbi Meir Kahane: "War is war."[50]

Juergensmeyer has shown convincingly that a specific argument is crucial to various violent religious activists, from U.S. antiabortion activists bombing clinics and killing staff to Jewish, Islamic, and Sikh radicals to the Buddhist Aum Shinrikyo sect killing twelve and injuring thousands by releasing poison gas in the Tokyo subway. They believe they are already at war, and therefore merely responding to a great ongoing struggle, reacting defensively to a threat to religion and faith. For example, the very term "terrorist" "depends on one's worldview: If the world is perceived as peaceful, violent acts appear as terrorism. If the world is thought to be at war, violent acts may be regarded as legitimate."[51] A *fatwa* delivered by Osama bin Laden in February 1998, months before the bombing of the American embassies in Kenya and Tanzania, proclaimed: "The world is at war."[52]

Both sides to this process securitize religion; they simultaneously draw on the particular character of religious referent objects and violate their religious core. The gap between the transcendental and the immanent is denied, and doubt is replaced by the certainty of war. The nature of such transformation of religion through securitization will be clearer with the more extreme examples of securitization of quasi-religious ideologies in the next section.

Understanding the Religion of Politics

So far we have analyzed the nature and dynamics of securitization of explicitly religious referent objects, i.e., what happens when an object is simultaneously constituted by a religious discourse *and* a security discourse. This is the religious sector of securitization studies. However, religious as well as quasi-religious discourse is relevant in other sectors as well, notably the political and the societal.

One of the problems with much of the existing literature on religion is that it operates with vague definitions that make it unclear whether, for instance, ideologies are to be seen as religion (since they often fulfill the criteria). We have proposed an approach that singles out the distinctly religious about religion and therefore enables us to explore the specific dynamics of the religious sector. With this approach it is also possible to look beyond the explicitly religious to understand what role religious discourse plays in sectors that are ultimately about something else, such as political rule or societal identity.

The Religious Dimensions of Political Ideologies

It has already been shown elsewhere that the concepts and the thinking of IR are influenced by religious semantics, that concepts like sovereignty, state, and nation have (often rather obvious) religious roots.[53] Here, we will deal with the importance of religion in politics in a more direct way. In a simplified version the argument goes like this: *Religion plus securitization equals ideology.* Ideologies can be seen as attempts to legitimize a given polity and policy by the use of quasi-religious semantics. By overlaying a religious discourse with a political one (securitization), certain favored political options are presented as the only ones, as political actions understood as prescribed by a transcendent power and hence as necessary, imperative. Ideology is religion securitized.

It is important to stress that securitizing religion means impoverishing it. By using religion for political gains, one denies the transcendence of the divine call. Instead of being based on fear and trembling, religion becomes a source of absolute certainty. Religious behavior stops being driven by, for instance, the acknowledgement of sin (or, more broadly conceptualized, the distance between the earthly and the transcendental realm), and becomes political behavior carried out as though one were God. *Ideology is quasi-religion, not religion per se.* Ideology resembles Kierkegaard's second stage: the ethical stage. Being "religious" in the political domain implies following a "law," that is, the will of the political ruler. In contrast, the will of God in Kierkegaard's third stage is known only in a negative way, through the experience of sin. Ideology is "religious" by staging the subject's attempt at overcoming the primordial separation (negation) in the striving for divine immanence. As religion, it attempts to mediate between the earthly and the transcendent realm. This is done through heterogeneous activities (secondary negations as described by Bataille: orgiastic meetings, rage, burning of books). But in ideology, transgression and suspension are subsumed as work in the Bataillian sense. It works for the upholding of a hegemonic project.

Describing ideology as a way of securitizing religion helps us to stress that politics does something to religion. De-securitization then means de-securitizing ideology, or in other words respecting religion as it is. It implies the acceptance of a lack of being, or in other words the acceptance of the fact that being in religious discourse is essentially being before a transcendental realm.

Ideology as a Way of Securitizing Religion

In following Žižek, we claim that ideology has three main dimensions. First, ideology is, as commonly acknowledged, a system of more or less coherent ideas. Hence, to investigate ideology (as political religion), one should map the semantic used. Second, ideology has the character of fantasies, i.e., basic scenarios channeling desires that provide ways of mobilizing an audience and hence legitimizing a given policy. Third, ideologies are used in creating relations of submission. These three concerns correspond to the focus in the Copenhagen School on fixation of meaning (semantics), securitizing moves, audience and mobilization (economies of desire), and extraordinary measures (use of power). Let us briefly investigate these three aspects and stress the similarities and differences between religion and ideology, and accordingly how religion is securitized through the use of ideology. First, semantics.

As commonly argued within the structuralist camp, meaning is not given through ostentation—through, for instance, reference to the intrinsic sacredness of objects. Rather, meaning is given in a web of signifiers that can be combined and recombined in a potentially unlimited number of ways. How they are actually fixed is a matter of strategies, previous use, and the like. Religious semantics are often highly stable and thus can be used to fix and stabilize meaning. Second, the role of master signifiers should be mentioned. Master signifiers are those signifiers that knot others together. In knotting together a range of signifiers, the master signifier itself must remain empty. The best example is God. In being transcendent, God can be that which everything can gain existence by standing before. As a synonym for the highest good, the highest of being, that which cannot be questioned, it easily pervades other signifiers.

The parallel to the process of securitizing an object should be evident. Securitization stops the sliding of signifiers, or, perhaps better still, annuls the "political" character of politics, arguing that there is only one feasible option, only one interpretation of the current state of affairs. Security works as a master signifier in much the same way as 'God' and other master signifiers do in an ideological discourse. All being becomes a being referring to an ultimate political goal, such as the defense of sovereignty. Hence, the signifier 'God' can be and is often used in securitizing an issue. Fixation of meaning through a security move nevertheless indirectly makes signifiers refer to a specific political project. They are not really empty signifiers, like those found in religious discourse—they only pretend to be. In this sense securitization impoverishes religion.

In Žižek's view, ideology anchors being. It is not a secondary phenomenon, but rather the possibility of signification as such. To describe this phenomenon, Lacan (Žižek's main source of inspiration) coined the concept of "fantasy."[54] Fantasies are scenarios constructing objects of desire. These fantasies answer the question: Why desire this object? Or, more basically, why this desire? Why desire the relics of Lazar? Because, the fantasy answers, they contain the essence of being Serbian. Fantasy aims at providing a ground, laying a foundation; and one thus cannot step outside fantasy, just as one cannot leave religion. Both deal with the constitution of being.

But again, it is necessary to distinguish between religion and ideology. Religion constitutes the naked subject who essentially is as a being facing an abyss: the transcendental realm. In contrast, ideology constitutes identity and thus, for instance, dresses the subject in Serbian nationalist clothes. Not unlike religious identities, these identities are presented as a matter of being, as existential. The subject of religion and the subject of ideology are, however, different: Ideologies create an illusion of a fullness of being, while religion stresses that there is always a higher being barring the subject. The case is that ideology aims to fool us on that point.

Like Bataille, Žižek argues that negation (law) is primary. He claims that this primary separation creates a desire to overcome it.[55] Fantasies, and hence ideologies, are scenarios of such an overcoming of the bar separating the subject from his "primordial" being. The parallel to Bataille's understanding of religion should be clear. For Bataille, religion is also about overcoming a split (primary negation, law) through a transgression (secondary negation, sacrifice). For both, the goal is "divine" immanence, the overcoming of the subject/object split.

Fantasy lives by desires. These desires are different from needs. A need can be fulfilled, and accordingly disappears when satisfied, while a desire remains unfulfilled.[56] Any desired object is basically just a substitute for the primordially lost object.[57] In other words, we project our lack onto objects and create illusive fantasies of (re)gaining them. These posited objects are sublime in the sense of being perceived as a filler that can heal the subject. To construct an object as threatened is a prime example of how this is done.[58] In other words, ideology commonly works through securitization. It uses the security-insecurity nexus.

It is worth noting the similarities between the sublime object of ideology and the sacred object of religion. Both objects belong to the heterogeneous realm. They are objects with extraordinary qualities. But again, it is also important to stress differences as well. Sacred objects become sacred primarily through acts of faith, while the sublime objects of ideology gain their qualities primarily by becoming objects of desire. The difference is thus that religious objects are seen as mediators, while ideological objects are seen as the thing itself. In ideology no transcendence is involved, only distance qua projection. Finally, the confrontation with the sublime object of ideology aims at ontological security, while confrontation in religion produces anxiety (fear and trembling).

The third aspect of the definition of ideology concerns its function in sustaining relations of dominance. Not much can be said in theoretical terms. It is a matter of historical investigation. Within the Marxist tradition it has been argued that ideology serves the ruling class of owners of the means of production. We do not want to make such an a priori claim, but only stress the importance of focusing on the maker of the security move.

So far, we have argued that ideology abuses religious discourse by presenting itself as religion. It speaks of faith, transcendence, and mediation. And, just as important, it uses the same signifiers as religion does. Or perhaps better still, it uses these signifiers precisely because they belong to religious semantics. In general, ideology flattens the transcendence of religious discourse.[59]

The distinction between religion and ideology is, as argued, crucial. We do not find, as Huntington does, that religions are necessarily securitized. But, on the other hand, they easily become so due to the nature of religious discourse. Religion has fundamental "structural affinities" to securitization through the existential question and the role of decision/leap. If religion is present in politics, the crucial task is to prevent it from becoming ideology. Hence, the task is to de-securitize ideology.

Bringing Religion "Back In"

The above analysis also has implications for theory, first of all for the Copenhagen School theory of securitization. One was addressed already in the first section. The need to open up to an additional sector: religion. The reasonableness of this has been reinforced by the analysis. A second set of implications are more interesting and of more general import outside the school itself.

First, our analysis has shown that religion should be respected as religion. Much literature on religion is not really on religion but, for instance, on the *political functions* of religion or (like previous writings by the Copenhagen School) on religious communities *as communities*. In order to include the religiosity of religion, it is necessary to open oneself to what the academic tradition prefers to avoid or suppress.

Second, in line with the general ethics of the Copenhagen School, the aim is de-securitization, which in this case means to let religion be *religion*, and avoid ideologization.

Third, the concept of securitization has a structural affinity to religion: The decisionistic nature of securitization is similar to the leap of Kierkegaard. This was recognized by the leading decisionistic theorist, Carl Schmitt: "The exception in jurisprudence is analogous to the miracle in theology."[60] And so are other performative political acts, since they by definition include an element of "social magic," creating something out of nothing.[61] Thus, it might be that the theory of securitization itself draws on political theology. Could and should the approach accept that religion is not only an external object studied by it but that it is in some sense present within the theory itself? To understand what kind of IR theory this would produce, we must look briefly at religion in IR theory.

Classical IR and Religion

Explicitly religious elements in IR theory have appeared mainly in two places: debates on "ethics and IR" and in classical realism (including the early English School). The first is the application of various ethical traditions to questions in IR, especially to questions of war and peace.[62] When religion is mentioned in the context of IR, this will probably be the connotation that it has to most IR scholars. However, there are often limits to how far this thinking penetrates into the religious nature of international thought, because, as R. B. J. Walker has noticed, this literature usually takes the form of ethics *and* international relations, i.e., an external relationship.[63] Religious thought exists somewhere else; IR is in itself areligious, and then we try to bring religious-based ethics to IR. More interesting is whether there are traditions that claim religious dimensions of international relations or IR theory as such.

Many classical realists did this, and so did the early English School (Martin Wight and Herbert Butterfield). Religious realism begins with Augustine, who is "often called the first political realist because of his emphasis on human limitations."[64] In modern IR, Augustinian thought was introduced first and foremost by Reinhold Niebuhr. One of the aspects he upgrades is the *tragic* element of human action, the inevitable difference between action and aspiration.[65] Partly through Niebuhr's influence, Hans Morgenthau also makes explicit arguments about the implications of religion for IR thinking. The tragic meaning of life in his version is simply the argument that due to the complex constellations of interests among actors and the drive for power, we will inevitably sin whenever we act toward our fellow beings (including nonaction).[66] Partly, this argument is based on a recognition of the limits to human knowledge and understanding, and again is based on a contrast between full knowledge that only God can have and the limited nature of humans. Up against scientific aspirations for an unrealistic level of knowledge (which he associates with liberalism), Morgenthau pleads for the tragic art of the statesman.

In addition to Morgenthau's explicit, self-declared use of religious arguments, Véronique Pin-Fat has shown in an excellent analysis how

Morgenthau's whole theory, and particularly his ethics, hinges on a basic ("grammatical") separation of the transcendent and the actual.[67] There are universal knowledge and ethics that man senses and longs for, yet he can in action realize only the particular. What she calls "the imperfectability thesis" in Morgenthau is possible only with absolute standards to judge against, and therefore the distinction between the actual and the transcendental is necessary. Although Morgenthau has said about his relationship to Niebuhr's thought that "Reinie and I come out about the same on politics, but I do not need all his metaphysics to get where we both get,"[68] Pin-Fat shows that Morgenthau's realism is still a "Christian realism," not a fully secular realism. Similarly, the two founders of the English School, Butterfield and Wight, were led to humility and a sense of history as drama and tragedy by their Christian inspiration.

In all these cases, the religious impulse led to important differences between this classical thought and much of current mainstream, rationalist IR, including contemporary realism. This explains much of the otherwise quite surprising parallel between realism and the English School on the one hand and poststructuralism on the other. Religion for the former produces parallel effects to the view of language in the latter.[69] Our realists and early English School writers emphasize that structural ironies and tragedy are built into the nature of international relations. Also, poststructuralism operates with an ultimate paradoxicality by which attempts to fix meaning produce strange effects. To both it is impossible to subsume the world into thought or speech. The realists locate their ironies in the constellations of the social, and to a lesser or greater extent, then derive this from religious assumptions about the nature of man. The poststructuralists either follow a Nietzschean abundance of life or, more radically, stress the complex dynamics and mechanisms of language, which operate not only logically but through, for example, homonyms and are more generally influenced by the presence of the unconscious.

Most current IR scholarship—be it "rationalist" or "constructivist"—is comparatively much more optimistic about the possibility of knowledge and the "rationality" of practice. When classical realists and early English School thinkers exhibited a modesty and sensitivity that is today represented mainly by poststructuralists, it was to a large extent due to the influence of religious thought on their theorizing.

In this section we have argued as if poststructuralism in a "secular" way reached parallel effects to the "religious" realism of previous decades. The pressing question is, however, whether these parallels are not caused by the religious roots of poststructuralism itself.

Poststructuralism and Religion

In recent years, poststructuralist philosophy has increasingly opened itself to religion. This is probably due at least partly to poststructuralism's well-known penchant for provocation. But more importantly, there are good reasons within poststructuralist thinking for exploring connections to religious thinking. According to John Caputo, the increasingly obvious religious pronouncements from Jacques Derrida are derived from deconstruction's overarching passion for transgression, which is religious or prophetic. Deconstruction aims at the unimaginable and unforeseeable. "Deconstruction is a passion and a prayer for the impossible. By religion, I mean a pact with the impossible, a covenant with the unrepresentable," and then Caputo goes on to discuss Kierkegaard, not unlike our argument above.[70]

Caputo is right in pointing out the increasing importance of religion in Derrida's oeuvre. However, his interpretation is problematic in overemphasizing the specifically Jewish nature of Derrida's thought: its eschatology and messianism. More important is the relationship between religion and the limit to symbolization that Derrida shares with much poststructuralist philosophy. Thus, we better return to Bataille (and Derrida's reading of him).[71] In contrast to almost all prior philosophical systems (epitomized by Hegel), poststructuralism does not try to subsume everything into one system, but to respect true negativity. A major task is therefore to prevent any dialectical *Aufhebung*. "To be indifferent to the comedy of the *Aufhebung*, as was Hegel, is to blind oneself to the experience of the sacred, to the heedless sacrifice of presence and meaning."[72]

The argument is similar to the role of the Real in Lacan as that which cannot be represented and which forces its way upon us nevertheless (punctuating speech, upsetting the identification by subjects), and to Derrida's recent writings on politics and ethics. The argument of the latter can be exemplified by the distinction between law and justice.[73] Law is the concrete historical product, whereas justice is the indeterminate reference to wider ethical considerations. Thus, the distinction between law and justice corresponds to the distinction between a law given by man and a law given by God(s). Even when justice is no longer explicitly stated as divine, it is universal and in contrast to the always particular law. Any given, concrete law always rests on violence, while the necessary distance to the law is created by the concept of justice. Justice is a call, a reminder of our obligation to a responsibility without limits, a responsibility that can never be institutionalized. The call of justice has to be interpreted by the subject. Or in Žižek's formulation:

> The moral Law does not tell me *what* my duty is, it merely tells me *that* I should accomplish my duty—which means that the subject himself has to assume the responsibility of "translating" the abstract injunction of the moral Law into a series of concrete obligations.[74]

As we explained above, traditional ethics within a moral system is part of Bataille's homogeneous sphere, in contrast to the call for the sovereign decision of the subject to act on an ethics beyond this system, which takes us into the heterogeneous (closely linked to religion). Our argument still follows the logic of the leap in Kierkegaard's scheme. To move from the aesthetic to the ethical stage is to succumb to the law; to move on to the religious, one has to face the abyss, the lack, the unfounded leap. Poststructuralism is open to religion in this sense due to its general recognition of a constitutive abyss, acceptance of the lack, and taking tragedy as the basis for an ethics.

Toward an IR Theory That Acknowledges Its Own Religion

Derrida:

> And there are signs. It is like a new International, but without a party, or organization, or membership. It is searching and suffering, it believes that something is wrong, it does not accept the "new world order."[75]

With Derrida's concept of justice, one is constantly exposed to a double bind. On the one hand, there is an inescapable call to act; on the other hand, any attempt to answer this will be different from the absoluteness of the call itself. It is never "justice" that acts, only some human acting with reference to it.[76] Ultimately, each concrete manifestation of "justice" becomes "law" and has to be criticized as such. Conversely, it is not possible to let go of the law and just act in "a spirit of justice"; rather, one has to "go through the aporia and *perform the contradiction*."[77] The tension between the universal and the particular is what keeps ethics alive. Morgenthau half a century ago formulated it like this:

> Whenever we act with reference to our fellow men, we must sin, and we must still sin when we refuse to act; for the refusal to be involved in the evil of action carries with it the breach of the obligation to do one's duty.[78]

This is even more relevant in relation to so-called fundamentalism. The Western perception is that "we" are secularized and they are "fundamentalists." But "we" too are religious in the sense that we are not the products of abstract universality but substantially given from *our* basis. When we act in humanitarian interventions, we hold certain things sacred (life, human rights). Our fundament too is constituted in a religious way. Probably, it is easier to meet other religions if we do not see *them* as fundamentalist religionists and ourselves as secular rationalists. De-securitization is easier if we see the parallelism in our differences. This demands that we open up to the religious in our reflections on ourselves, not only on the Other.

Recently, William E. Connolly has argued in *Why I Am Not a Secularist* that modern secularism acting in the name of pluralism actually restricts pluralism by its exclusion of religious forms of subjectivity, intersubjectivity, and thinking. Against the dogmatism of secularism, Connolly wants to promote an openness to more diverse traditions, each of which "contributes something to an appreciation of the indispensability and constitutive fragility of ethics in political life."[79] A similar argument was made in the context of IR two decades before:

> It has become fashionable for secular political writers and political scientists to speak of religious writers as mere preachers. These judgements throw a shadow as much on those who make them as upon religionists. Having broken the shackles of religious orthodoxy, modern secular thinkers run the risk of blinding themselves to what religious thought has to offer. It is as incumbent on an open intellectual society to draw upon the truths contributed by the giants in the major religious traditions as it is to recognize the wisdom of the best secular thinking. Freedom of thought is imperiled both by religious and secular dogmatism; those who seek a viable political ethic must follow truth wherever it leads them.[80]

Conclusion: Who's Afraid of Religion?

Religion deals with the constitution of being through acts of faith. It contains narratives about that which, according to Bataille's thinking, could be called the primary negation. And it gives prescriptions for approaching God. Religion is a fundamental discourse answering questions like, why being, why law, why existence? It is difficult not to pose such questions. Answers to such questions have the character of transcendental justification, and as such anchor being (and societies).

If religion is an inescapable discourse, the question is not whether religion is important and present in modern societies—it is—but rather which form it takes. Perhaps the church is no longer the most important institution in articulating faith. To detect the work of religious discourse outside what is commonly seen as the religious sector, that is, churches and the like, one needs to understand what characterizes religion as a discourse. This we established through the theories of Kierkegaard and Bataille, and in the second section we showed how ideologies are the product of a securitization on the basis of quasi-religious semantics. Such securitization of religion means impoverishing it. When mobilized as politics, religion represses the transcendence of the divine. Fear and trembling is replaced by absolute certainty. In relation to more straightforward security policy in defense of religion, we also find clear patterns: Faith (religion) is a particularly strong referent object and therefore easily securitized, because it is *already existential*. It is not a sphere of a little more, a little less. Whenever there are challenges, these are easily seen as threats. Furthermore, religiously based securitizations have a special proclivity for violence due especially to the logic of cosmic war.

Our discussion, especially in the first section, was structured by securitization, where the *referent object* is religious (and in the second section quasi-religious); but equally important are *religious threats to nonreligious referent objects*. Especially securitization on behalf of secularization against fundamentalism justifies many violations of democracy and civil liberties around the world. From a secularist platform, religion as such can be depicted as a threat to political culture. On this issue, IR theory is not the neutral observer it pretends to be; it is implicated by its own secularist self-perception. Despite the religious inspiration in classical IR realism, the rejection of religion has become even stronger in IR than in most other disciplines. One reason for this has been explored by Michael Williams.[81] The state, the state system, the narrow concept of security, and philosophical materialism and positivism are a package deal established in early modern Europe on the basis of a *security argument:* to end the wars of religion. Therefore, politics—and especially *security* policy—with reference to identity and worst of all to religion is the ultimate threat to order, security, and civility.

It is thus a major challenge for IR theory to open itself to religion as *religion* and to acknowledge its own religion. To avoid the most violent and ideologized conflicts is a task that demands first of all de-securitization, which in the present case means to respect religion as *religion*.

However, at this point, we might ourselves have become too schematic and formulaic, more taxonomy than transcendence. There is no simple "solution," no way to save religion and avoid conflict by just keeping categories apart and defining decently. Securitization and de-securitization are political processes, not stable formulas. The drawing of distinctions is a constant political battle. Ayatollah Khomeini was probably right: "Life is faith and struggle."[82]

Notes

For helpful criticism and suggestions, we would like to thank Ulla Holm, Vibeke Schou Petersen, Mikkel Vedby Rasmussen, Stefano Guzzini, Pertti Joenniemi, Lene Hansen, Barry Buzan, Birgitta Frello, and Katalin Sarvary, participants in the workshop on Holy Places in Modern Global Societies at the Danish Convention of Sociologists, August 2000, and the two anonymous reviewers of the journal.

1. Samuel P. Huntington, *The Clash of Civilizations and the Remaking of World Order* (London: Simon and Schuster, 1997); Douglas Johnston, "Introduction: Beyond Power Politics," in *Religion, the Missing Dimension of Statecraft,* eds. Douglas Johnston and Cynthia Sampson (Oxford: Oxford University Press, 1994); and Barry Rubin, "Religion and International Affairs," in *Religion, the Missing Dimension.*

2. "Religion is a central defining characteristic of civilizations, and, as Christopher Dawson said, 'the great religions are the foundations on which the great civilizations rest.'" Huntington, *The Clash of Civilizations,* 47.

3. Ibid., 28f.

4. Ibid., 95ff. "The revenge of god" is a phrase borrowed from Gilles Kepel, *The Revenge of God: The Resurgence of Islam, Christianity and Judaism in the Modern World* (Cambridge: Polity Press, 1994).

5. Martin E. Marty and R. Scott Appleby, eds., *The Fundamentalism Project,* vols. 1–5 (Chicago: The University of Chicago Press, 1991–1995).

6. Bernard Lewis, "The Roots of Muslim Rage," *Atlantic Monthly* 226, no. 3, (1990): 47–54; Abdullahi A. An-Na'im, "Political Islam in National Politics and International Relations," in *The Desecularization of the World: Resurgent Religion and World Politics,* ed. Peter L. Berger (Grand Rapids, MI: William B. Eerdmans Publishing Company, 1999); and William Martin, "The Christian Right and American Foreign Policy," *Foreign Policy,* no. 114, (1999): 66–80.

7. Peter L. Berger, "Secularism in Retreat," *The National Interest,* no. 46, (1996/97): 12.

8. See Edward Luttwak, "The Missing Dimension," in *Religion, the Missing Dimension.*

9. Kalevi J. Holsti, *Peace and War: Armed Conflicts and International Order, 1648–1989* (Cambridge: Cambridge University Press, 1991), 149.

10. The name "Copenhagen School" was coined by Bill McSweeney in the critical review essay "Identity and Security: Buzan and the Copenhagen School," *Review of International Studies* 2, no. 1 (1996): 81–94.

For these other elements, see Barry Buzan, Ole Wæver, and Jaap de Wilde, *Security: A New Framework for Analysis* (Boulder, CO: Lynne Rienner, 1998).

11. J. L. Austin, *How to Do Things with Words,* 2d ed. (Oxford: Oxford University Press, 1975), and John R. Searle, *Speech Acts* (Cambridge: Cambridge University Press, 1969). For analyses closer to our understanding of speech acts, see Jacques Derrida, *Limited Inc.* (Evanston, IL: Northwestern University Press, 1988); Judith Butler, *Excitable Speech: A Politics of the Performative* (London: Routledge, 1997); and John Forrester, *The Seductions of Psychoanalysis: Freud, Lacan, and Derrida* (Cambridge: Cambridge University Press, 1990).

12. Ole Wæver, "Insécurité, Identité: Une Dialectique sans Fin," in *Entre Union et Nations: L'État en Europe,* ed. Anne-Marie Le Gloannec (Paris: Presses de Sciences Po, 1998).

13. Ole Wæver, Barry Buzan, Morten Kelstrup, and Pierre Lemaitre with David Carlton et al, *Identity, Migration, and the New Security Agenda in Europe* (London: Pinter, 1993), 22f, 44, 132ff. See also Buzan et al, *Security,* 123f.

14. Slavoj Žižek, "Holding the Place," in *Contingency, Hegemony, Universality—Contemporary Dialogues on the Left,* eds. Judith Butler, Ernesto Laclau, and Slavoj Žižek (London: Verso, 2000), 315–16.

15. For the concept, see Peter L. Berger, *The Sacred Canopy—Elements of a Sociological Theory of Religion* (New York: Anchor Books, 1967), 100, 110, 180.

16. A problem arising from the tendency to understand religion as integration is the tendency to overlook religion as a source of conflict. See Niklas Luhmann, *Funktion der Religion* (Frankfurt am Main: Suhrkamp, 1977), 10f.

17. George Bataille, *Theory of Religion* (New York: Zone Books, 1989).

18. Søren Kierkegaard, "Afsluttende uvidenskabelig Efterskrift," in *Samlede Værker,* vol. 9 (København: Gyldendal, 1962), 80–90.

19. The absurdity of faith is discussed in Kierkegaard, "Afsluttende uvidenskabelig Efterskrift," vol. 10, 224–47.

20. Søren Kierkegaard, "Frygt og Bæven," *Samlede Værker,* vol. 5 (København: Gyldendal, 1962), 7–111.

21. For the most systematic exposition of the three stages, see Søren Kierkegaard, "Enten Eller," in *Samlede Værker,* vols. 1–2.

22. Søren Kierkegaard, "Sygdommen til Døden: En Christelig Psychologisk Udvikling til Opbyggelse og Opvækkelse," in *Samlede Værker,* vol. 15.

23. Kierkegaard, "Enten Eller," vol. 1.

24. Kierkegaard, "Frygt og Bæven," 51–62.

25. Niklas Luhmann, "Kontingenz als Eigenwert der Modernen Gesellschaft," in *Beobachtungen der Moderne* (Braunschweig: Der Westdeutsche Verlag, 1992).

26. Georges Bataille, "La Structure Psychologique du Fascisme," in *Oeuvres Complètes de Georges Batailles* (Paris: Gallimard, 1970).

27. George Bataille, *The Accursed Share,* vols. II-III (New York: Zone Books, 1991), 61–86.
28. Bataille, *Theory of Religion.*
29. Ibid., 17–18, 24.
30. Ibid., 18.
31. Ibid., 49.
32. Kierkegaard, "Frygt og Bæven," 7–111.
33. Mark Juergensmeyer, "Antifundamentalism," in *Fundamentalisms Comprehended,* eds. Martin E. Marty and R. Scott Appleby (Chicago: University of Chicago Press, 1995), 353.
34. Ibid., 354.
35. Ibid., 354
36. Gabriel A. Almond, Emmanuel Sivan, and R. Scott Appleby, "Fundamentalism: Genus and Species," in *Fundamentalisms Comprehended.*
37. Ibid., 402.
38. Mark Juergensmeyer, *The New Cold War? Religious Nationalism Confronts the Secular State* (Berkeley and Los Angeles: University of California Press, 1994).
39. Marty and Appleby, "Introduction," 1.
40. Ibid., 1.
41. Juergensmeyer, *The New Cold War?* 2.
42. Sonia L. Alianak, "The Mentality of Messianic Assassins," *Orbis* 44, no. 2 (2000): 283–94.
43. Charles K. Bellinger, "'The Crowd Is Untruth': A Comparison of Kierkegaard and Girard," *Contagion: A Journal of Violence, Mimesis, and Culture* 3 (1996): 103–20.
44. René Girard, *Violence and the Sacred* (Baltimore, MD: Johns Hopkins University Press, 1977) and *The Scapegoat* (Baltimore, MD: Johns Hopkins University Press, 1986).
45. Juergensmeyer, *The New Cold War,* 160.
46. Ibid., 155.
47. Ibid., 158.
48. Juergensmeyer, *Terror in the Mind of God: The Global Rise of Religious Violence* (Berkeley and Los Angeles: University of California Press, 2000), 11.
49. Carl von Clausewitz, *Vom Kriege* (Frankfurt: Ullstein Materialen, 1980), esp. book I, chap. 1. See also Ole Wæver, *Concepts of Security* (Copenhagen: University of Copenhagen, 1997), 219–20, 321–23.
50. Quoted by Juergensmeyer, *The New Cold War,* 165.
51. Ibid., 9.
52. Ibid., 145.
53. Carl Schmitt, *Politische Theologie: Vier Kapitel zur Lehre von der Souveränität* (Berlin: Duncker and Humblot, 1990) and *Politische Theologie II: Die Legende von der Erleidigung jeder Politischen Theologie* (Berlin: Duncker and Humblot, 1970); Ernst H. Kantorowicz, "Mysteries of State: An Absolutist Concept and Its Late Medieval Ori-

gin," *Harvard Theological Review* XLVIII, no. 1 (1955): 65–91, and *The King's Two Bodies: A Study in Medieval Political Theology* (Princeton, NJ: Princeton University Press, 1957); Anthony D. Smith, "Ethnic Election and National Destiny: Some Religious Origins of Nationalist Ideals," *Nations and Nationalism* 5, no. 3 (1999): 331–56.

54. Jacques Lacan, *The Seminar. Book XI: The Four Fundamental Concepts of Psychoanalysis, 1964* (London: Hogaarth Press and Institute of Psychoanalysis, 1977), 185.

55. Slavoj Žižek, *The Indivisible Remainder—Essays on Schelling and Related Matters* (London: Verso, 1996), 189–90.

56. Jacques Lacan, *Écrits: A Selection* (London: Tavistock Publications, 1977), 311.

57. Slavoj Žižek, *Looking Awry: An Introduction to Lacan through Popular Culture* (Cambridge, MA: MIT Press, 1991), 12.

58. Slavoj Žižek, *Tarrying with the Negative: Kant, Hegel, and the Critique of Ideology* (Durham, NC: Duke University Press, 1993), 201–5.

59. The original version of this article published in the special issue of *Millennium* (vol. 29: 3) contained here an illustrative case study of German National Socialism, pp. 729–733.

60. Carl Schmitt, *Politische Theologie*, 49. We partly follow the translation by George Schwab, *Political Theology: Four Chapters on the Concept of Sovereignty* (Cambridge, MA: MIT Press, 1985), 36.

61. Pierre Bourdieu, *Language and Symbolic Power* (Cambridge, MA: Harvard University Press, 1991).

62. See, for example, Terry Nardin, ed., *The Ethics of War and Peace: Religious and Secular Perspectives* (Princeton, NJ: Princeton University Press, 1996).

63. R. B. J. Walker, *Inside/Outside: International Relations as Political Theory* (Cambridge: Cambridge University Press, 1993), 50f.

64. Kenneth W. Thompson, *Fathers of International Thought: The Legacy of Political Theory* (Baton Rouge: Louisiana State University Press, 1994), 44.

65. Kenneth W. Thompson, *Masters of International Thought: Major Twentieth-Century Theorists and the World Crisis* (Baton Rouge: Louisiana State University Press, 1980), 21f. See also Reinhold Niebuhr, *Moral Man and Immoral Society: A Study in Ethics and Politics* (New York: Charles Scribner's, 1932).

66. Hans J. Morgenthau, *Scientific Man vs Power Politics* (Chicago: University of Chicago Press, 1946), 201–3.

67. Véronique Pin-Fat, "'Words are Deeds': Grammar and the Limits of Ethics in Hans J. Morgenthau" (paper presented at the annual meeting of British International Studies Association, Southampton, 1995).

68. Quoted by Pin-Fat, "'Words are Deeds,'" 5.

69. Ole Wæver, "Does the English School's Via Media Equal the Contemporary Constructivist Middle Ground? Or, on the Difference between Philosophical Scepticism and Sociological Theory" (paper presented

at the 24th Annual Conference of the British International Studies Association, Manchester, 1999).

70. John D. Caputo, *The Prayers and Tears of Jacques Derrida: Religion without Religion* (Bloomington: Indiana University Press, 1997), xx.

71. Jacques Derrida, *Writing and Difference* (London: Routledge, 1978), chap. 9.

72. Derrida, *Writing and Difference,* 257.

73. Jacques Derrida, "Force of Law: The 'Mystical Foundation of Authority,'" in *Deconstruction and the Possibility of Justice,* eds. Drucilla Cornell, Michel Rosenfeld, and David Gray Carlson (London: Routledge, 1992).

74. Slavoj Žižek, "The Unconscious Law: Toward an Ethics Beyond the Good," in *The Plague of Fantasies* (London: Verso, 1997).

75. Jacques Derrida, "The Deconstruction of Actuality," *Radical Philosophy,* no. 68 (1994): 39. For a fuller version of this argument/vision, see Jacques Derrida, *Specters of Marx: The State of the Debt, the Work of Mourning, and the New International* (London: Routledge, 1994), chap. 4.

76. Cf. Reinhold Niebuhr, *Christianity and Power Politics* (New York: Charles Scribner's, 1940), 23 and 216–19.

77. Hent de Vries, *Philosophy and the Turn to Religion* (Baltimore, MD: Johns Hopkins University Press, 1999), 414 emphasis in original.

78. Morgenthau, *Scientific Man,* 201

79. William E. Connolly, *Why I Am Not a Secularist* (Minneapolis: Minnesota University Press, 1999), 17; see also Lynch and Thomas in this volume.

80. Thompson, *Masters of International Thought,* 2.

81. Michael C. Williams, "Comment on the 'Copenhagen Controversy,'" *Review of International Studies* 24, no. 3 (1998): 435–41, and "Security and the Politics of Identity," *European Journal of International Relations* 4, no. 2 (1998): 204–25.

82. Quoted in Juergensmeyer, *The New Cold War,* 161.

PART III

POLITICIZING RELIGION: TOWARD A NEW GLOBAL ETHOS?

CHAPTER 6

A WORLDWIDE RELIGIOUS RESURGENCE IN AN ERA OF GLOBALIZATION AND APOCALYPTIC TERRORISM

Richard Falk

Points of Departure

Even before the September 11 attacks, the relevance of religion to global governance was a subject of controversy and confusion: After the Cold War, it was the energies of Islam that mounted the greatest threat to the sort of world order that the West was championing, which rested on a domestic governance model of constitutionalism and a strong private sector economy. The role of governmental institutions was to become mainly a facilitative one, especially with respect to the smooth operations of the world economy. This vision of a future based on liberal values of moderate states and robust markets was widely promoted as the best path to progress and prosperity, especially as underpinned by a growing willingness of governments to acknowledge the authority of human rights. Such a vision was no longer challenged by Marxist/Leninist ideology or by a bloc of states under the dominion of a nuclear superpower. Indeed, the collapse of the

Soviet Union, the embrace of the liberal model by the successor states, and the incredible rate of capitalist growth achieved by Communist China in the 1990s seemed to confirm the historical weight of a post-Marxist materialist approach to global politics.

In retrospect, it is evident that such an outlook was a mixture of wishful thinking and blinkered perception. There were clear indications even before the end of the Cold War that this Western model was not universally acceptable, especially in the countries of the South. The Iranian Revolution in 1978–79 against the Shah's White Revolution was one sign of trouble. The emergence on the world stage of Ayatollah Khomeini suggested the potency of another way of envisioning governance and human destiny that rested on traditional values and the primacy of religious leaders and institutions in shaping the life of society. Beyond this, Khomeini enunciated what amounted to a declaration of war against the United States and its worldview, calling America "the Great Satan." What was most significant about this challenge was that it mobilized Iranian society to rise en masse and overthrow a leader who had previously been regarded as strong and secure. It is worth recalling that the government of the Shah of Iran enjoyed the ardent patronage of the United States, as well as having managed to have positive diplomatic relations with neighboring states including the Soviet Union. Khomeini's message seemed also to resonate powerfully beyond Iran, with "the Islamic street," the peoples of the Islamic world, even as it frightened their secular leaders. When youthful Islamic radicals seized the American embassy in Tehran in late 1979, embarrassing and frustrating the U.S. government as the TV cameras churned day after day for well over a year, the impression that political Islam conceived of America as its main enemy intensified.

The Iranian Revolution had these two goals: to Islamicize the structure of domestic governance and to define the historical situation by reference to a postcolonial struggle of Third World countries against American-led globalization. Both of these faces found varying parallel expressions in other circumstances. Even authoritarian China, with its long antimetaphysical tradition, seemed most challenged from within by the religious movement known as the Fulan Gong and by the Muslim separatist Uigur movement in Xinjiang province seeking to establish an independent East Turkistan and alleged to have close relations with Usama bin Laden and Al Qaeda. Elsewhere also, as in Turkey, Pakistan, Russia, the Philippines, Indonesia, and Malaysia, extremist opposition and separatist movements inspired by Islam pose the main challenge to public order.

In the West—especially in the United States—the political leverage of the religious right was more strongly felt than ever before in the central citadels of governance, although this influence has been largely concealed, and the main global perceptions have involved anxieties about American empire building and global reach. The fear of American cultural and economic primacy was paramount in Asia, where economic globalization was being uncritically pursued by most of the governments, at least until the roadblocks of the Asian financial crisis of 1997, and the most visible resistance was to be found there, in mainly a cultural form. Moves to stress "Asian values," which thinly masked concerns about U.S. dominance, were seen as upholding civilizational identities while reaping the benefit of the world economy. Shortly thereafter, first at Seattle and later at various meetings associated with the management of globalization, climaxing at the Genoa meeting of the G–8 in the summer of 2001, an antiglobalization movement took shape at the grassroots that went further, and challenged the American-led market-driven view of global policy as unfair in its impacts, especially on the poor in the South, and antidemocratic in its management.

Against such a background it is not surprising that the Huntington thesis of "a clash of civilizations" caused a stir when it first appeared in 1992, provoking a strong countertendency in ensuing years beneath the banner of "a dialogue of civilizations."[1] The clash thesis seemed dangerous and simplistic, drawing ethnic and religious battle lines that anticipated a new epoch of cultural wars based on intercivilizational enmity, culminating in the slogan "the West against the rest." Such an outlook was at odds with the globalization thesis as well as with the liberal idea that the American model of state and global governance was the only relevant model for the achievement of a human rights culture, and could and should be exported to non-Western countries. By emphasizing civilizational identities, the clash thesis also rejected the economic determinism of the globalization model, which seemed to make markets the new driving force of history, thereby perversely adopting the basic Marxist hypothesis of materialism at the very moment when Marxism had lost its historical relevance as an ideological weapon wielded against capitalism. To counterpose culture to economics created an opening for religion that had seemed closed by reference to either economistic or highly rationalistic worldviews that were essential features of modernity as shaped by the West. And finally, by asserting "civilizations" as the unit of primary relevance to the future, Huntington encouraged the view that the long period of dominance exercised by territorial sovereign states was in the process of being superseded, which put into question traditional state-centric forms of global governance.[2] But by linking civilizational identities with the intensification of conflict, the clash thesis cast a shadow over the resurgence of non-Western cultural and religious identities, seeming to suggest that a more peaceful world would result from an embrace of the technological gifts of modernity and the organizational benefits of a networked world, the alleged wave of a humanistic future.[3]

It is against this complex background that the events of September 11 and their aftermath must be taken into account. The character of the attack, its inspiration deriving from Usama bin Laden's extremist views of Islamic faith and his genocidal hostility directed against Americans, Jews, and "Crusaders" gave this experience of apocalyptic terrorism religious overtones.[4] These were reinforced due to the identity of the hijackers as militant foot soldiers of Islam fully prepared to engage in suicidal missions of mega-terrorism. In fashioning a response, the U.S. government has been generally careful to designate the enemy as "terrorism," and not Islam, and to emphasize that Arab Americans, and adherents of Islam, should not be singled out for discrimination. At the same time, the wider sympathies evoked by bin Laden's outlook, especially its castigation of the United States for its policies toward Palestinians, its maintenance of sanctions against Iraq a decade after the Gulf War ceasefire, and its general military encroachment on the most sacred Islamic sites, suggest that the risk of provoking a civilization war and the relevance of religion to this potential encounter cannot be ignored.

Indeed, an unfortunate aspect of the current world setting is the polarization of views about the relevance of religion to humane forms of global governance. There are those who view religion as disposed toward extremism, even terrorism, as soon as it abandons its proper modernist role as a matter of private faith and is allowed to intrude upon public space, and especially upon governance. Their most ardent antisecular opponents insist on the opposite view, which contends that without basing governance on the dictates of religious doctrine and values, the inevitable result is decadence, decline, and impotence. This essay seeks to advance a different view of the relevance of religion. It argues that all great religions have two broad tendencies (and many shades of variation in each) within their traditions: the first is to be universalistic and tolerant toward those who hold other convictions and identities; the second is to be exclusivist and insistent that there exists only one true path to salvation, which if not taken results in failure and futility, if not evil.

From such a standpoint, the first orientation of religion is constructive, useful, and essential if the world is to find its way toward humane global governance in the decades ahead, while the second is regressive and carries with it a genuine danger of a new cycle of religious warfare carried out on a civilizational scale. The best hope for the future is to give prominence and support to this universalizing influence of religion and, at the same time, to marginalize and discredit religious extremism based on a variety of alleged dualisms between good and evil.

It should also be noted that secular views that hold the line against the hostile perception of religion also can adopt fundamentalist canons of belief and view religious affiliation as intrinsically evil. Such secular intolerance is as unwelcome with respect to informing patterns of global governance as is its religious counterpart.[5] This regressive secularist trope has resulted in the suppression of religious freedom in a number of countries, including Turkey and China, where the established order perceives any collective expression of religious identity as dangerous and subversive. Both religious and secular traditions can contribute to the emergence of humane forms of global governance if they jointly adhere to an ethos of tolerance, abandon rival metaphysical claims of certitude, and seek from distinct vantage points to address the deep causes of human despair and discontent. It is these claims that provide the foundation for intolerance and repression of "the other," as well as a variety of extremisms enacted in the lifeworld of political engagement.

While establishing the present context of religious relevance is necessary, it is also essential to take into account antecedent conditions and longer-term trends. At this point it is difficult to assess the degree to which the revived preoccupation with "security," along with its accompanying recourse to global war by the United States to address "terrorism," will bend these trends in enduring ways. It is currently impossible to discern the scope and disorienting effects of the war on global terror, partly because its goals have not been clearly defined and partly because the degree and success of terrorist countermoves have not been established. The remainder of this essay proceeds on the assumption that global normalcy will reemerge within the next year or so, and with it a renewed preoccupation with global governance in an era of globalization, almost as if September 11 had not occurred. Possibly, the traumatizing impact of this unanticipated war experience will even make leaders and social forces more attentive to the reconciliation of markets and human well-being, the greatest challenge of worldwide significance before September 11.

Narrating the Interplay of Religion and Politics: The Emergence of Modernity

The religious dimension of human experience has been generally excluded from the serious study and practice of governance for several centuries, especially in the West. This exclusion is primarily a consequence of the European Enlightenment and its endorsement of autonomous reason as the only reliable guide for human affairs, as well as its general tendency to ground politics upon a secular ethos, a principal feature of which is the separation of church and state. Of course, as with many questionable moves in history, this development had positive aspects and was rooted in a particular set of historical circumstances in Europe at the time of the formation of the modern states system, a process whose origin is difficult to locate with precision but is often, although somewhat arbitrarily, dated to coincide with the Peace of Westphalia in 1648.[6]

Without entering into this complex story in any detail, religion was regarded as inimical to the rise of science and material progress in human affairs and as the cause of a series of terrible religious wars that marked the split of Christendom. So, it is first necessary to understand that the exclusion of religion from political life was seen as a vital step in the ongoing struggle to establish humane governance, that is, governance based on reason, religious and ethnic tolerance, and the individual and collective dignity of the human species, as well as encouraging scientific inquiry and technological innovation. In many respects Hugo Grotius, a typical Renaissance figure of Protestant Europe, embodied the passing of medieval Europe to the new Europe of independent, sovereign, territorial states. Grotius was, in one sense, seeking to restore the religious possibility for human life by removing it from the violent rivalries of the political realm. In his vivid, often-quoted words,

> Throughout the Christian world I observed a lack of restraint in relation to war, such as even barbarous races should be ashamed of; I observed that men rush to arms for slight causes, or no cause at all, and that when arms have once been taken up there is no longer any respect for law, divine or human; it is as if, in accordance with a general decree, frenzy had openly been let loose for the committing of all crimes.[7]

In adopting this critical stance, Grotius combined two of the defining characteristics of modernity: a claim of moral superiority associated with the specific identity of "the Christian world" that should inform political life wherever possible and an implicit deprecation of non-Christian societies as the vast domain of "barbarous races."[8] The first impulse led to the idea that the relations among states are to some extent governed by law, while the second gave a sort of underpinning to the Eurocentric conceptions of world order and hierarchical relations between Western and non-Western peoples that came to flourish in the colonial age. Such liberal rationalizations for the politics and structures of domination were later produced by the most admired Enlightenment figures: Hegel, Kant, and John Stuart Mill among others. Neither led to humane governance for the peoples of the world: International law was too weak to contain the passions of nationalism or dreams of empire, and the validation of colonial rule amounted to little more than a rationalization for the exploitation and domination of non-Western peoples and generated in many instances deep patterns of resentment and frustration that surfaced in the form of intense intrasocietal violence in postcolonial settings.

There have been recent attempts to draw normative orientations from existing political realities and pave the way toward more humane governance on a global level. Hedley Bull, for instance, depicted an international society of states that sustained a balance between sovereign rule within territorial limits and a kind of prudent moderation, safeguarded by the benevolence of leading military powers.[9] Myres McDougal, the founder of the New Haven School of Jurisprudence and International Law, depicted, with a group of collaborators, the spread of Enlightenment values through the commitment to democratic types of public order systems as an evolving foundation for a humane intercivilizational pattern of governance that had the capacity to produce, by stages, peaceful and equitable governance structures of benefit to the entire world.[10]

Both of these normative approaches were premised on the persistence of the states system as the basis of world order and on the role of power in managing relations among states, and were in these respects rooted in the antiutopian traditions of political realism.[11] Additionally, building on the heritage of Woodrow Wilson and the experiments in world organization represented by the League of Nations and the United Nations, there emerged a more utopian strain of secular thought that fundamentally believed that the only secure and legitimate form of world order depended upon the establishment of juridical universalism in the form of world government, a body of thought that came to be associated with world federalism and is probably still best represented by the work of Grenville Clark and Louis B. Sohn in the form of *World Peace through World Law*.[12]

Even the World Order Models Project (WOMP), with its explicit undertaking to consider the diverse world order perspectives representative of the leading regions and ideologies of the 1980s and 1990s, failed to include in any serious or systematic manner the relevance of religion, although it did acknowledge that world order values, widely shared on an intercivilizational basis, provided the normative framing of any successful project to establish, or even to envisage, humane global governance.[13]

Although the perspectives arising from the work of Bull and McDougal remain useful within the existing framework of world order, their regulative capabilities and potentialities seem far too modest to address the deficiencies of international political life that arise from the persistence of war and militarism, from the pervasiveness of poverty and economic deprivation, from the circumstances of political oppression and religious extremism, from the disregard of environmental decay and danger, and from the neglect of the spiritual sides of human nature and aspiration, and from predatory market forces associated with transnational finance and corporate operations. The advocacy of world government as a normative project seems strangely discordant with the current weakening of support for even the feeble efforts to sustain existing world political organizations.[14] Such decline is epitomized by the recent travails of the United Nations, and although there is an increasingly frequent framing of political life through the metaphor of the "global village," this is seen primarily as an expression of the potency of economic globalization, or it embodies intense preoccupations with transnational terrorism, criminality, and drug trafficking.[15] In effect, the best of secular thinking falls short of providing either a plausible path to travel in pursuit of humane global governance or a sufficiently inspiring vision of its elements that would mobilize a popular grassroots movement for drastic global reform.[16] The paucity of alternatives to capital-driven globalization and American global hegemony exhibits the absence of plausible agency for constructive social change; the nihilistic efforts of Islamic extremists merely reinforce the point both by their dismal image of an alternative public order (as prefigured by the Taliban regime in Afghanistan) and by consolidating, rather than weakening, the American drive toward global dominance.

This failure of political imagination is partially due to the exclusion of religious and spiritual dimensions of human experience from the shaping of the vision and practices associated with the quest for global humane governance. This chapter presents an overview: first, a section on dominant world order trends and tendencies with respect to global governance; then some consideration of the extent to which these recent world order trends, which are shaping the historical situation at the start of the third millennium, are also creating new, unexpected openings for religious and spiritual energies, a development that also, as with the secularist era of exclusion, has deeply disturbing, as well as encouraging, aspects. This religious resurgence is discussed as part of the double-edged relevance of religion for the kind of global governance most likely to emerge. The final section argues for the inclusion of emancipatory religious and spiritual perspectives in world order thinking and practice, along with an enumeration of their potential contributions.[17]

Current World Order Trends, or Pathways to Inhumane Governance

Without entering into a detailed inquiry, it seems evident that there are several dominant world order trends that are converging in such a way as to generate a more integrated form of governance at the global level, but through the emergence of "inhumane" social patterns. Such an indictment is not meant to be a total condemnation.[18] There are aspects of these globalizing developments that represent normative improvements on prior conditions (for instance, a reduction in the prospect for large-scale nuclear war, a diminishing likelihood of traditional warfare among states in general, and the alleviation of poverty and economic deprivation for hundreds of millions of people, particularly those living in several of the most populous, and previously some of the most severely and hopelessly impoverished, countries of the Pacific Rim), but the overall impact has been to fracture the peoples of the world, to neglect the plight of those who are most deprived and vulnerable, to place nonsustainable burdens on the environment that seem likely to diminish the life quality of future generations, to deepen over time the disparities between rich and poor, and to engender an ethos of consumerism that forecloses the most fulfilling forms of individual and social self-realization.[19] Despite the mixed picture that emerges, it seems appropriate to label the current arrangements of global governance as cumulatively contributing to a variant of "global inhumane governance." This assessment is reinforced by the severity and durability of the terrorist backlash, which in turn has produced a renewed phase of global militarism that is taking shape as a continuing war without geographical limits and lacking in a discernible endpoint, being waged by an American-led coalition of states against the nonstate, transnational, and nonterritorial Al Qaeda network with operations in as many as sixty countries. Such a war of territorial versus nonterritorial political actors is creating an unprecedented crisis of sovereign rights, where states become targets of potential military intervention because perceived as havens of terrorists.

To some extent, the preceding paragraphs explain why economic globalization, while clearly improving the material and social conditions of life for many millions, is still properly viewed as responsible for a dangerous momentum that is leading in the direction of "inhumane global governance." Four clusters of adverse normative effects identify this drift toward inhumane global governance: (1) polarization and global apartheid: It is undeniable that globalization has fostered widening income, wealth, and skill gaps, whether these are measured by class, region, gender, or race;[20] (2) neglect of human suffering and world poverty: While economic growth in recent decades has moved mainly ahead, the commitment of resources to eliminate poverty and related deprivations has declined; (3) undermining global public goods: There has been evident an unwillingness to devote adequate resources to the protection of the global commons or to provide regulatory capabilities to avoid the excesses of both the world economy and domestic oppression; (4) menacing technological horizons: the failure to address the deep problems posed by human cloning, super-intelligent machines, robots mobilized for violence, and generally to regulate private sector initiatives that pose dangers to the human condition.

These negative developments confront us with the likelihood that the third millennium will witness the fashioning of durable forms of inhumane governance that include severe risks of ecological and social catastrophe. This disturbing prospect is the latest, purest, and most ambitious phase of the fundamental application of the Enlightenment Project to human affairs, accentuated by the strength of market forces. The continuous stream of technological innovations adapt to secularized political space in order to achieve the greatest profits for the owners of capital goods. To be sure, there are important contradictory tendencies and progressive varieties of resistance, described by the rubric of globalization from below, but the political leverage of such forces is likely to remain limited to local battlegrounds and has the nuisance value of global gadfly unless such dispositions are reinforced by religious commitments and by support from important sectors of the organized religious communities around the world. It is this possibility of a religiously grounded transnational movement for a just world order that alone gives hope that humane global governance can become a reality. This hope is, of course, currently clouded by the perceived dangers to minimum order and stability associated with religious extremism in all its forms. In the West this situation encourages efforts to put religion back in the box constructed by secularism over the centuries, thereby confusing religious extremism with religion generally, and failing to recognize that religion generates both intolerance and an ethos of human solidarity.

Why Religion? Openings and Regressions

Among the surprises of the last several decades has been a multifaceted worldwide resurgence of religion as a potent force in human affairs. From the perspective of humane governance, this religious resurgence has a double-coded message: portending the hopeful possibility and necessity of transcending the constraints of economistic secularism, which has become the signature of a disturbing interface between late modernity and a nihilistic postmodernity, but also simultaneously disclosing a range of regressions in the form of extreme variants of inhumane governance that arguably, in certain instances, make the repudiation of secularism a terrifying descent into political extremism, repression, and violence. On the negative side, I have in mind the regressive politics that religion has brought to such countries as Iran, Afghanistan, Algeria, and, to some extent, India and Sudan in recent years, but also the tragic and gruesome behavior of religious cults such as Heaven's Gate and Aum Shinrikyō, which have been seemingly incubated in the midst of secularized contemporary modernity[21] — and most of all, of course, the startlingly potent Al Qaeda network apparently formed and led by Usama bin Laden, operating, as noted, in many different countries, which possesses the will and demonstrated capacity to shake the foundation of the existing structures of world order. Historically, then, it would appear that the outer limits of secularism are giving rise to transformative possibilities that lead in opposite directions, both toward humane governance and toward regressive potentialities that mix in various ways the most severe deficiencies of premodernity with the most frightening sequels to modernity. The dialectical implications of these developments must not be discounted, giving rise to a space-governed imperial control system that is entrusted with facilitating the extension of globalization from above in its most predatory attributes, while crushing the challenges of the mega-terrorists.

It is, of course, difficult to give an account of this religious resurgence that adequately situates it in the present, but this resurgence seems closely related to an exhaustion of the creative capacity of the secular project, especially as it is embodied in the political domain. It is within this domain, of course, that modernity has been so closely associated with the preeminence of the territorial sovereign state.[22] The principle of sovereignty has been virtually unchallenged in this century with respect to the organization of governance and is powerfully, if imperfectly, reinforced by nationalism, by far the strongest ideology of modern times.[23] Even the innovations associated with the establishment of the League of Nations and the United Nations were deeply rooted in a statist system of world order, as epitomized by their membership rules and participatory procedures. These institutional experiments represented mainly extensions of statism that perpetuated the allocation of governance capabilities to territorial sovereigns, although idealistic segments of the public have always believed that more was possible, or that the League, and later the UN, could be morphed in the direction of humane global governance. In actuality, the management of the whole was entrusted to geopolitical arrangements that continued to rely on the special governance role of leading states, what political scientists have called "hegemonic actors." In other words, a statist world order, although claiming to respect sovereign equality, was always based on a series of hierarchies, especially strong against weak, center versus periphery, Western or Eurocentric versus non-Western, and, most recently, North versus South.[24] It also presupposed the availability of war as a geopolitical instrument of dominant sovereign states, despite a certain lip service given to legal and moral restraints on the use of force in this century.

But although this statist world order validated many patterns of abuse, either by way of immunizing domestic political order from scrutiny or through the interventionary and exploitative behavior of dominant states, it also gave rise to important normative ideas: limitations on the legitimate use of force, human rights, humanitarian intervention, asylum, criminal accountability of leaders. These normative ideas have been often subordinated to geopolitical manipulations of various sorts, but they provided some encouragement for liberal perspectives, which were imbued with the idea of progress in human affairs, and anticipated a gradual evolution of this statist world in the direction of peace and harmony. This approach to humane global governance is associated with the "democratic peace" hypothesis, which asserts that the spread of constitutional democracy brings an assurance of peaceful relations among democratic states. And by extension, if buttressed by an effective international law of human rights that include economic and social rights (and not just civil and political), this world would fulfill the requirements of humane governance for the planet without requiring either disarmament or the centralization of political authority in international institutions.[25]

The main problem, however, with the democratic peace theory is that it neglects the social impact of economic globalization as enacted in an ideological climate shaped by neoliberalism and reinforced by geopolitical militarism. To connect this analysis with my wider argument, then, the secular imagination has long been dependent on the problem-solving capacities of the state, but these have been increasingly transferred to the main arenas of economistic authority (that is, the World Economic Forum, G–7, WTO, etc.). In the present setting, the restructuring of governance comes by way of the market, and, to some extent, is reinforced by the self-organizing, globalist ethos of the digitalized sensibility that shapes the Internet world picture. It is generally opposed to the social functions of government, to public goods, and to any deliberate effort to achieve humane governance. In opposition to this trend lies the diverse transnational array of networks, coalitions, associations, and initiatives that has been earlier labeled here as "globalization from below."[26] It is my contention that this effort to construct a democratic global civil society is informed by religious and spiritual inspiration, and if it is to move from the margins of political reality and challenge entrenched constellations of power in a more effective way, it will have to acquire some of the characteristics and concerns of a religious movement, including building positive connections with the emancipatory aspects of the great world religions.[27] Without religion, prospects for global humane governance appear to lack a credible social or political foundation and, more important, miss the spiritual character that can mobilize and motivate people much more potently than can "the market," "secular reason," or even "nationalism."

What is meant by 'religion' here requires considerable clarification in the course of constructing a global civil society and recasting the meaning of citizenship and democratic practice.[28] It is evident that religion cannot be reduced to any single religious tradition, although it can draw strength from their collaborative support, and also that some aspects of certain religious traditions are antithetical, especially those concerning claims of "the chosen people," or revealing "exclusive" instruments of a divine or sacred design or of the enactment of some apocalyptic scenario for the ascendance to higher or purer forms of existence, especially when these are thought to be achieved by way of holy war or jihad involving struggle to crush the infidels and nonbelievers. Such aspects of the overall religious heritage may authentically engage the lives and sensibilities of persons of genuine faith, but they offer nothing constructive in relation to the struggle to create patterns of humane global governance for all the peoples on earth. As the global terror of Al Qaeda exemplifies, exclusivist initiatives are particularly damaging to the potential contributions of religion, and may strengthen a regressive statism under the banners of increased national security and counterterrorism.

Religious Pillars of Humane Global Governance

Having identified the forms of religious expression inimical to the quest for humane governance, it remains to consider the potentially positive contributions of religion.[29] In setting forth these contributions, it is necessary that we allow considerable cultural space for a wide spectrum of interpretations of specific religiously based undertakings. It is also important to acknowledge that secular thought is also capable of reaching parallel points of ethical and political reference but lacks the deep historical foundations and universal roots of religion in the collective memories and traditions of peoples of varied backgrounds. The relevance of religion cannot be separated from its persistence in human consciousness and its historical role in the social construction of human nature. Religion is understood here as encompassing not only the teachings, beliefs, and practices of organized religions but also all spiritual outlooks that interpret the meaning of life by reference to faith and to the commitment to that which cannot be explained by empirical science or sensory observation and is usually associated with an acceptance of the reality of the divine, the sacred, the holy, the transcendent, the mysterious, the ultimate. Religion is also the source of limits, suggesting outer boundaries of acceptable behavior for the human species, a guidance that has great current relevance with respect to imposing limits on scientific inquiry and technological innovation, as in the instance of human cloning. Religion, then, must be understood as providing a rationale for the unconditional, for the refusal to accept limits to the extent that the divine is being served. In these respects, religion encompasses belief in God and gods, but does not depend on such theistic convictions, or for that matter, theological dogma of any kind.

The introduction to the complex matter of *positive* religious relevance offered here is intended only to be suggestive and is designed mainly to stimulate discussion, reflection, and dialogue in the context of building a global democratic movement for humane governance. The *negative* relevance of religion is not considered, although, as earlier sections suggest, these detrimental aspects bear upon any comprehensive evaluation of religion and its impact on human well-being, past, present, and future. In a heuristic spirit, a series of domains associated with religion and its practice can be identified and described, without sufficient elaboration at this point, nor will reference be made to a wide spectrum of intercivilizational and intracivilizational variations.

Appreciation of Suffering

The religious path can be strongly associated with a Gandhian acknowledgment of the "least man" (or woman), of the lowliest class, caste, race, and with a central commitment to lift up those who suffer acutely, a dedication to those most acutely victimized—it was Gandhi's insistence that politics be practiced so as, above all, to lift up persons at the bottom of the social, economic, and political hierarchy in society. Jesus and the Buddha were also particularly oriented toward enhancing the life and stature of those who were poor and outcasts. Along these lines, religion can embody a social revolution against worldly injustice, against the societal myths that convey the impression that hierarchy is intrinsic to the human condition and itself part of the divine plan.

In contrast, the Marxist rejection of religion was based on its role as an "opiate," falsely reconciling the poor and the exploited workers of the early Industrial Revolution to the cruelties of the human condition. In many occasions, the religious establishment of the day defends the status quo, and is itself part of the oppressive social and political order. Religious institutions find the more radical visions of social reformers who interpret the religious path as necessitating justice on earth for the poor as extremely disruptive and threatening, and tend to marginalize their impact, or even to align religion against such claims of justice.

These inherent tensions are important at the present time. To what extent can religion be a force in the struggle against global poverty, social injustice, and the inequities of globalization? And, if a positive force, can religion avoid mobilizing movements that challenge injustice, but from the perspective of rigid premodern traditionalism (as with the Taliban in Afghanistan or the hardline Islamicists in the unfolding of the Iranian Revolution)? Much of the recent intellectual turmoil in Iran, for instance, has been between those who seek to interpret the Islamic tradition as consistent with modernity, democracy, and cosmopolitanism (for example, Abdolkarim Sorush) and those who view the Islamic orientation of the state as entailing ultraliteral religious practice and constraint.

Civilizational Resonance

Whereas secular transformative thought tends to appeal mainly to intellectuals not strongly bonded with existing structures of governance, religious revolutionary language and utopian aspirations enjoy a sense of legitimacy in popular culture and possess great mobilizing potentials. What the religious resurgence has demonstrated, against all predictions flowing from Western Enlightenment circles, including its revolutionary Marxist expressions, is the persistence of religious outlooks in the body politic of even the most "modern" states—and beyond this, the susceptibility of the postcolonial world to a variety of religiously framed alternatives to the adoption of Western secular modernism. Part of this susceptibility needs to be understood as the expression of disillusionment with a series of deforming encounters with modernity: corruption, the selling out of the national economy to global capitalists, geopolitical servitude toward the West, the betrayal of the just causes of their own civilizational brethren.

Iran under Pahlevi rule was the perfect example. The Shah's White Revolution promised the people of Iran the benefits of secular modernity, following roughly the path taken more successfully by Atatürk in Turkey two generations earlier. This path involved major investments in science and education, the marginalization of Islam, an adoption of Western lifestyles and popular culture, the subordination of regional identifications to the foreign policy priorities of the United States (e.g., supplying oil to such regional pariahs as Israel and apartheid South Africa), major deployments of American military forces in the country, and public displays of corruption and decadence by the royal family and its entourage. The Iranian Revolution, under the inspiration of Khomeini, organized mass discontent around the symbols and convictions of Islam, revealing to a stunned world the mobilizing power of religion in the postcolonial world of the late 1970s and 1980s.

An Ethos of Solidarity

Closely related is the uniting feature of religious consciousness, the oneness of the human family that can give rise to an ethos of human solidarity, the unity of all creation, and, with it, the sense of both the wholeness of human experience and the dignity of the individual. Such solidarity is a sign of religious inclusiveness and celebration of religious diversity, contrasting with the narrow paths of intolerance traveled by exclusivist religiosity. Such an inclusive view also bonds the human spirit with the stranger and the guest, dissolving the sharp boundaries of political community engendered by nationalism and patriotic fervor. This inclusivity is particularly important in strengthening globalization from below and countering the Westphalian tradition that overwhelmingly associates solidarity with territorial sovereign states. The religious vision provides a potential political grounding for humane global governance that cannot arise otherwise.

Inclusivity that is bounded by culture and religion could induce positive trends toward regional political arrangements, thereby weakening the statist character of world order. Of course, regionalism as in Europe rests primarily on functional considerations of competitiveness and war prevention, but its viability as an approach is undoubtedly based also on the premodern collective heritage of Christendom. In Asia, Latin America, and Africa, religious identities both facilitate and obstruct efforts to forge regionalism. Part of what has made the postcolonial period so anguishing for Africa is the relative weakness of transnational, and even national, religious identities, and the comparative strength of ethnic and tribal ties. Such weakness has been accentuated in Africa by the difficulties of postcolonial state building.

As with other aspects of the religious resurgence, a counterproductive religious ethic may seem to be of greater relevance today. Religious exclusivism has captured the political imagination, especially in the aftermath of the Iranian Revolution, and even more so, in the wake of September 11. To the extent that the central issue of human destiny is posed as resistance to the West (and specifically, to the United States) and to globalization rather than the wider challenge of global transformation and humane global governance, the militancy of exclusivist religious orientations is eschewing some fundamental struggles. As a consequence, Western powers have mobilized their own nontransformative response against "terrorism," and there is a tendency for their apologists to frame the struggle as one of emancipatory modernity against repressive religious fundamentalism. Such an interpretation, while responsive to aspects of the religious resurgence, overlooks its wider role in preparing political consciousness for humane globalization by encouraging an awareness of human solidarity. Thinking dialectically, the greater the salience of exclusivist religious outlooks, the more historically significant will be the opportunities for religious inclusivism.

Normative Horizons

A compassionate response to suffering and the affirmation of human solidarity imply a belief in the normative horizons that affirm human potentialities. Religion thus endorses the transcendence of present conditions, including the market ethos, which neglects many forms of acute human suffering. The market ethos tends to elevate the claims of the part or the fragment over those of the whole, of winners over losers, and is fraught with the sort of consumerist and materialist preoccupations nurtured by mass advertising and franchise capitalism. Religiously oriented normative horizons embody and converge in many respects with the secularly defined priorities of a human rights culture, especially with regard to the economic and social needs of the most materially disadvantaged individuals and peoples. Such normative horizons also incline toward the replacement of power as the regulative basis of order with law and ethics.

It appears to be the case, especially given the seeming irrelevance of socialist modes of political analysis and influence, as well as the strength of market forces, that only religion has the possibility of filling the normative vacuum that exists in settings where extreme versions of capitalism seem unchallenged. There are other reactions to this reality, including a rightist backlash that blames adverse change on immigration and loss of identity, and a religious exclusivist backlash that promises to restore purity by institutionalizing ultra-orthodoxy. Only inclusivist religion, with its sense of the sacredness of all human beings, can provide the political foundation for a global humane governance. Only inclusivist religion can give primacy to the fundamental needs of humanity: food, shelter, health, sustainable environment, peace, meaningful life.

Although some humanists have advanced the idea that "a law of peoples" or "a human rights culture" provides the ethical basis of humane global governance, there has been no convincing way of identifying these agencies of change and reform. References to human rights as "a secular religion" also miss the point. It is the "nonsecular" character of religion that accounts for its continuing mobilizing appeal, that speaks to the human quest for an account of human existence whereby some sort of reconciliation with mortality is achieved.

Faith and Power

A belief in the transformative capacities of an idea that is sustained by spiritual energy lends itself to nonviolent forms of struggle and sacrifice, thereby challenging most secular views of human history as shaped primarily by governing elites, warfare, and a command over innovative military technology. Especially in the disillusioning aftermath of Marxist experiments in governance and in the face of subsequent outbursts of religious fanaticism, the secular imagination is suspicious of and hostile toward any advocacy of utopian solutions, whereas the religious consciousness is not so constrained. The religious framing of reality is rooted in the present, but is also hopeful about deliverance from suffering and privation. Indeed, the central founding narratives of the world's great religions are preoccupied with liberation from oppressive social and political arrangements, promising that by adhering to faith, emancipation will be attained. It is also true that the institutionalization of religions often suppresses their emancipatory potential.

What has been happening around the world in the last several decades suggests that a new set of oppressive circumstances for humanity cannot be addressed by secular authority. In this global setting, the opportunity for and responsibility of religion becomes evident: to provide hope for emancipation, and in effect give a spiritual grounding to efforts to move toward global democracy and humane globalization. Religious hope of this nature can be influential on all levels of social interaction, from the very local to the global.

Human Limits

Religion, in its inclusivist modes, is capable of contributing profound humility in relation to human thought and action. This modesty is particularly sensitive to human fallibility, and appreciates the limited capacity of the inquiring mind to grasp the fullness of reality or to claim the truthfulness and correctness of any particular interpretation of what needs to be done in the world. Religion can induce humans to remain open at all stages of dialogue with strangers and apparent adversaries, which can serve to correct mistakes and insensitivities, and to experience a sense of awe in face of the divine, which can protect humanity from idolatry and from a false sense of human autonomy.

The primacy of human autonomy was always questioned to some degree by prophetic cultural voices drawing on ancient myths, such as the Prometheus story. Goethe's *Faust* and William Blake's "dark satanic mills" were warnings about the dire consequences of this modern pact with the devil to replace the spiritual for the worldly promise of knowledge. These critiques became much more acute after the explosions of the atomic bombs at Hiroshima and Nagasaki, raising the question of whether limits had been exceeded in a manner that threatened human survival, and of how to find a way to restore such constraints. Current debates about genetic engineering and the prospects for superior robots and elaborate cyborgs give added currency to these concerns. The most valuable cultural resources for striking balances between competing values of gaining knowledge, extending life, improving economic performance, and respecting limits are situated mainly within religious frameworks. Even the possibilities (on the Western side) of casualty-free wars, first apparent in the 1990s, raises profound issues of limits that secular civilization has little to say about, especially as it has endorsed the idea that whatever power a warring state can mobilize in support of its security can be introduced onto the battlefield so long as it satisfies minimal notions of "military necessity" (provided only that the force relied upon conforms to the rather modest restraints of international humanitarian law). Again, the absence of a vital political alternative means that such issues go unquestioned unless the religious perspective is brought into play.

Identity

Inclusivism strives for a religious identity that transcends the locus of the sovereign state and the time frame of the present; it alternatively rests on a future fulfillment. This can be articulated and explored by replacing the idea of "citizen" with that of "citizen pilgrim": the distinctly religious understanding of political identity by reference to a spiritual journey that is unseen and unlikely to be completed within the span of this lifetime. Identity is, in other words, a human process, the value of which is an object of intense faith and dedication that extends beyond prescribed and instinctive loyalties to nation and state. It embraces temporal loyalties to a future that bring justice and peace to the entire human family. The citizen pilgrim can find a home either within established religious traditions or by a more personalized spirituality, but the essence of such an exemplary identity is to move energies and hopes from structure to process, from present to future, from state to world.

But the challenge of identity is far more complex than this image of the citizen pilgrim suggests, embracing all forms of participation in collective experience and responding to the appeals of social movements and regional restructuring, especially for the sake of democratizing the world economy and finding ways to extend the rule of law beyond the reach of sovereignty. European experience is suggestive of what is possible under certain conditions. The global efforts to establish a functioning International Criminal Court and to build support for a global parliament are indications of the relevance of identities that can no longer be reduced to state/society relations. Religion fits into this dynamic by providing support for such efforts through its conceptualization of community and authority without being doctrinally tied to statist definitions.

Reconciliation

Inclusivist religion can help to diminish the obstacles to a needed and desirable reconciliation of science, reason, and spirituality. Whether this reconciling process occurs within the domain of formal religion, outside it, or in both spheres, is of secondary significance. The need for reconciliation in the setting of severe conflict is pressing today, and must be associated with mechanisms of accountability that can ground gestures of forgiveness in prior political recognition, and within a process of justice. These complex issues have surfaced in a range of efforts to facilitate a transition from an abusive past to a more democratic future at the level of the state. Truth and reconciliation commissions in Latin America and South Africa have tried to find ways to acknowledge past criminalities without relying on punitive and vindictive responses, but such efforts involve delicate balancings of competing concerns, especially when past abuse was conducted on a large scale, for a long time, and had a severe character. Religious traditions and respected religious leaders have a special capacity to lend legitimacy to such efforts by articulating both sets of objectives in a convincing and resonant language.

The challenge is posed more explicitly in cases of conflicts where the rival parties have a religious character, as in Palestine/Israel, Kashmir, and Northern Ireland. There, the role of religion is open; it can either fuel the conflictual energies of either or both sides, making reconciliation an impossibility, or pave the way toward mutual recognition. It is not evident that religious leaders will often play a constructive role, being themselves often the voices of polarization, but the opportunity exists to an unprecedented degree because the struggles are being defined by reference to religious identity, and secular solutions are not fully responsive to the goals of the warring parties.

Finally, religion can bring clarity and charity to debates about a range of grievances regarding past abuses. There has been much attention given lately to claims associated with the lost wealth and uncompensated labor of Holocaust victims in Europe and cases related to Japanese militarism in Asia. Also, reparations claims have been raised concerning the dispossession of indigenous peoples throughout the Western Hemisphere and the Pacific and the pain and suffering wrought by the institution of slavery. Although religion cannot provide a definitive response to such efforts to reconcile the past and present, it can offer a setting in which such issues can be addressed in a manner that moves toward a terrain of reconciliation rather than recrimination and mutual dismissal. These are difficult issues that may require symbolic solutions by way of apologies, museums, or trust funds that acknowledge the past without burdening and embittering the present. Religious institutions and modes of thought can encourage such approaches more readily than can the adversarial character of Western law, which tends toward either/or outcomes that validate one side while rejecting the other.

These positive contributions of inclusive religious outlooks provide an intercivilizational grounding for transnational efforts to improve the normative and institutional governance of human affairs. Patterns of governance are situated at all levels of social interaction, from local efforts to challenge the construction of high dams and nuclear power plants to planetary concerns about global warming and human cloning. Religious dialogue can facilitate understanding and the development of the sort of ethically sensitive consensus that engages popular participation in ways that cannot be achieved by intergovernmental diplomacy and treaty making.

Religion and Humane Global Governance: Concluding Observations

The perspective proposed is that a religious/spiritual orientation needs to inform the energies of globalization from below if it is to have any serious prospect of effectively launching a political project that offers an alternative to that being foreshadowed and actualized by the largely economistic and collaborative geopolitical forces associated with globalization from above. It is not a matter of repudiating state or market but of insisting that these organizing arenas of authority and influence be spiritualized in accordance with the generalized attributes of religion. But it is also not expecting a miraculous rescue from above (a *deus ex machina*), whether in the form of a sudden embrace of world government or the emergence of regional institutions and the United Nations as political actors no longer constrained by geopolitics and the reigning neoliberal world picture.

Humane global governance will occur only as the outcome of human struggle, and in this sense is similar to past efforts to overcome slavery, colonialism, and apartheid. Each of these struggles was substantially inspired by direct and indirect religious thought as embodied in the lives and works of devout adherents. Each undertaking seemed "impossible" at its point of origin, given the array of opposed social forces, fixed beliefs, and institutional supports affirmed by the conventional wisdom of the day to validate and uphold inhumane practices. In the recent past we have witnessed successful struggles against oppression carried out by the peoples of Eastern Europe and the Soviet Union, of many countries in Asia, and of the victims of apartheid in South Africa. They have enjoyed limited or overall success against great historical odds, although following through with humane patterns of reconstruction has not proved easy in any of these historical instances.

We do not now know enough to conclude pessimistically that humane global governance is an impossibility. We do know enough to understand that such an outcome, if it occurs, will not come about spontaneously or without anguishing struggles, and that given the historical ascendancy of market forces and the widespread acceptance of the economistic world picture, an alternative orientation can hope to emerge only if nurtured and guided by inclusive religious energies creatively adapted to the specific problems and concerns that exist at all levels of social reality. Religion is crucial if the agency problem is to be solved in the course of seeking justice and sustainability for the peoples of the planet.

The complexity and precariousness of a globalizing world is bringing into being an unprecedented degree of global governance. The forms of this governance cannot be understood by reference to the United Nations but are related above all to the efforts by market forces to coordinate and stabilize their operations on a regional and global basis, and to some extent by their geopolitical allies, especially the United States, which provide protection via global policing mechanisms. The extension of this type of global governance is threatening to human well-being and to the quality of social and political life at the level of the state. The religious challenge is to infuse the struggles of the peoples of the world for democracy, equity, and sustainability with a vision of human existence that is human-centered yet conscious of the relevance of a surrounding nature, of the sacred, and of mysteries beyond the grasp of reason and machines. In a sense, religion remains the best and primary custodian of premodern wisdom that has been almost entirely forgotten throughout the experience of modernity.

The difficulty of this undertaking is heightened by September 11 and its aftermath, which has diverted energies and resources from the policy agenda associated with alternative patterns of globalization and revived a paralyzing preoccupation with the dynamics of war. Such a preoccupation freezes the structural character of global governance, and leads to an underestimation of threats to stability and justice that fall outside the domain of the war effort. Such observations seem particularly true with respect to the war against global terror, which lacks a clear definition of goals and whose limits cannot be geographically specified. The territorial base of terrorist activities is fluid, if not nonexistent. The locus of terrorism can be situated anywhere, even within the country leading the antiterrorist campaign. A further difficulty relating to the inquiry of this essay is the linkage, real and projected, between Al Qaeda terrorism and religious commitment. Bin Laden's rationale for political extremism is premised on his particular interpretation of Islam, which Islamic scholars overwhelmingly reject as wrong and perverse. Despite this, what saves bin Laden's version from dismissal as the ravings of a demented and death-fixated mind is that his words evoke a wide and potent resonance in the Islamic world, especially with respect to its animating message of anti-Americanism.

This ambiguous reality provides ammunition for those who would generalize the response to September 11 by taking on the entire Islamic world, especially its Arab sectors, and use this context as an occasion to confront religion as the enemy of modernity and democracy. From such a vantage point Turkey was until now mindlessly celebrated for its secularism, generally understood as epitomized by its containment of political Islam, and no inquiry is made as to whether positive or negative dispositions of religion, or both, are being opposed in Turkey. Here, we need to stress that when secular energies suppress inclusive religious expression, they operate to diminish the emancipatory forces at the disposal of societies.

In this setting the most sinister renderings of the implications of September 11 attain a quality of plausibility. An erudite and influential Middle East specialist has put forward the idea that bin Laden's challenge has been mounted so formidably because he was encouraged by the alleged reluctance of the United States during the 1990s to use its military power fully to crush any opposition to its strategic goals. Without a word of criticism of the US role in relation to either the Israel/Palestine conflict or the maintenance of indiscriminate sanctions against Iraq, Bernard Lewis encourages a maximal approach to antiterrorist war in the Middle East, specifically Iraq and Iran. He writes: "It is difficult for Middle Easterners to resist the idea that this refusal to implicate Saddam Hussein is due less to a concern for legality than to a fear of confronting him."[30] According to Lewis, American "squeamishness" with respect to the use of force against its challengers pushes Islam into the arms of the bin Laden worldview, and thus ends up with a mighty clash of civilizations. This type of thinking effectively argues that the two alternatives prefigured by September 11 are either an expansive war now against hostile forces in the Islamic world or a massive religious war later.

This sort of counterapocalyptic reading of September 11 is dangerous and unnecessary. The Al Qaeda attack needs to be addressed by an effective response that includes warmaking in Afghanistan and intense law enforcement wherever else the network operates. It also should be extended to peacemaking with the wider Islamic world, which will depend on a fair solution to the Palestinian ordeal, the internationalization of Jerusalem, the elimination of all weapons of mass destruction from the military arsenals of all countries, and a credible effort to make globalization operate in a manner that is more equitable and protective of the most vulnerable peoples in the world. Lifting the gaze beyond the battlefield will also enable a recovery of the degree to which Islam, and religion generally, is part of the solution, and not only of the problem. With consideration of these more distant horizons, the challenge of establishing humane global governance takes on the importance it deserves, as well as contributes to our understanding that defeating terrorism in the world is associated with justice as well as with the weaponry of counterterrorism and war.

Unfortunately, the September 11 attacks appear to eclipse democratizing tendencies of the 1990s and give ascendancy to a strengthened marriage of economic and state power, taking the unprecedented form of a nonterritorial counterterrorist crusade that asserts its interventionist claims throughout the world and seeks to perpetuate this commanding role through monopoly control over the militarization of space. Only the great world religions have the credibility and legitimacy to identify and reject the idolatry that seems to lie at the core of this American project of planetary domination.

Notes

1. Samuel Huntington, *The Clash of Civilizations and the Remaking of the World Order* (New York: Simon and Schuster, 1996); for a collection of essays on the "Dialogue of Civilizations," see the *Global Dialogue*'s Special Issue, vol. 3, no. 1 (2001).

2. Others, of course, had also pointed out the emergence of a post-Westphalian world. For an astute appraisal along these lines see Joseph A. Camilleri and Jim Falk, *The End of Sovereignty? The Politics of a Shrinking and Fragmenting World* (Aldershot: Edward Elgar, 1992); see also Jean-Marie Geuihenro, *The End of the Nation-State* (Minneapolis: University of Minnesota Press, 1993).

3. This thesis is stated in a popular form in Thomas Friedman, *The Lexus and the Olive Tree: Understanding Globalization* (New York: Farrar,

Straus, Giroux, 2000); for a more academic perspective, see Mehdi Mozaffari, *A Triangle of International Ethics, Law and Politics: Global Standard of Civilization* (Aarhus: Department of Political Science, University of Aarhus, 2000).

4. There is reported a scholarly initiative under way to show that bin Laden's campaign violates fundamental Islamic principles regulating the use of force against innocent civilians and the authority to issue *fatwas* (religious decrees). See Alan Cooperman, "Scholars Plan to Show How Attacks Violated Islamic Law," *Washington Post,* 20 January 2002, A15.

5. Comprehensive anti-fundamentalism is well articulated in relation to the United States and Islam by Tariq Ali, *The Clash of Fundamentalisms: Crusades, Jidhads and Modernity* (London: Verso, 2002).

6. This interplay of religion, politics, and world order as established within the Westphalian frame is a theme of Scott M. Thomas' chapter in this volume.

7. Hugo Grotius, "Prolegomena," in *On the Law of War and Peace* (New York: Bobbs Merrill, 1925), 20.

8. For general assessments of the Grotian impact, especially as facilitator of the transition to modernity by way of the passage from religious to secular authority, see Hedley Bull, Benedict Kingsbury, and Adam Roberts, eds., *Hugo Grotius and International Relations* (Oxford: Oxford University Press, 1990); see also Yasuaki Onuma, ed., *A Normative Approach to International Relations: Peace, War, and Justice in Hugo Grotius* (Oxford: Oxford University Press, 1993).

9. Hedley Bull, *The Anarchic Society: A Study of Order in World Politics* (New York: Columbia University Press, 1977).

10. See Myres McDougal and associates, *Studies in World Public Order* (New Haven, CT: Yale University Press, 1960) and Myres McDougal and Harold D. Lasswell, *Jurisprudence for a Free Society,* 2 vols. (New Haven, CT: New Haven Publishers, 1992), esp. vol. 2.

11. The antiutopian outlook was, perhaps, best articulated by E. H. Carr in response to the peace settlement of World War I, in *The Twenty Years' Crisis, 1919–1939* (New York: Harper & Row, 1946).

12. Grenville Clark and Louis B. Sohn, *World Peace through World Law,* 3d ed. (Cambridge, MA: Harvard University Press, 1966).

13. For representative works from WOMP over the period of its existence, see Saul H. Mendlovitz, ed., *On the Creation of a Just World Order* (New York: Free Press, 1975); R. B. J. Walker, *One World/Many Worlds: Struggles for a Just World Peace* (Boulder, CO: Lynne Rienner, 1988); Richard Falk, *On Humane Governance: Toward a New Global Politics* (University Park, PA: Penn State University Press, 1995); and Ali Mazrui, *A World Federation of Cultures* (New York: Free Press, 1976).

14. For one assessment of this UN weakness, especially relative to the strength of international financial institutions and European regional-

ism, see Richard Falk, "Meeting the Challenge of Multilateralism," in *Foreign Policy for America in the Twenty-first Century: Alternative Perspectives,* ed. Thomas H. Hendriksen (Stanford, CA: Hoover Institution Press, 2001).

15. But see articulate argument in favor of world government in David Ray Griffin, "Global Government: Objections Considered," in *Toward Genuine Global Governance: Critical Reactions to Our Global Neighborhood,* eds. Errol E. Harris and James A. Yunker (Westport, CT: Praeger, 1999).

16. A more obscure secular theme focuses on the European regional experience as a prelude to a "world of regions." Such an image, while more promising than world government, remains a dim and remote prospect at present.

17. The emphasis on "emancipatory religious and spiritual perspectives" is premised on a distinction between "inclusive" and "exclusive" interpretations of the meaning of human existence. Inclusive interpretations are nondogmatic, allowing moral and political space for alternative interpretations and worldviews. Exclusive interpretations are insistent that there is only one true path and that the embrace of alternatives is inherently false, immoral, and worthy of destruction. This endeavor is similar in intention to the chapter in this volume by Fred Dallmayr, who anchors his concern less in extremist interpretation than in the possibilities that religion becomes commodified by the cultural hegemony exerted through the capitalist marketplace.

18. In this respect, I share the view in Michael Hardt and Antonio Negri, *Empire* (Cambridge: Harvard University Press, 2000) that globalizing tendencies have greater emancipatory potential than did a Westphalian world, and that the way forward for progressive thinking is not to suffocate within the straws of a revived statism.

19. For negative assessments of globalization, see John Gray, *False Dawn: The Delusions of Global Capitalism* (New York: New Press, 1998); Richard Falk, *Predatory Globalization: A Critique* (Cambridge: Polity, 1999); and George Soros, *On Globalization* (New York: Public Affairs, 2002).

20. For documentation, see United Nations Development Program, *Human Development Reports* (New York: Oxford University Press, 1990–1999).

21. Robert Jay Lifton, *Destroying the World to Save It: Aum Shinrikyō, Apocalyptic Violence, and the New Global Terrorism* (New York: Metropolitan Books, 1999); Mark Juergensmeyer, *Terror in the Mind of God: The Global Rise of Religious Violence* (Berkeley and Los Angeles: University of California Press, 2000).

22. See Stephen Toulmin, *Cosmopolis: The Hidden Agenda of Modernity* (New York: Free Press, 1990); R. B. J. Walker, *Inside/Outside: International Relations as Political Theory* (Cambridge: Cambridge University

Press, 1993); and Hendrick Spruyt, *The Sovereign State and Its Competitors* (Princeton, NJ: Princeton University Press, 1994).

23. "Imperfectly" to the extent that national identities do not necessarily correspond with state boundaries.

24. See Immanuel Wallerstein, *The Modern World-System,* 3 vols. (New York: Academic Press, 1974–1989); Samir Amin, *Eurocentrism* (New York: Monthly Review, 1989); and Samir Amin, *Rereading the Postwar Period: An Intellectual Itinerary* (New York: Monthly Review, 1994).

25. See, for example, Bruce Russett, *Controlling the Sword: the Democratic Governance of National Security* (Cambridge, MA: Harvard University Press, 1990), esp. 119–145; and Bruce Russett, *Grasping the Democratic Peace for a Post–Cold War World* (Princeton, NJ: Princeton University Press, 1993); for a critical view, see Joanne S. Gowa, *Ballots and Bullets: The Elusive Democratic Peace* (Princeton, NJ: Princeton University Press, 1999).

26. For further clarification, see Paul Wapner, *Environmental Activism and World Civic Politics* (Albany: SUNY Press, 1996); Ronnie D. Lipschutz, *Global Civil Society and Global Environmental Governance* (Albany: SUNY Press, 1996); and Richard Falk, *Explorations at the Edge of Time: The Prospects for World Order* (Philadelphia, PA: Temple University Press, 1992).

27. The work of Hans Küng has moved in this direction in recent years. See Hans Küng, *Global Responsibility: In Search of a New World Ethic* (New York: Crossroads, 1991), esp. chap. 6.

28. For a closely comparable revisioning of religious consciousness, see the important book by Charlene Spretnak, *The Resurgence of the Real: Body, Nature, and Place in a Hypermodern World* (Reading, PA: Addison-Wesley, 1997).

29. In many respects the approach adopted in this section is complementary to and parallel with what Scott M. Thomas is proposing under the rubric of "virtue-ethics" as embodied in the great world religions, which is also seeking to turn the energies of the religious resurgence in the direction of what I have been calling humane global governance. It is also similar in intention to the chapter by Fred Dallmayr, who depicts vividly the ways in which religion in practice can shape behavior and outlook in humanly positive directions.

30. Bernard Lewis, "The Revolt of Islam," *The New Yorker,* 19 November 2001, 63.

CHAPTER 7

A GLOBAL SPIRITUAL RESURGENCE?

On Christian and Islamic Spiritualities

Fred Dallmayr

At the time of his visit to the 1893 Parliament of the World's Religions in Chicago, the great Indian swami Vivekananda is reported to have told a journalist inquiring about his impressions: "I bring you spirit, you give me cash." His response reflected the sentiment of a deep cultural divide between East and West, a sentiment according to which Western culture is synonymous with a crass materialism, while Eastern culture is deeply imbued with spirit or spirituality. One can doubt that the cultural divide between East and West was historically ever as neat and rigid as Vivekananda suggested; it certainly no longer corresponds to experiences in our time. Under the aegis of globalization, Eastern or Asian societies—without entirely abandoning their traditions—have been anxious to develop their material resources and thereby to catch up with Western lifestyles; on the other hand, Western societies in recent times have been invaded and literally inundated by new forms of spiritualism promising to satisfy peoples' deeper needs for meaning beyond the material cash-nexus. Perhaps one can say that, on a global level, we witness today both a striving for material "development" and a resurgence and growing fusion of spiritual aspirations—a fusion that, in the North American context, has been described as the emergence of a "spiritual marketplace."

In an essay on contemporary religiosity in North America, the theologian Matthew Ashley reaches some discomforting conclusions. "If one peruses the sections on 'spirituality' or 'inspiration' in a Barnes and Noble or Borders bookstore," he writes, "one comes away with the impression that spirituality is something that relatively secure middle- or upper-middle-class North Americans do in their spare time." As part of the pervasive culture of consumerism, spirituality appears here as another marketable item designed to relieve a lingering sense of boredom—an item readily supplied by a culture industry that has discovered that "spirituality sells."[1] Although not without a point, the theologian's assessment appears overly harsh and dismissive. While capturing some trendy features, it fails to grasp a more recessed motivation and significance: the deep (albeit inchoate) sense of longing or yearning for meaning pervading large numbers of people in our world today. A hundred years after Vivekananda's statement, in 1993, another meeting of the Parliament of the World's Religions took place in Chicago, attended by nearly seven thousand delegates from nearly all the religions around the world. In a declaration adopted at the end of the meeting, the delegates pledged themselves to work for a worldwide "transformation in individual and collective consciousness," for "the reawakening of our spiritual powers through reflection, meditation, prayer, or positive thinking"; in sum, for "a conversion of the heart." The sense of this pledge was more clearly spelled out by Robert Muller (a former deputy secretary-general of the United Nations) in his keynote address, which pleaded for "a world cathedral of spirituality and religiosity." As Muller stated at the time, in part paraphrasing an earlier leader of the United Nations, Dag Hammarskjöld:

> Religions and spiritual traditions: the world needs you very much! You, more than anyone else, have experience, wisdom, insights, and feeling for the miracle of life, of the earth, and of the universe. After having been sidelined in many fields of human endeavor, you must again be the lighthouse, the guides, the prophets and messengers of the one and final mysteries of the universe and eternity. You must set up the procedures to agree, and you must give humanity the divine or cosmic rules for behavior on this planet.[2]

The statements cast a different light on the upsurge of spirituality in our time, by underscoring its possible contribution to the fostering of global or cosmopolitan peace. To be sure, recognition of this contribution does not entirely obviate Ashley's misgivings. Even while appreciating the unleashing of new spiritual energies in our time, one may still wish to guard against their commodification and especially against a possible slippage into "pop" psychology and private self-indulgence. In an effort to avoid or reduce this danger, the following presentation seeks to retrieve a sense of "spirituality" as it has been handed down and preserved in older traditions of religious and mystical experience. From the vantage of these traditions, spirituality is not (or not principally) a form of psychic subjectivism, but rather involves a mode of transcendence and self-transgression—more precisely, an effort to rupture self-centeredness by opening the self toward "otherness" (which is variously described as God, the world-soul, or the ground of being and nonbeing). For the sake of brevity, my discussion will focus on the two traditions of Christianity and Islam, with only a few side-glances devoted to other religious legacies. Within the confines of the two selected traditions, a distinction will be introduced between two major and often competing types of spirituality—a distinction that inevitably shortchanges the rich diversity of spiritual life over the centuries. The two types will be described here as "gnostic" spirituality on the one hand, and "erotic-mystical," or *agape,* spirituality on the other. Following some initial comments on the meaning of "spirituality" and its major forms, the presentation will explore prominent examples of the two kinds of spirituality taken from the traditions of Christianity and Islam. Returning to the contemporary "spiritual marketplace," the concluding section asks which mode of spirituality may be most commendable in our present, globalizing context.

Traditional Meaning of Spirituality

Before proceeding to concrete examples of spirituality, it seems advisable to reflect briefly on its meaning. As the word indicates, spirituality derives from "spirit" and hence designates (or is meant to designate) some manifestation of the work of spirit. Most of the great world religions have terms akin to "spirit" or that capture some aspect of it. Thus, we find in the Hebrew Bible the term *ruach,* in the Arabic of the Qur'an *ruh,* in the Greek version of the New Testament the word *pneuma* (and/or *logos*), translated in the Latin Vulgate as *spiritus*—and the list could probably be expanded to include the Sanskrit *brahman* and the East Asian *tao.* Unfortunately, this concordance or parallelism of terms does not yet offer clues for unraveling their meaning. All the mentioned words are inherently ambivalent and open to diverse readings. Thus, to take the nearest example, the English "spirit" is closely related to "spirited," "spiritistic," and even to "spirit" in the sense of an alcoholic beverage; in turn, the French equivalent *esprit* conjures up other connotations (of wittiness, intellectual cleverness, or virtuosity)—not to mention here the profusion of meanings associated with the German *Geist*.[3] How to make headway in this multivocity? Here it is good to remember the core feature of religion or religious experience: the transgression from self to other, from immanence to transcendence. When viewed from this properly religious angle, spirit and spirituality must somehow participate in this transgressive or transformative movement. Differently put: They must be seen as bridges or—better still—as vehicles or vessels suited for navigating the transgressive journey.

Descending from the level of metaphor, it should be clear that spirit and spirituality cannot simply be equated with or reduced to a human "faculty," as the latter term has been understood in traditional anthropology and psychology. Traditional teachings about "human nature" commonly distinguish between at least three main faculties or attributes: the faculties of reason (or mind), will (or willpower), and emotion or sensation (a tripartition reflected, for example, in the Platonic division of the human *psyche* into *nous, thymos,* and appetite). While reason enables us to "know," will—in this scheme—enables us to "act," and emotion or sensation to "feel."[4] Located squarely in human nature, none of these faculties can be directly identified with spirit or spirituality—although none of them should be construed as its simple negation or antithesis. Thus, without being antirational or irrational, religious spirit cannot be equated with human rationality because it is the work or breath of the spirit that allows reason to reason and to know anything in the first place. Likewise, spirit cannot be collapsed into will, for the simple reason that divine grace and transformation cannot merely be willed or unwilled (although it may require a certain human willingness or readiness). Finally, spirit cannot or should not be leveled into sentimentality or emotionalism—despite the fact that it cannot operate without engaging human sentiment or feeling in some way. It is in order to guard against such equations that the religious traditions previously invoked typically insist on terminological distinctions. Thus, the Hebrew *ruach* is set over against *binah* (rational mind) and *nephesh* (organic life); the Arabic *ruh* over against '*aql* (reason or intellect) and *nafs* (desire); the Greek *pneuma* over against *nous* and *thymos;* the Latin *spiritus* over against *ratio* and *voluntas.* None of these distinctions, it is important to note, should be taken in the sense that spirit is elevated into a kind of super- or hyperfaculty: Far from being another, though higher, property or attribute, spirit basically supervenes and unsettles all properties by virtue of its transformative-transgressive potency.

What this means is that spirit not only resists terminological uni-vocity; it also unsettles ontological and anthropological categories or compartments. As a transgressive agency, spirit addresses and trans-fuses not only this or that faculty, but the entire human being, body and mind, from the ground up. In traditional language, the core of the entire human being tends to be located in the "heart" or the "soul" (corresponding to the Chinese *hsin*, meaning "heart-and-mind")—pro-vided these terms are not in turn substantialized or erected into stable properties. To this extent, one might say that spirit and spirituality are, first of all, affairs of the heart (or heart-and-mind).[5] This means that, without being an attribute or faculty, spirit also cannot be defined as a purely external or heteronomous impulse; rather, to perform its work, it necessarily has to find a resonance or responsiveness "inside" human beings—which is the reason why spirituality, quite legitimately, is com-monly associated with a certain kind of human inwardness. Looking at the development of religious traditions, one can probably say that re-ligious history shows a steady deepening and also a growing complex-ity of inwardness.

Thus, during the early phases of Christianity, spirituality was closely linked with doctrinal theology, which, in turn, was mainly the province of a clerical or ecclesiastic elite. Church historians speak in this con-text of a "spiritual" or "mystical" theology linking this term with such names as Pseudo-Dionysius and Jerome, and later, Bernard of Clair-vaux and St. Bonaventure.[6] In many ways, the Reformation brought an intensification and also a growing popular dissemination of spiritual-ity. Martin Luther, for example, differentiated between an "external" and an "inner" man (or human being) and clearly associated spirit—chiefly the Holy Spirit—with human inwardness.[7] At the same time, the Reformation released spirituality from its earlier clerical confine-ment (in accordance with the motto of "the priesthood of all believ-ers"). Still more recently, partly as a result of Romanticism and progressivism, spirituality has been further democratized. Leaving aside fashionable forms of contemporary spiritualism (criticized at the beginning of this chapter), Charles Taylor is surely correct when he states that religion cannot simply be an external form or constraint, but has to find some kind of personal "resonance" among people today.[8] Viewed from this angle, the heart (or heart-and-mind) might be described as the great resonance chamber constantly open or attuned to new religious or mystical experiences (in a mode of fine tuning or "high fidelity").

To be sure, to perform its task, this resonance chamber cannot be self-contained or resonate only within itself, but must remain attentive to an address or supervening appeal. Here we need to return to the central point of spirituality: its role as a great vessel (or *mahayana*) navigating the straits between immanence and transcendence, between the human and the divine.[9] Obviously, there are different ways of navigating these straits; in fact, the history of religions reveals a great variety of spiritualities. For present purposes, two kinds are singled out for special attention: What I previously called the gnostic and erotic-mystical varieties. To grasp their difference, one needs to recall again the "in-between" character of spirituality, its placement between the two shores of worldly finitude and infinity. Basically, one can interpret the image of the two shores in two different and even opposite ways. One can construe their relation as starkly hierarchical or vertical; in this construal, the divine shore (so to speak) differs from the worldly shore in the same manner as higher relates to lower, or as light stands over against darkness, spirit against matter. On the other hand, one can construe the two shores as more analogous and laterally differentiated; in this case, the finite and infinity are linked in the mode not of negation or strict subordination, but of sublimation and transformative analogy. As one should note, both varieties affirm a kind of distinction or difference; but in the first case, the distinction is radical and ontological (or cosmological), while in the second case it is mediated and dialectical. Notwithstanding the shared assumption of a certain duality, both versions also endorse a certain kind of "monism"—though it is important to recognize its different meanings. In the one case, it is precisely the insistence on hierarchy that ultimately leads to the victory of one shore over the other, the absolute triumph of the divine over the finite world; in the other case, the duality is bridged and mediated through the unifying bond of love.

The idea of spiritual hierarchy—combined with the insistence on oneness through ultimate divine victory—is chiefly linked with the traditional teachings of gnosticism (or at least prominent strands in gnosticism).[10] Most of the great world religions evince traces of gnostic beliefs; however, as a full-fledged doctrine, gnosticism seems to be a specialty of the Middle East or of West and South Asia. As is well known, a major example of gnostic spirituality was Manichaeism, which can be traced to the Babylonian sage/prophet Mani; but its origins seem to be much older and to go back to ancient Middle Eastern and Persian forms of light worship. During the Hellenistic period, older types of gnosticism became fused or infused with elements of Neoplatonism as well as Jewish and Christian forms of *logos*-mysticism. A basic assumption in traditional gnosticism is the notion of an initial division or contradiction in the divine or the godhead, a division that became manifest with the creation of the outer world, a creation ascribed to a Demiurge. Since the time of this creation, a basic duality (or "dyotheism") has operated: the distinction between the hidden, unknown, and nonmanifest God and the overt, knowable, and manifest world. Hellenistic gnostic texts described God variously as the Great Absence, the Supreme Void, or the Abyss (*bythos*)—a void covered over by the manifest world (the creation of the Demiurge) and into which that world eventually needs to be "emptied." Corresponding to this cosmic duality is a division of modes of knowledge: While the manifest or external world can be known exoterically by everybody, knowledge of the godhead is necessarily esoteric and reserved in stages only to the select few endowed with the divine spark or spirit—a feature that tends to lend to gnostic movements a secretive or hermetic character.[11]

In essence, gnostic spirituality culminates in the recognition of one's own basic unity or identity with the godhead, hence in a form of deification. It is chiefly on this point that erotic-mystical or, *agape,* spirituality demurs. By not accepting the radical dualistic scenario, erotic spirituality also refuses to endorse its telos or cosmic teleology. In lieu of the eventual conquest or erasure of the world by the divine, *agape* stresses the mediated and covenantal relation between the two shores; accordingly, the gnostic path of deification or self-deification is here replaced by the ascending path of loving redemption.

Christian Spiritualities

Throughout its history, Christianity has provided a fertile ground for many kinds of spirituality.[12] To be sure, relations with the official church (or churches) have always been uneasy or tense, frequently giving rise to oppression or persecution. As a form of personal religious resonance, spirituality by its nature tends to be suspect in the eyes of scriptural literalists and clerical traditionalists. Suspicion and hostility overshadowed the lives of most of the illustrious medieval and early modern mystics. Thus, the great mystic and Dominican preacher Meister Eckhart (1260–1328) was accused of heresy by Rome and subjected to Inquisition proceedings, first in Cologne and later in Avignon (then the papal residence); after his death a large number of his views were condemned as heretical. Likewise, the Spanish Carmelite mystic John of the Cross (1542–1591) was harassed by the higher clergy and finally imprisoned in a cloister, just as at an earlier time Mechtilde of Magdeburg (1207–1282) was hounded by the same clergy whom she criticized for their worldly ambitions. Even such a relatively orthodox

thinker as Ignatius of Loyola (1491–1556) was interrogated by the Inquisition and accused of being a member of the Alumbrados (a sect of
free thinkers). Tensional relations continued after the Reformation
and gave rise to recriminations between orthodox Lutherans and
Calvinists, on the one side, and Pietists, free sects, and *Schwärmer* (en-
thusiasts), on the other. Still more recently, recriminations took on a
confessional or denominational slant. Thus, the Protestant theologian
Adolf von Harnack denounced mystical spirituality as a typical out-
growth of Catholic faith; intensifying the invective, the Swiss Emil
Brunner wrote even more pointedly: "Christian mysticism is a blending of faith and mystification, of Christianity and paganism—a blending which characterizes Catholicism as a whole."[13]

Leaving aside surface skirmishes or polemics, it seems advisable to
return to the two main types of spirituality mentioned before. Of the
two types, gnostic spirituality has undoubtedly suffered most severely
at the hands of official Christianity (or Christendom). Although there
were many motives, this hostility was chiefly due to the official view regarding the centrality of Jesus as the Christ and redeemer—a centrality
that is likely to be sidelined by an accent on esoteric illumination. This
does not mean that Christianity is devoid of gnostic strands. As one will
recall, early Christianity emerged in the context of late Roman and Hellenistic civilization, which, in many ways, was a vast spiritual marketplace bringing together a multitude of religious traditions and beliefs;
one of the prominent currents in this marketplace was gnosticism. As
historians have shown, the very birth of Christianity was attended, and
even assisted, by a host of sectarian movements (inside and outside of
Judaism) with gnostic or semignostic leanings. Students of the period
are familiar with the Merkaba mystics of Palestinian Judaism, with the
teachings of the Essenes (known through the Dead Sea Scrolls), and
with the Nag Hammadi documents discovered in upper Egypt (in
1940). These and other findings give evidence of a broad illuminationist ferment gripping the Middle East at the time. Surrounded by this
ferment, the early Christian church was the arena of intense struggles
dedicated to sorting out official from unofficial or heretical beliefs.

These struggles proved difficult because of the absence of clear
boundaries and the frequent intermingling of religious ideas. Sometimes
gnostic views were propounded by reputable church leaders, such as
Basilides in the East and Valentinus and Marcion in the West.[14] Slowly
solidifying their doctrinal position, the early church fathers—led by Ire-
naeus and Tertullian—launched a concerted offensive against heretical
beliefs and successfully expunged or marginalized gnostic spirituality
(Marcion and Valentinus were excommunicated around A.D. 150).

This, of course, was not the end of Christian gnosticism. During the Middle Ages and early modernity, many new gnostic or semignostic movements arose in Western and Eastern Christianity. Students of history recall such names as Catharism and Bogomilism, and also such sects as the Albigensians, Waldenses, and the aforementioned Alumbrados. Links with gnostic teachings can also be detected in the spirituality of the Knights Templar (Knights of the Temple of Solomon) and of the Rosicrucians—movements that in later centuries were succeeded by Masonic lodges and, still more recently, by the networks of theosophy and anthroposophy. It was chiefly in the fight against medieval and early modern gnostic sects that the Inquisition gained its reputation of persecutionary zeal and religious intolerance. During the thirteenth century, larger-scale crusades were mounted by the church against heretical sects, in the course of which large numbers of Cathars, Albigensians, and others were massacred. Often the church could rely on the complicity of temporal rulers, especially in France. Thus, during the reign of Philip le Bel (1268–1314), Jacques de Molay, Grand Master of the Templars, and thousands of other Templars were arrested throughout France (Friday, 13 October 1307). A few years later, the Grand Master and another leading Templar figure were publicly burnt on a slow fire as heretics.[15] In this respect, the Protestant Reformation signaled an end to large-scale physical persecution, but not an end to polemical invective. It was against the semignostic spirituality of the *Schwärmer* that the Pietist and student of Luther, Count Zinzendorf (1700–1760) uttered his scathing words of condemnation (which probably should not be extended to Christian spirituality as such). Such mystical spirituality, he stated harshly, leads to "arrogant conceit" [*Einbildung von sich selbst*] and "self-righteousness" without Christ, and hence to a form of human "self deification," which is "a dangerous and miserable doctrine opposed to the very core of creation."[16]

Although generally hostile to gnostic teachings, Christianity—despite many reservations—has always been relatively hospitable to erotic mysticism, or *agape* spirituality. Notwithstanding his strong denunciation of the *Schwärmer,* Martin Luther himself repeatedly resorted to erotic symbolism to portray the relation between Jesus and Christian inwardness: namely, the image of bridegroom and bride. This symbolism, of course, is much older than Luther and, throughout the Middle Ages, served as a vehicle for expressing the relation between Jesus and the community of believers.[17] In Christian *agape* spirituality, the loving relation between bridegroom and bride is first initiated by Jesus and only then reciprocated by human beings. As we read already in St. Paul's letter to the Galatians (2:20): "I live by faith in the son of God who loved me and has given Himself for me." A similar sentiment is expressed in the fourteenth-century text *Imitatio Christi*, which states: "If you rely on yourself alone, nothing is accomplished; but if you rely on God, heaven's grace redeems you." Heaven's grace here is Jesus, the suffering redeemer whose love invites us to share in his suffering (again in the words of the *Imitatio:* "For without pain you do not live in love").[18] In every case, Christian *agape* spirituality involves a loving relationship between an "I" and a "You" or "Thou," between humans and the divine. And like every genuine love, this relationship is basically ambivalent and cannot be captured either in a rigidly dualistic or a synthetic or monistic formula. "I and You" here implies a twoness or duality (or difference) that can be mediated or bridged through love, but cannot be abolished, either through appropriation of the "other" by the self or the dissolution of the self in the "other." As Gerhard Ebeling has correctly noted: "Even in the most intimate union with Christ a difference remains. For although genuine love unites, it does not cancel duality in an indiscriminate fusion devoid of language and communication."[19]

These comments can be illustrated by a brief glance at some prominent Christian *agape* mystics. Thus, the "spiritual poetry" of John of the Cross is in essence a series of love songs exploring the depth and ecstasy of the human encounter with the divine. As he states in one of these songs:

> Oblivious of created things,
> recollecting the Creator alone,
> the depths of inwardness we plumb,
> by loving lovingly the Beloved.

"Plumbing inwardness," one should note, signifies here neither a retreat into solipsism nor a gnostic-intellectual union with the divine. As John himself elaborates: "Our soul becomes unified with God not through cognition or mental representations, nor through passive enjoyment or anything sensual, but intellectually only through faith, recollectively through hope, and actively through love"—where *love* means an ek-static movement toward the "You" of God and also laterally toward the "You" of fellow human beings (again in John's words: With love of God, "love for fellow beings likewise grows").[20] A similar orientation is manifest in John's compatriot Teresa of Avila (1509–1582). In Teresa's case, love of God means love for the crucified Jesus—which translates concretely into loving care for the needy and the sufferings of humankind. As it happens, this linkage or translation was not present from the beginning. In fact, during her early monastic life, Teresa was strongly attracted to a kind of superspiritual (and quasi-gnostic) union with the divine, disdainful of worldly concerns. However, in 1554 a religious experience of the "mortally wounded Jesus" changed her outlook. The impact of this experience is recorded in her *Autobiography,* where she writes that under the influence of certain spiritual teachers, she had initially believed

> that everything bodily [or worldly] was only an obstacle to complete contemplation, which is a purely spiritual exercise. . . . God willing, this [contemplative] mode of prayer is indeed very tasty and pleasurable. . . . Hence, nobody could have prompted me to return to a consideration of the humanity of Jesus which appeared to me then as a mere distraction. . . . Had I remained in this stance, I would never have reached my present position; for I now consider that [earlier] stance an error. . . . Lord of my soul and my highest good: crucified Jesus! I never remember without pain my earlier delusion which now appears to me as a great betrayal of you.[21]

Examples of this kind could be multiplied; for present purposes, however, a few additional illustrations must suffice. As indicated, for Christians—whether Catholic or Protestant—*agape* spirituality is centered on the encounter with Jesus, and, in light of Jesus' suffering and death, this love relation spills over into a loving engagement with fellow humans and their sufferings. For the Dominican Johannes Tauler (fourteenth century), love involved a radical transformation (or *periagoge*), a move through self-denial and mortification to a rebirth affected by Christ's love. This rebirth in and through Christ, however, could not lead to a complete fusion—which would negate human humility and longing. At the same time, abandonment of selfish attachments freed the heart for the *imitatio Christi* and for the co-suffering with Jesus and the world (the mystical *compassio* taught earlier by Bernard of Clairvaux). As Josef Zapf concisely formulates Tauler's teaching: "Abandon self-centeredness and be guided by the life and suffering of Christ. . . . Ponder God's will and your own nothingness. . . . Then God works in all your works and deeds."[22] In a similar vein, Count Zinzendorf emphasized the need to anchor Christian spirituality in the life and suffering of Jesus. After an initial flirtation with mystical enthusiasm, Zinzendorf returned to the more sober Lutheran conception of Jesus as bridegroom and the redemptive quality of his suffering. As he wrote at one point: "If there is a genuine mystic, it is Jesus. For a mystic is someone who lives a hidden life. . . . which one might call a *statum mortis,* away from the praise and vituperation of this world." In order to share in this mystical life, it is necessary to die and be reborn in Christ, a rebirth through which—as in a feast of love—the soul joins Jesus as "your redeemer, your best, your first and last friend." By gaining Jesus as best friend, however, the soul also joins in his suffering and the suffering of the world: "All one can do in this life is to have daily contact with the crucified."[23]

Before proceeding, a few additional comments seem in order. An important point to note is that the distinction between gnostic and *agape* spirituality is not watertight (and probably not as categorical as the preceding discussion suggests). As mentioned before, Christian spirituality through the centuries is not devoid of gnostic or semi-gnostic strands; occasionally, the two kinds are mingled or interpene-trating—although, on the whole, the *agape* theme tends to prevail. A case in point are the writings and teachings of Meister Eckhart. What might be considered gnostic or semignostic features in Eckhart's work have to do mainly with his notion of a hidden godhead beyond or be-neath the personal God, a godhead variously described as Being or be-yond Being, or else as Emptiness and Abyss; closely linked with this notion is the accent on an intellectual plunge, a self-emptying submer-gence of the intellect in the divine abyss.[24] Although prominent, these features probably should not be taken in isolation or as a denial of practical *agape.* What one can hardly forget is that Eckhart was also a Dominican cleric and as such deeply involved in preaching and pas-toral care. Some of his finest insights are to be found in his Latin and German sermons. Thus, his famous sermon "Beati pauperes spiritu" calls into question precisely the gnostic ambition to "know" and fully plumb God's mystery through our rational intellect or "spirit"; at the same time, it questions our ability to reach God through willpower and mental exercises—counseling instead a "releasement," allowing God to work in and through us. It is in this sense that one should probably also understand his celebrated sermon on the respective merits of con-templation versus active life—or, biblically expressed, the respective merits of Mary and Martha (Luke 10:38–42). Deviating from tradi-tional treatments eulogizing Mary, Eckhart gave the palm of piety to Martha; for, while Mary desired to be unified with Jesus through pas-sive illumination, Martha was content to do God's work in everyday life. Through her unpretentious "business," Eckhart stated, "Jesus is united with her and she with Him, and she shines and glows with Him . . . as a pure light in the fatherly heart."[25]

The other Christian mystic frequently associated with gnostic spiri-tuality is the Silesian Johannes Scheffler, who wrote under the name of

"Angelus Silesius" (1624–1677). In his long and meditative essay titled *Sauf le Nom,* Jacques Derrida devotes considerable attention to Scheffler's work, emphasizing particularly its more intellectualist or quasi-gnostic features. Thus, he gives pride of place to such (gnostic-sounding) verses of Scheffler as these:

> To become nothing is to become God.
> Nothingness swallows everything before it:
> And if it does not swallow you,
> You can never be born in eternal light.

Or again these lines:

> I am like God, and God like me.
> I am as great as God; He as small as I;
> He cannot be above me, I not under Him.

Derrida expressly accentuates this quasi-gnostic outlook—called here an "apophatic" mysticism—while distancing it as far as possible from Christian *philia,* or charity or love. As he states pointedly:

> The question arises here: what does friendship of a friend mean if one frees friendship—together with negative theology as such—from all the dominant definitions of Greek or Christian origin, that is, from the fraternal and "phallocentric" scheme of *philia* or charity?[26]

As in the case of Eckhart, one needs to guard here against a certain one-sidedness that would sideline or neglect Scheffler's deeply Christian (or Christ-centered) spirituality in favor of pure contemplation. As it happens, Scheffler himself distinguished between two kinds of spirituality, an intellectual and an erotic-mystical type, and he associated these two kinds with two angelic choirs: the Cherubim, representing knowledge or intellect, and the Seraphim, representing love. Although one of his main collections of poems is called *Cherubinic Wanderer* [*Cherubinischer Wandersmann*], he basically wanted to keep the two spiritual paths tied together. As he wrote: "Blessed are you if you are able to make room for both and if, in your earthly life, you sometimes burn with heavenly love like Seraphim, and sometimes focus your mental eye steadily on God like Cherubim." As a wanderer or pilgrim, Scheffler basically followed in the footsteps of St. Bonaventure's *itinerarium mentis in Deum;* this path, for him, involved a purifying movement, an itinerary from humanity to divinity ("durch die Menschheit zu der Gottheit")—but in a manner that never forgets human finitude and the mediating role of Jesus. Thus, the bold sentence "I am like God, and God like me" needs to be balanced against these other lines:

> The mediator is Jesus alone.
> I know no other medium but my Jesus Christ;
> It is His blood through which God flows into me.

And probably one should also not forget the following lines, so far removed from gnostic illumination:

> Highest knowledge it is
> Not to know anything
> But Jesus Christ
> And Him as Crucified and Risen.[27]

Islamic Spiritualities

When turning from Christian to Islamic spirituality, one notices many familiar themes, but also a kind of sea change. A prominent similarity resides in the rich profusion of different spiritualities—varieties that are only loosely bundled together under the umbrella label of Sufism. Another similarity derives from the Abrahamic legacy shared by the two religions, a congruence manifest in the invocation of similar biblical stories and religious symbolisms. The sea change, on the other hand, has to do with the relatively greater prominence of gnostic or quasi-gnostic tendencies in the Islamic context. Several reasons may account for this divergence. One may be the relatively late arrival of Islam in the Middle East, at a time when gnosticism had already taken firm roots and acquired a broad religious following. Another important reason has to do with the centrality of divine oneness (*tawhid*) and the absence of mediating features in Islam—a centrality that may encourage gnostic aspirations toward ultimate unification or fusion. Closely connected with this aspect is the different statuses of Jesus and the Prophet Muhammad in the two religious traditions. On this score, it is perhaps more difficult to link the messenger of Islam with *agape*-style spirituality—although resources for such a linkage are surely not lacking. In this context, greater attention should probably be given to the Prophet's recorded sayings (*hadith*) than is often done in Islamic theology. Thus, precisely with regard to the nature of faith and spirituality, one might usefully remember his response to the question "what is faith?": "self-restraint and gentleness"—a response that exudes sympathy but makes no claim to esoteric knowledge.[28]

As indicated, Islam has historically displayed a variety of spiritual orientations; however, as in the Christian case, two stand out: a knowledge-based and a love-based variety. Notwithstanding numerous internal modulations, gnostic spirituality aims at the unification or identification of the human knower with divine Being or else with the empty "abyss" of the divine—an identification that, by its nature, is reserved for a select group endowed with the spark of gnosis. Given the restrictedness of this spark and its separation from the ordinary world of ignorance (*jahiliyya*), gnostic spirituality favors esotericism and a relatively secret transmission of doctrines, in accord with its accent on privileged insight or knowledge (*ma'rifa*). In contrast with this restrictive type, ordinary Muslim spirituality comprises and relies on a number of ingredients. In mainstream Sufism, knowledge or illumination is by no means ignored, but it is amplified and counterbalanced by reverence for God (*makhafa*) and compassionate love (*mahabbah*). Generally speaking, one might say that the latter two ingredients take the place of the focus on Jesus and his suffering in Christian *agape* mysticism. Fear or reverence of God, in particular, guards against intellectual conceit and a self-righteous self-deification or identification with the divine. Pride of place in ordinary Sufism, however, goes to love (*mahabbah*), a love whose target—God or fellow human beings—remains ambivalent and undecided, since sensible and supersensible, visible and invisible realms are here seen as analogous and lovingly reconciled in their difference.

In the Islamic (as in the Christian) context, intellectual spirituality is not a compact movement, nor does it subscribe to a unified doctrine (such as Manichaeism). Moreover, its social stance varies, adopting sometimes a more reclusive or purely contemplative and sometimes a more activist or intrusive (occasionally even millenarian) cast. An exemplar of the former kind is the Great Sheikh: Abu Bakr Muhammad Muhyi-d-Din, known as Ibn Arabi (1165–1240). The point here is not to claim that Ibn Arabi was a gnostic in any formal sense of the term, nor that his spirituality was exclusively of an intellectual or illuminationist type. The opposite is the case. As in the case of some Christian mystics, one can say that Ibn Arabi's outlook was multifaceted and comprised a variety of strands, including the strand of love mysticism. As he actually stated at one point, for him love (*mahabbah*) and not knowledge (*ma'rifa*) was the summit of mysticism, because it is love and not knowledge that truly reflects divine union (*tawhid*). And in his *Tarjuman al-Ashwaq* we read:

> Mine is the religion of love.
> Wherever His [God's] caravans turn,
> The religion of love
> Shall be my religion and my faith.[29]

Yet, it is commonly agreed that among Muslim mystics, Ibn Arabi is the most intellectual or that his thought places a strong, perhaps preeminent accent on intellectualism. This accent is evident in his key concept of *wahdat al-wujud* (unity of Being) according to which there is only one divine reality in comparison with which all other finite beings are ultimately nothing or nonexistent. The task of the Sufi mystic honoring this doctrine is to recognize his/her nonexistence as a finite being and to accept his/her fusion with the divine.[30]

For present purposes, it must suffice to consider briefly one text in which the intellectual element clearly prevails. The text is "Whoso knoweth Himself . . ." taken from Ibn Arabi's *Treatise on Being* [*Risale-t-ul-wujudiyyah*]. The point of the title is that "whosoever knows himself" properly knows himself as integral to, and coterminous with, divine reality or Being. Commenting on the saying of the Prophet: "I know my Lord by my Lord," Ibn Arabi states:

> The Prophet points out by that saying that thou art not thou: thou art He, without thou; not He entering into thee, nor thou entering into Him, nor He proceeding forth from thee, nor thou proceeding forth from Him. And it is not meant by this that thou art anything that exists or thine attributes anything that exists; but it is meant by it that thou never wast nor wilt be, whether by thyself or through Him or in Him or along with Him. Thou art neither ceasing to be nor still existing. *Thou art He,* without any of these limitations. Then if you know thine existence thus, then thou knowest God; and if not, then not.

In this text, in his zeal to celebrate the absolute unity (*tawhid*) of divine being, Ibn Arabi goes even beyond traditional gnostic formulas, stressing the need for a self-emptying or a cessation of self in God. "Most of those 'who know God [*al 'urraf*],'" he writes,

> make ceasing of existence and the ceasing of that ceasing a condition of attaining the knowledge of God; but that is an error and a clear oversight. For the knowledge of God does not presuppose the ceasing of existence nor the ceasing of that ceasing. For things have *no* existence, and what does not exist cannot cease to exist. . . . Then if thou knoweth thyself without existence or ceasing to be, then thou knoweth God; and if not, then not.[31]

Aware of the boldness of these formulations, Ibn Arabi's text proceeds to answer some questions raised by skeptically inclined readers. One such question concerns precisely the idea of an absolute unity devoid of duality, twoness, or difference. "How," the questioner asks, "lies the way to union, when thou affirmest that there is no other beside Him, and a thing cannot be united to itself?" Ibn Arabi answers:

> No doubt, there is in reality no union nor disunion, neither far nor near. For union is not possible except between two, and if there be but one, there can be no union nor division. For union requires two either similar or dissimilar. Then, if they are similar, they are equals, and if they are dissimilar, they are opposites; but He (whose name be exalted) spurns to have either an equal or an opposite. . . . So there is union without union, and nearness without nearness, and farness without farness.

Elaborating further on this thought, he explains:

> Understand, therefore, that the knower's knowledge of himself is God's knowledge of Himself, because his soul is nothing but He. . . . And whoever attains to this state, his existence is no more, outwardly or inwardly, any but the existence of Him (whose name be exalted). . . . So if one say "I am God," then hearken to him, for it is God (whose name be exalted) saying "I am God," not he. . . . [Here] our discourse is only with him who has sight and is not born blind; for he who does not know himself is blind and cannot see. And until the blindness departs, he will not attain to these spiritual matters.[32]

What one may notice in this statement is the surreptitious reemergence of a duality or difference: the duality between knowledge and ignorance, between the knowledgeable few and the unknowing multitude. But even assuming radical nonduality, how can divine self-knowledge—as celebrated by Ibn Arabi—be reconciled with *makhafa* and *mahabbah* (reverence for God and compassionate love)? Does God fear and revere Himself? And more importantly: Does love here mean God's self-love or love for Himself—and how far is this kind of love removed from narcissism and self-indulgence?

Ibn Arabi's teachings have left a strong imprint on Islamic spirituality over the centuries. For the most part, his legacy has been contemplative and reclusive, giving rise mainly to esoteric Sufi orders hermetically sheltered from, and disdainful of, the mundane world. However, intellectual (*ma'rifa*) spirituality can also take a different turn: Especially under the impact of a more traditional gnostic dualism, the distinction between the "knowers" and the ignorant, between the "godlike" and the ungodly, can foster violent aggression and quasi-millenarian militancy. An example is an early version of Ismailism, a gnostic-dualistic branch that flourished mainly during the late Abbasid reign. In line with older Manichaean teachings, this sect—according to some historians—sharply distinguished between the hidden, unknowable God, or divine abyss, on the one hand, and the material-bodily world seen as the work of an inferior Demiurge, on the other. The task of gnostic believers was to achieve deification through affirming their superior knowledge while attacking and, if possible, eradicating the inferior world. The latter aim was particularly the goal of the esoteric order of the so-called Assassins, a secretive group of militants (also known as *batiniyyah* ["people of the inner truth"] or *fida'iyyah* ["self-sacrificers"]). According to historical reports—which are perhaps biased and certainly contested—the Assassins wreaked havoc throughout the Muslim world, killing two Abbasid caliphs, several sultans, and hundreds, perhaps thousands, of others. Whatever the historical accuracy, the great al-Ghazali (1058–1111)—though himself a Sufi mystic, but of a very different persuasion—felt moved to denounce the teachings of this sect and their leaders.[33] During more recent centuries, *ma'rifa* spirituality has assumed many diverse shapes, often entering into symbiosis with more recent intellectual developments, such as theosophy. An example of the mingling of Islamic gnosticism and newer theosophical teachings is the work of Frithjof Schuon, especially his book *Gnosis: Divine Wisdom* (first published in French under the title *Sentiers de gnose*). As Schuon writes in that book, in a passage reminiscent of Ibn Arabi and other *ma'rifa* mystics: "Esotericism looks to the nature of things and not merely to our human eschatology; it views the universe not from the human standpoint but from the standpoint of God."[34]

Without denying the role of intellectual insight or *ma'rifa,* major strands in Islamic Sufi spirituality have always accorded a central role to *makhafa* and *mahabbah*. For present purposes, it must suffice to focus briefly on the mystical poetry of Jalal ad-Din Rumi, the great and justly revered "mevlana," or "maulana" (1207–1273, a bare generation after Ibn Arabi). Rumi's work, especially his *Mathnawi,* is a rich and multidimensional tapestry of ideas, symbols, and metaphors. Some of these ideas are surely gnostic or intellectual (perhaps Neoplatonic) in character. Thus, one recalls his famous statement: "Every form you see has its archetype in the divine world, beyond space. If the form perishes, what does it matter, since its heavenly model is indestructible?" Or this other statement: "Appear as you are, be as you appear. You are not this body, but a spiritual eye—what the eye of man contemplates, it becomes." Occasionally, one also finds in Rumi traces of the doctrine of the unity of ultimate reality (*wahdat al-wujud*). Thus, we read:

> I am filled with you—
> Skin, blood, bone, brain, and soul.
> There's no room for lack of trust, or trust.
> Nothing in this existence but that existence.

Or consider these Zen-like phrases, echoing Meister Eckhart:

> Praise to the emptiness that blanks out existence. Existence:
> This place made from our love for that emptiness.
> Yet somehow comes emptiness,
> This existence goes.
> Praise to that happening, over and over!

Or again:

> Dissolver of sugar, dissolve me,
> If this is the time.[35]

Yet, as in Eckhart's case, this is not the whole story. In Rumi's work, celebration of unity and of ultimate disappearance in the divine is always counterbalanced, and perhaps outweighed, by *mahabbah*—a loving devotion that never forgets a remaining twoness or difference, even in the very urgency of overcoming separation. For without a recognition of twoness, and hence of human finitude, how could Rumi have written: "Love must have a little pain?" Or these lines: "O love, everyone gives thee names and titles—last night I named thee once more: 'Pain without remedy.'" In this connection, we may also wish to remember these verses:

> When I remember your love,
> I weep, and when I hear people
> Talking of you, something in my chest,
> where nothing much happens now,
> moves as in sleep.

And here is his celebration of unity in twoness, a poem dedicated to his beloved friend, Shams of Tabriz:

> All our lives we've looked
> into each other's faces.

> That was the case today too.
> How do we keep our love-secret?
> We speak from brow to brow
> and hear with our eyes.[36]

As is clear from his poetry, Rumi's mysticism—his *agape* spirituality—
was all-consuming and all-embracive. Setting aside rigid boundaries,
he did not confine his love to God, nor to his friend Shams (who ultimately vanished), but allowed his love to grow and percolate and ultimately include all his fellow creatures in the world. As he stated at one
point: "How can one profess love for God if one does not love and actively show love to fellow-beings?" Love (*mahabbah*) here begins to
shade over into service and compassion—an engaged commitment to
the well-being of humanity at large. Here are some of Rumi's truly ecumenical verses, reflecting an ecumenism of loving service—though
verses unlikely to be well received by clerical literalists in any religion:

> Tell me, Muslims, what should be done?
> I don't know how to identify myself. I am
> neither Christian nor Jew, neither Pagan nor Muslim.
> I don't hail from the East or from the West.
> I am neither from land nor sea . . .
> This being human is a guest house:
> every morning a new arrival . . .
> Be grateful for whoever comes,
> because each has been sent
> as a guide from beyond.[37]

Toward Global Spirituality?

By way of conclusion, it seems appropriate to reflect briefly on competing spiritualities and their social relevance, especially in the context
of the contemporary spiritual marketplace on a global scale. The issue
at this point is not so much the compatibility or incompatibility of
Christian and Islamic spiritualities (although one might wish to explore this in greater detail). The main issue emerging from the preceding discussion is the comparison and respective assessment of gnosis
and *agape,* of esoteric-intellectual spirituality and of love- or service-
based spirituality, respectively. Loosely speaking, one might say that
the former is more vertical and inner-directed, while the latter is more
horizontal and other-directed. Still speaking very loosely—and neglecting possible overlaps—gnostic spirituality may be said to invite
solitary contemplation and a solitary merger with the divine (a merger

reserved for the privileged few); by contrast, *agape* spirituality has a more active and outgoing slant, a slant potentially rupturing or transgressing all boundaries based on status, race, and ethnic or religious background. The former type insists on a worldly division or hierarchy (hence the pronounced dualism of traditional gnosticism), while the latter type seeks to combine or balance integration and difference.

Both kinds of spirituality have merits and also demerits. Esoteric spirituality fosters a withdrawal from social bonds, from the busyness of worldly affairs; it encourages a retreat into the kind of *Abgeschiedenheit* so dear to Eckhart, Angelus Silesius, and many other mystics—a retreat that alone seems able to shield the human spirit against consumerism and rampant commodification. Seen from this esoteric vantage, *agape* spirituality stands accused of promoting a meddlesome, managerial attitude—a danger that indeed inhabits many contemporary forms of pragmatism and social "welfarism." Still, the respective dangers are probably not equal or symmetrical. Although valuable in many ways, retreat into inner solitude can also shade over into solipsism, which in turn can engender selfishness or haughty self-indulgence. Martin Luther's and Zinzendorf's invectives against the arrogant conceit of self-righteous "knowers" should probably not be forgotten in this context—and actually deserve increased attention in an age exposed to the lure of technocracy and "expertocracy." Moreover, in our globalizing era, technocratic rule tends to be compounded by the worldwide prevalence of neo-liberalism, with its stress on rugged economic individualism—an emphasis that, in the eyes of many observers, conjures up the danger of a global class division between North and South, rich and poor (a division resonating uncannily with a radical gnostic dualism between good and evil). In the prevailing global situation, gnostic retreat also signals—or can be perceived to signal—an exit from global moral and political responsibility. In the words of Matthew Ashley (the theologian quoted at the beginning of this chapter), such an outlook readily becomes "a spirituality of the status quo, a spirituality that has very little good news for the poor."[38]

In light of these and related perils, intellectual or *ma'rifa* spirituality, in my view, urgently needs to be counterbalanced by, and perhaps subordinated to, more sober and world-open perspectives—especially the demands of *makhafa* and *mahabbah*. Regarding the linkage between knowledge and *makhafa*, it is well to remember the words of the Psalmist (III:10): "Initium sapientiae timor domini" [fear/reverence of God is the beginning of wisdom]—words that act as a firm barrier against gnostic conceit. Fear/reverence of God, however, quickly opens up the wellspring of love, *agape* or *mahabbah*—a wellspring that, for most Christian and Muslim mystics, constitutes the core of genuine spirituality. In the words of St. Paul again (1 Corinthians 13:2): "And if I have prophetic powers, and understand all mysteries and all knowledge, and if I have all faith, so as to remove mountains, but have not love, I am nothing." As readers of his letter know, this statement is followed almost instantly by Paul's great paean to love/*agape* (1 Corinthians 13:4–13), which begins with these words: "Love is patient and kind; love is not jealous or boastful; it is not arrogant or rude"— and continues with these lines: "Love never ends. As for prophecies, they will pass away; as for tongues, they will cease; as for knowledge, it will pass away."

There is an old Christian tradition—with clear parallels in Islam— called contemplation in action or mysticism of everyday life. In the words of Ashley, such comtemplative action deserves affirmation, especially in our world today, insofar as it is able to overcome social barriers between rich and poor and also to break down an "elitist division of labor" that privileges the life of monks or clerics while leaving ordinary lay people religiously or spiritually destitute or unemployed.[39] Fortunately, there are many examples in recent history illustrating the breakdown of this kind of division. One particularly prominent example of contemplation in action or mysticism of everyday life is the work of Dag Hammarskjöld, the renowned secretary-general of the United Nations (1953–1961). Addressing an assembly of the World Council of Churches soon after assuming office, Hammarskjöld pinpointed the meaning of contemplative action by stating that we must approach global issues from two angles: first, there is "a need for practical action, helping underdeveloped countries to achieve such economic progress as would give them their proper share in the wealth of the world"; and second, there is an equal "need for inspiration, for the creation of a spirit among the leaders of peoples which helps them to use the forces which they have to muster, for peace and not for war." Roughly at the same time, Hammarskjöld penned a statement of personal faith that admirably linked traditional *agape* spirituality with commitment to contemporary service. "The explanation," he wrote,

> of how man should live a life of active social service in full harmony with himself as a member of the community of spirit, I found in the writings of those great medieval mystics for whom "self-surrender" had been the way of self-realization, and who in "singleness of mind" and "inwardness" had found strength to say *yes* to every demand which the needs of their neighbors made them face, and to say *yes* also to every fate life had

in store for them. Love . . . for them meant simply an overflowing of the strength with which they felt themselves filled when living in true self-oblivion. And this love found natural expression in an unhesitant fulfillment of duty and in an unreserved acceptance of life, whatever it brought them personally of toil, suffering or happiness.[40]

Notes

1. J. Matthew Ashley, "Contemplation in Action: Oscar Romero's Challenge to Spirituality in North America," in *Monseñor Oscar Romero: Human Rights Apostle* (Notre Dame, IN: Helen Kellogg Institute for International Studies, 2000), 25, 30. As Ashley notes, the phrase "spiritual marketplace" was coined by Wade Clark Roof. For a similar assessment, see Peter Toon, *What Is Spirituality? And Is It for Me?* (London: Daybreak, 1989), who writes (p. ix): "Spirituality has become an 'in' word. Inside and outside the churches people are talking about it—or at least using the word. Publishers are listing a growing number of volumes under the heading 'Books on Spirituality.'"

2. See Hans Küng and Karl-Josef Kuschel, eds., *A Global Ethic: The Declaration of the Parliament of the World's Religions* (New York: Continuum, 1995), 36, 101. Muller also quoted the remark by André Malraux that either the third millennium will be "spiritual" or there will be no third millennium.

3. Regarding the meaning of "spirit" in different traditions see, for example, the article on "Soul, Spirit," in Keith Grim et al., eds., *The Perennial Dictionary of World Religions* (San Francisco: Harper & Row, 1989), 699–702.

4. See Plato, *Republic,* Book IV, 435b–441c. In modified form, the tripartition persists in Kant's three Critiques and, still more recently, in the sociological (Weberian) distinction of the three "value spheres" of science, ethics, and aesthetics (or art).

5. On the Chinese tradition of *hsin,* see especially William Theodore de Bary, *Neo-Confucian Orthodoxy and the Learning of the Mind-and-Heart* (New York: Columbia University Press, 1981).

6. See Philip Sheldrake, "What is Spirituality?" in *Exploring Christian Spirituality: An Ecumenical Reader,* ed. Kenneth J. Collins (Grand Rapids, MI: Baker Books, 2000), 26–30. In Sheldrake's words, it would be most fruitful "to study the 'mysticism' of the Fathers as the very heart of their theology." Ibid., 27. Compare also Jordan Aumann, *Spiritual Theology* (London: Sheed and Ward, 1980).

7. Martin Luther, "The Freedom of a Christian," in *Martin Luther's Basic Theological Writings,* ed. Timothy F. Lull (Minneapolis, MN: Fortress Press, 1989), 344–46. Compare also Bengt Hoffman, "Lutheran Spirituality," in *Exploring Christian Spirituality,* 122–37.

8. Charles Taylor, *Sources of the Self: The Making of the Modern Identity* (Cambridge, MA: Harvard University Press, 1989), 512–13. From an explicitly Christian perspective Sheldrake writes: "I would suggest that what the word 'spirituality' seeks to express is the conscious human response to God that is both personal and ecclesial'. Sheldrake, 'What is Spirituality?" 25. Compare also Karl Rahner's comments: "It has been said that the Christian of the future will be either a mystic or no longer a Christian. If we mean by mysticism not peculiar para-psychological phenomena but rather a genuine experience of God arising from the heart of existence, then the statement is correct and its truth and depth will become clearer in the spirituality of the future." Rahner, "In Sorge um die Kirche," in *Schriften zur Theologie,* vol. 14 (Einsiedeln: Benziger, 1960), 375.

9. As Wolfgang Böhme writes: "Christian mysticism [or spirituality] cannot be grounded entirely in 'inner' experience or reflect a pure inwardness. There must also be an impulse from beyond, an appeal in some kind of mundane form." Wolfang Böhme, ed., *Zu Dir Hin: Über mystische Lebenserfahrung, von Meister Eckhart to Paul Celan* (Frankfurt-Main: Insel Verlag, 1987), 12. For further definitional clarifications, see Walter Principe, "Toward Defining Spirituality," *Exploring Christian Spirituality,* 43–59, and Alister E. McGrath, *Christian Spirituality: An Introduction* (Oxford: Blackwell, 1999). For a broader comparative perspective, see Eliot Deutsch, *Religion and Spirituality* (Albany: State University of New York Press, 1995).

10. In some versions of gnosticism, dualism, or "dyotheism," is greatly attenuated in favor of an ascending scale of insight available to a select group. What links the various branches of gnosticism is mainly the stress on *sophia,* or intellectual illumination, leading to knowledge of the divine.

11. On gnostic traditions and teachings, see especially Hans Jonas, *The Gnostic Religion* (Boston: Beacon Press, 1963); *Gnosis und spätantiker Geist,* 2 vols. (Göttingen: Vanderhoeck & Ruprecht, 1934–35); and Gilles Quispel, *Gnosis als Weltreligion* (Zürich: Origo, 1951). In view of the tendency to hermeticism, Eric Voegelin's association of gnosticism with modern political mass movements appears odd and unconvincing; see *Science, Politics and Gnosticism* (Chicago: Regnery, 1968).

12. The following presentation stays largely on an ecumenical level, thus bypassing denominational differences. For a discussion of Orthodox, Anglican, Methodist, Evangelical, and similar forms of Christian spirituality, see Collins, ed., *Exploring Christian Spirituality,* Part 3, 93–226.

13. Emil Brunner, *Die Mystik und das Wort* (Tübingen: Mohr, 1924), 387, cited in Böhme, *Zu Dir Hin,* 12.

14. At that time, Christian gnosticism often took the form of "docetism," a doctrine according to which Jesus was only seemingly human and his death on the cross only an apparent death, but actually an illusion.

15. See Malcolm Barber, *The Trial of the Templars* (Oxford: Cambridge University Press, 1994), 46; Trevor Ravenscroft and Tim Wallace-Murphy, *The Mark of the Beast* (London: Sphere Books, 1990), 53; and Tim Wallace-Murphy and Marilyn Hopkins, *Rosslyn: Guardian of the Secrets of the Holy Grail* (Shaftesbury: Element Books, 2000), 103–04.

16. Otto Uttendörfer, *Zinzendorfs religiöse Grundgedanken* (Herrnhut: Bruderhof, 1935), 161, cited in Dietrich Meyer, "Christus mein ander Ich: Zu Zinzendorfs Verhältnis zur Mystik," *Zu Dir Hin*, 213.

17. In fact, the symbolism can be traced back even further to Jewish "wisdom" literature, in which God and humankind were seen as linked in covenantal love.

18. Thomas à Kempis, *The Imitation of Christ* (New York: Penguin, 1952); also *De imitatione Christi*, vol. 2 (Paris: Duprey, 1860), 38, cited in Josef Sudbrack, "Christliche Begegnungsmystik," in *Zu Dir Hin*, 142–43.

19. Gerhard Ebeling, *Die Wahrheit des Evangeliums* (Tübingen: Mohr, 1981), 207. Similarly Wolfgang Böhme observes: "Love is possible only when there is a Thou or You *toward* whom we can move, who addresses us, and with whom we can have a 'loving dialogue.' . . . Hence, the divine You remains the reference point, which militates against a [gnostic or pantheistic] submergence or disappearance in the cosmos [or in nothingness]." Böhme, *Zu Dir Hin*, 11. Böhme also cites Martin Buber's rejection of a cosmic union or fusion, which, for Buber, only reflected human conceit and self-aggrandizement; *I and Thou*, trans. Ronald G. Smith (Edinburgh: T. & T. Clark, 1958), 109–23.

20. For the passages from John of the Cross, see Sudbrack, "Christliche Begegnungsmystik," in *Zu Dir Hin*, 146–48. As Sudbrack comments: "There is here no fusion with the godhead, no expansion of consciousness to cosmic dimensions, no insinuation of ultimate convergence, nor any submergence in private subjectivity. . . . With indisputable clarity John of the Cross stresses the unbridgeable distance from God on the level of knowledge and sensation, while finding a possible union only through active love." Ibid., 148, 150 (I bypass here John's and Sudbrack's linkage of loving with "willing"). Cf. also Marilyn M. Mallory, *Christian Mysticism—Transcending Techniques: A Theological Reflection on the Teaching of St. John of the Cross* (Amsterdam: Van Gorcum, 1977).

21. Teresa of Avila, *The Autobiography of St. Teresa of Avila* (Rockford, IL: Tan Books, 1997), cited by Sudbrack in *Zu Dir Hin*, 152–53. In Sudbrack's view, it is impossible to understand Teresa's life and work without attention to the congruence of devotion to God and care for humans, of contemplation and commitment to social responsibility. Ultimately, the "encounter with Jesus" was for her the "touchstone" of spirituality. Ibid., 151, 153. See also Sudbrack, *Erfahrung einer Liebe: Teresa von Avilas Mystik als Begegnung mit Gott* (Freiburg: Herder, 1979).

22. Josef Zapf, "Die Geburt Gottes im Menschen: Nach Johannes Tauler," in *Zu Dir Hin*, 89. Cf. also Georg Hofmann, ed., *Johannes Tauler: Predigten* (Einsiedeln: Johannes Verlag, 1979).

23. For the above, see Dietrich Meyer, "Christus mein ander Ich," *Zu Dir Hin,* 214–15, 217, 219. In Meyer's words: Zinzendorf's spirituality involves "union with Christ as personal encounter and friendship." For him, this personal relation is primary, in contrast to any kind of "mystical fusion." Ibid., 225. Cf. also Dietrich Meyer, *Der Christozentrismus des späten Zinzendorf* (Bern: Herbert Lang, 1973).

24. For some philosophical discussion of Eckhart's thought, see Martin Heidegger, *Der Satz vom Grund* (Pfullingen: Neske, 1957), 71–74; *Gelassenheit,* 2d ed. (Pfullingen: Neske, 1970); and John D. Caputo, *The Mystical Element in Heidegger's Thought* (Columbus: Ohio University Press, 1978).

25. Meister Eckhart, *Deutsche Predigten und Traktate,* ed. Josef Quint (Munich: Hanser, 1979), 53–57 and 303–306; and *Meister Eckhart: The Essential Sermons, Commentaries, Treatises and Defenses,* trans. Edmund College and Bernard McGinn (New York: Paulist Press, 1981), 177–81. For a discussion of the sermon "Beati pauperes spiritu," see Otto Pöggeler, "Sein und Nichts: Mystische Elemente bei Heidegger und Celan," in *Zu Dir Hin,* 282–83. For a discussion of the sermon on Mary and Martha, see Ashley, "Contemplation in Prophetic Action," 28–29. As Ashley comments, in his sermon Eckhart showed himself as a proponent of medieval "contemplation in action" and as a forerunner of the "mysticism of everyday life" favored by later Protestant Pietists.

26. Jacques Derrida, *Sauf le Nom* (Paris: Editions Galileé, 1993), 15–16, 31, 39, 76. See also Angelus Silesius, *Cherubinischer Wandersmann/Pélerin cherubinique* (Paris: Aubier, 1946).

27. For the above citations, see Alois M. Haas, "Christförmig sein: Die Christusmystik des Angelus Silesius," in *Zu Dir Hin,* 181–83, 185, 188. Haas relies on H. L. Held, *Angelus Silesius: Sämtliche Poetische Werke in drei Bänden* (Munich: Hanser, 1949–53).

28. See Maulana Wahiduddin Khan, ed., *Words of the Prophet Muhammad: Selections from the Hadith* (New Delhi: Islamic Centre, 1966), 7. To be sure, there are also some more gnostic-sounding statements attributed to the Prophet. Famous among these statements is: "I am an Arab without the letter *ayn* [i.e., a *rabb* or Lord]; I am Ahmad without the *mim* [mortality]; he who has seen me has seen the Truth." See the entry "*al-Insan al-Kamil*" [The Perfect Man] in Cyril Glassé, ed., *The Concise Encyclopedia of Islam* (San Francisco: Harper Press, 1989), 189.

29. Cited in Glassé, ed., *The Concise Encyclopedia of Islam,* 168. (*Tarjumán al-Ashwaq* means "the Interpreter of Longings"). Among Ibn Arabi's most celebrated writings are *al-Futúhát al-Makkiyyah* [The Meccan Revelations] and *Fusus al-Hikam* [Bezels of Wisdom].

30. There is a sprawling literature surrounding Ibn Arabi's work. Cf. especially Rom Landau, *The Philosophy of Ibn Arabi* (London: Allen and Unwin, 1959); Ibn al-Arabi, *Sufis of Andalusia* (Berkeley and Los Angeles: University of California Press, 1972); and Claude Addas, *Ibn Arabi ou, La quête du soufre rouge* (Paris: Gallimard, 1989).

31. Ibn Arabi, *Whoso Knoweth Himself . . .* , trans. T. H. Weir (Gloucestershire: Beshara Press, 1976), 4–5.

32. Ibid., 15 and 20–23. A famous esoteric mystic who had claimed "I am God" long before Ibn Arabi was the Persian Husayn ibn Mansur, known as al-Hallaj (857–922). He was put to death by the Abbasid authorities in Baghdad.

33. See the entries on "Ismailis" and "Assassins" in Glassé, ed., *The Concise Encyclopedia of Islam,* 53–55, and 194–200. In accordance with their dualistic doctrine, some Ismailis ascribed to the Prophet Muhammad a merely exoteric knowledge, while crediting Ali (the fourth caliph and first Imam) with esoteric or "ineffable" knowledge. For a different and more favorable account, see Farhad Daftarg, *A Short History of the Ismailis* (Edinburgh: Edinburgh University Press, 1998), 15–16.

34. Frithjof Schuon, *Gnosis: Divine Wisdom,* trans. G. E. H. Palmer (London: John Murray, 1959), 80. Even more gnostic, in Ibn Arabi's vein, is this passage: "There are various ways of expressing or defining the difference between gnosis and love—or between *jñana* and *bhakti*—but here we wish to consider one criterion only, and it is this: for the 'volitional' or 'affective' man (the *bhakta*) God is 'He' and the ego is 'I,' whereas for the 'gnostic' or 'intellective' man (the *jñani*) God is 'I'—or 'Self'—and the ego is 'he' or 'other' . . . Most men are individualists and consequently but little suited to make 'a concrete abstraction' of their empirical 'I,' a process which is an intellectual and not a moral one: in other words, few have the gift of impersonal contemplation . . . such as will allow 'Got to think in us.'" Ibid., 77. Cf. also his *Esoterism as Principle and as Way,* trans. William Stoddart (Bedfont: Perennial Books, 1981). For arguments along lines similar to those of Schuon, see Sayyed Hossein Nasr, *Knowledge and the Sacred* (Albany: State University of New York Press, 1989).

35. *The Essential Rumi,* trans. Coleman Barks, with John Moyne et al. (Edison, NJ: Castle Books), 21, 33, 131; also the entry "Jalal ad-Din ar-Rumi," in Glassé, ed., *The Concise Encyclopedia of Islam,* 205.

36. *The Essential Rumi,* 199; also William C. Chittick, *The Sufi Path of Love: The Spiritual Teachings of Rumi* (Albany: State University of New York Press, 1983), 242.

37. *The Essential Rumi,* 109; and Glassé, ed., *The Concise Encyclopedia of Islam,* 205.

38. Ashley, "Contemplation in Action," 30. Regarding the danger of a global class division, see, for instance, Richard Falk, *Predatory Globalization: A Critique* (Cambridge: Polity Press, 1999). That altruism may occasionally lead to a meddlesome manipulation of other lives can readily be acknowledged. However, it is possible to distinguish between such an attitude and a caring orientation that precisely respects and nurtures the freedom and integrity of others. See in this respect Martin Heidegger's distinction between a "managerial" care and an

"anticipating-emancipatory" solicitude; Martin Heidegger, *Being and Time,* trans. Joan Stambaugh (Albany: State University of New York Press, 1996), 113–15.

39. Ashley, "Contemplation in Action," 29.

40. See Wilder Foote, ed., *Servant of Peace: A Selection of the Speeches and Statements of Dag Hammarskjöld* (New York: Harper & Row, 1977), 24 and 58. In this connection, one may also recall an address given by Czech president Václav Havel at Harvard University in 1996 under the title "A Challenge to Nourish Spiritual Roots Buried Under Our Thin Global Skin." In that address, Havel spoke of an "archetypal spirituality" implanted in humankind, beyond the confines of organized faiths, and "lying dormant in the deepest roots of most, if not all, cultures." See *Just Commentary,* no. 28 (1996): 3.

CHAPTER 8

ISLAM AND THE WEST

Muslim Voices of Dialogue

John L. Esposito and John O. Voll

Conflict and dialogue are frequently seen as the alternatives in relations between Islam and the West. In the months following the destruction of the World Trade Center by terrorists on 11 September 2001, conflict visions received much attention. The words of Muslims like Usama bin Ladin, who proclaim the necessity of violent conflict with the West, gained high visibility and were regularly repeated in the global mass media. Those Muslim voices advocating violent jihad were frequently matched by continuing Western pronouncements of a "clash of civilizations."

Beyond the visions of conflict, there are also significant advocates of dialogue in both the West and the Muslim world. The thought and political careers of three prominent Muslim activist intellectuals illustrate the transformations of Islamic visions of international politics and the high level of advocacy of global dialogue that exists in the Muslim world. Anwar Ibrahim, a former Islamic student activist, became deputy prime minister of Malayisa, and although he is now in jail, his ideas continue to be an important political force. The president of the Islamic Republic of Iran, Mohammad Khatami, is a scholar-politician whose policies reflect the rearticulation of the ideals and goals of the Islamic revolution in Iran. Abdurrahman Wahid, the intellectual leader of one of the largest Islamic organizations in the world, served as the elected president of Indonesia for a time in the transition to democracy following the end of the Suharto regime.

Activist religious intellectuals throughout the world have helped to transform the dynamics of international relations as well as the nature of politics within their own societies. As intellectuals, they are creating the new concepts and vocabulary in which policies and programs are articulated.

This chapter argues that Muslim activist intellectuals like Anwar, Khatami, and Wahid were especially significant in the final decades of the twentieth century in creating new perceptions of global interactions. In particular, reacting against the jihadist view of the world, they have been especially important in defining the terms of intercivilizational dialogue from an Islamic perspective. In differing ways, their ideas and careers reflect the major dynamics of both the clash of civilizations and intercivilizational dialogue.

Like other ideologically committed intellectuals throughout the world, thinkers in explicitly Islamic organizations and movements do not present a monolithic vision of the world. There is much disagreement and debate, and the lines of argument parallel the lines of intellectual conflict elsewhere. However, even in their disagreements, they provide an emerging Islamic discourse (not a single ideology) that works to redefine the international role and position of Muslim communities.

In policy debates and in the disagreements over interpretation of policies, two significant perspectives for viewing international relations have emerged. One can be defined as the "conflict vision" of global relations, and the other is the more complex vision of "dialogue." The most widely known expressions of these perspectives, especially as they relate to the place of the world of Islam in the international system, are portrayed in the debates over what Samuel Huntington argues is the inevitable clash of civilizations and what his critics advocate as the necessity for "the dialogue of civilizations." Among Islamic intellectuals in the second half of the twentieth century, advocates of both clash and dialogue visions had strong and highly visible voices. Their debates within the Muslim world are part of the broader dynamic of the significant role of religion and religious faith in defining the nature of international relations in the contemporary world.

Political Islam and International Relations

One of the major global developments of the late twentieth century was the "resurgence of religion," a major and highly visible part of the phenomena of civilizational clash and dialogue. This development ran counter to a vital part of what had been the accepted vision of the processes of modernization: The theory that described secularization—that is, the personalization of religion and the separation of "religious" activity from the secular/political public arena—as an inherent and inevitable part of the process of modernization. The secularization hypothesis has important implications for understanding the system of interstate relations that emerged by the middle of the seventeenth century. The Treaty of Westphalia (1648) "is generally recognized as the beginning of the modern system of nation-states."[1] Within this system, there is a "Westphalian presumption" that is fundamentally secular, assuming that "religious and cultural pluralism cannot be accommodated in international society, but must be privatized, marginalized, or even overcome."[2] There are now major challenges to this presumption. The recognition by prominent scholars like Peter Berger, who was a key figure in articulating secularization theory, that "a whole body of literature by historians and social scientists loosely labeled 'secularization theory' is essentially mistaken" has profound implications for understanding contemporary international relations.[3] This "desecularization" becomes an important dimension of the intellectual and historical context in which the

> very notion of 'international relations' seems obsolete in the face of the apparent trend in which more and more of the interactions that sustain world politics unfold without the direct involvement of nations or states.[4]

In this new context, religion becomes an increasingly important factor in transnational and "international" relations.

Because of the continuing and generally increasing significance of 'religion' in the public political arena, the Islamic resurgence in the final quarter of the twentieth century has been frequently viewed as the rise of "Political Islam." As a consequence, while the Islamic resurgence involves many different dimensions, its political impact has received the most attention. Political Islam involves many different types of movements. There have been movements advocating internal legal reform, the transformation of social institutions through legislation as well as social persuasion, and at times, revolutionary change of the political regime or political system. In these and other areas, resurgent Political Islam represents a direct challenge to the existing status quo. This is a challenge to political systems, socioeconomic institutions, and their moral and intellectual foundations. Islamically committed intellectuals were essential in defining and presenting these formidable challenges to the "secular-modern" status quo that had developed as a result of the "modernizing" reform programs of the nineteenth and twentieth centuries. The impact of their efforts is clearly visible in the policies of virtually every Muslim majority country and every Muslim minority community in the world. In other words, there has been a significant desecularization of politics and policies and a "re-Islamization" of the modes of political discourse.

This renewal of religious consciousness in the political arena is expressed in terms of international relations as well as domestic policies. The world visions of activists in Political Islam are directly tied to their goals and aspirations for Muslim societies. There are those who might be called the jihadists, whose vision of the world is similar to Huntington's. In the jihadist visions, the world is divided into two clearly definable camps: those who are true followers of Islam and those who are not. The latter includes both non-Muslims and those Muslims whose beliefs and practices are not in accord with the interpretations of the particular group defining the vision.

One of the most widely known expressions of this jihadist vision is in the writings of the Egyptian Islamist Sayyid Qutb. In this vision,

> Islam only knows of two types of societies: the Islamic society and the *jahili* [willfully ignorant of Islam] society. The "Islamic Society" is the society in which Islam is followed—in creed, practice, rules of life, institutions, morals, and behavior. The *jahili* society is the society in which Islam is not followed.[5]

In this perspective, the willful ignorance or active opposition to true Islam "surrounds" the true Muslim, and for that person, "the battle is continuous and jihad continues until the Day of Judgement."[6] Qutb presented this struggle, in the book that he wrote shortly before he was executed in 1966, explicitly in terms of the clash between civilizations, with Islam identified as the only truly "civilized" society, in conflict with false or incomplete civilizations.[7]

Qutb's articulation of a conflict vision of international relations did not initiate the jihadist vision in the Muslim world any more than Huntington's vision created the Manichaean perspective within Western policymaking communities. However, Qutb, like Huntington, *did* articulate the conflict vision in a distinctive way that has continuing influence. Each of them put religion at the heart of the definition of civilizations, and therefore, at the heart of the clash of civilizations. "Qutb is widely acknowledged as the father of militant jihad. . . . For those Muslims who, like bin Ladin, were educated in schools and universities with Islamist teachers, Sayyid Qutb was a staple of their Islamic education."[8] This religion-based conflict analysis stands in contrast to earlier discussions in which such global clashes might be defined in terms of economic systems—capitalism versus communism—or nationalism against imperialism. However, the basic framework of the conflict vision in which the world is divided into large clashing camps has deep roots in both the Muslim world and the West. A scholar's conclusion regarding the reliability of that vision is an essential part of the foundation of any interpretation of international relations. Among Muslim intellectuals, the issue is focused on the relationships between Islam and the West and Islam and modernity.

The alternative, dialogue vision also has deep roots in the Muslim world, as it does in the West. In medieval times, the spirit of Roger II's Sicily and those who made *convivencia* (constructive living together) between Muslim, Christian, and Jew possible in the Iberian Peninsula reflects the deep roots of cultures, communities, and civilizations in positive interaction. In the modern Muslim world, the Westernizing reformers clearly believed in civilizational dialogue, even though it usually meant one-directional "borrowing." Still, explicitly Islamic responses were not always articulated in the jihad mode. The influential Islamic modernist Muhammad Abduh affirmed that an effective synthesis between the Islamic tradition and Western modernity was possible. In the era of the late twentieth century Islamic resurgence, few Islamist intellectuals argued that Islam and modernity were incompatible, and even jihadists like Qutb noted, for example, the advantages of modern Western science. The issue for the jihadists, though, was the degree to which effective civilizational dialogue would undermine the authenticity of the faith, practice, and institutions of Muslims. In contrast, those supporting the dialogue vision oppose violence and argue that "an ethical and humane Islam is the only legitimate Islam."[9] In broad historical terms, the struggle is not between older tradition and modernity, but a conflictual process of defining "multiple modernities" in which "modernity and Westernization are not identical."[10]

The tension between the dialogue and conflict world visions provides an important foundation for the different understandings of international relations in the contemporary world. For most Islamic activist intellectuals, the understanding of international relations is just a part of a broader worldview related to the Islamic resurgence. Their lives and ideas reflect many of the factors that shape international politics in the Muslim world. None of the major politically active Muslim intellectuals set out to formulate a comprehensive theory of international relations, but each has contributed in important ways to the emergence of a new Islamic discourse on world politics.

Islamic Intellectuals and World Visions

Prominent activist intellectuals like Anwar, Khatami, and Wahid present very different individual histories. However, the international dimension of the life and work of each of these men reflects critical aspects of the development of international relations in the Muslim world and globally. There is a little jihadist in each of them as they provide a critique of unquestioning acceptance of Western concepts of development, especially as those concepts appear to demand a Western-style secularism in Muslim-majority societies. However, in their thinking, it is *not* civilizations that are in conflict, but lifestyles and attitudes toward religious faith. The broader community of Muslims (*ummah*) is seen as bringing together people from many different civilizations into a large community of faith. In this way, their world visions are conflictual primarily in terms of power conflicts among states or sensitivity to the moral impact of some aspects of contemporary globalization.

Dialogue is receiving increasing emphasis in the visions and policies of Islamically committed intellectuals at the beginning of the twenty-first century. Most have had important experience in Western societies and thus developed an informed understanding of the strengths and weaknesses of Western-style modernity. They are convinced, like Khatami, that this informed understanding is necessary and will strengthen rather than undermine the strength of authentically Islamic societies. This makes essential the establishment of an active two-way dialogue between civilizations, especially between Islam and the West. How this dialogue is defined represents one source of diversity among leading Islamic intellectuals.

A second source of diversity is the degree to which these intellectual leaders accept the context of global diversity and multiculturalism as a reality to live with, rather than as a *jahiliyyah* to oppose. This becomes crucial in determining the vision of international relations that underlies their recommendations for their respective countries' foreign policies and their general definition of their own political systems. The diversity and tensions reflect different understandings of the faith tradition and its relevance to contemporary conflicts. The importance of these differences becomes clear if we follow the "constructivist" approach to understanding the impact of faith on political conflict proposed in this volume by Hasenclever and Rittberger. In this theoretical perspective, "the impact of religious traditions on conflict behavior is deeply ambiguous: They can make violence more likely, insofar as a reading of holy texts prevails that justifies armed combat. On the other hand, they can make violence less likely, insofar as a reading of holy texts prevails that delegitimizes the use of violence in a given situation."[11] This defines quite clearly the mode of differences between the advocates of global jihad and the supporters of civilizational dialogue. Anwar, Khatami, and Wahid provide significant examples of the dialogue perspective and how it is defined.

Anwar Ibrahim:
Asian Values and Global *Convivencia*

Anwar played a significant role in the transformation of Malaysian politics and society both as a "charismatic fundamentalist" and a "liberal political reformer." When he organized a demonstration in Kuala Lumpur in 1980, he and his supporters were called "Malaysia's own Islamic zealots";[12] Anwar was described as the leader of one of the largest "fundamentalist" groups in the country.[13] Eighteen years later, when he was tried on politically inspired charges, Malaysia's former deputy prime minister had earned the reputation of "an unabashed globalist well suited to the modern world of markets and media"[14] and a liberal.[15] Anwar's transformation from the charismatic leader of an Islamic fundamentalist group into a globalist liberal advocating Southeast Asian *reformasi* (reform) appeared inconsistent and opportunistic to some but quite authentic and logical to others. In fact, it reflected the changing mainstream of Malaysian politics and identities. At the same time, Anwar was also a significant force in causing these changes, an almost prototypical activist intellectual, articulating new conceptualizations and paradigms, fulfilling the classic role of the intellectual in times of great historic changes.[16] As a leader of a significant student organization, a major Malaysian political figure and government official, and later the symbol of *reformasi* in his country, Anwar has also been the classic political activist.

Reformasi and Ijtihad

Anwar played a pivotal role through both his organizational leadership and his charismatic articulation of the goals and aspirations of Angkatan Belia Islam Malaysia (ABIM), founded in 1971. ABIM brought together students and younger professionals concerned as Malay Muslims with issues of social and economic justice in their country. During the 1970s, he also became more visible internationally, as a part of the developing global network of Muslim activist intellectuals. He served as a member of the United Nations Advisory Group on Youth (1973–74). After an interim two years (1974–76) in detention for his role in domestic political opposition, he served as a representative for Southeast Asia in the World Assembly of Muslim Youth (1976–82) and was among the first Muslim leaders to visit Iran after the revolution in 1979.

Like many Islamic activists, Anwar and the leadership of ABIM were influenced by the writings of major founders of twentieth-century international Islamic renewal movements, notably Hasan al-Banna, Sayyid Qutb, and Abu al-Ala Mawdudi. In particular, they embraced a belief in "the comprehensiveness of Islam as *ad-deen* (way of life)," a concept that is at the heart of the Islamist understanding of Islam.[17] He was influenced by others with whom he had personal contact, among them the prominent Malaysian scholar Naquib al-Attas and the Palestinian Ismail Ragi al-Faruqi of Temple University in Philadelphia, Taha Jabar Alawani of the International Institute of Islamic Thought and later the School of Islamic Social Sciences in Virginia, and Fathi Osman and Shaykh Yusuf Qardawi from Qatar.[18]

In the early 1980s, Anwar stunned friends and foes alike by suddenly joining the government of Mahathir Mohammed. In subsequent years, he evolved from an activist intellectual leader of opposition to a deputy prime minister and finance minister who defined policy principles and implemented national reforms. During that period, he was responsible for important conceptualizations of major domestic and global issues. Among the more prominent were: (1) the need for a broad new paradigm for sociopolitical and economic development, informed by religious and moral values; (2) a new understanding of the nature of pluralism in multireligious societies and the world as a whole; and (3) an emphasis on the importance of intercivilizational dialogue as the only possible alternative to a deadly clash of civilizations.

Convinced that the older Western understanding of the processes of development represented an outmoded paradigm, in the mid-1980s Anwar argued that "a new paradigm in development studies has slowly emerged," necessitated by the failure of both Marxist and secular materialist paradigms.[19] Following the collapse of communism in Eastern Europe, he developed this argument further, noting that

> Marxism failed precisely because of its flawed vision of man. It severs
> man from his moorings in faith, viewing him as nothing more than a ci-

pher, a cog in a brutal machine called the state. There was no place for ethics, morality or spirituality.[20]

Older Western modernization theory had a similar gap in its emphasis on the secular development of economics:

> Much of the definition of development originating from the West has rejected any reference to moral and ethical considerations. Cultural preservation is regarded as retrogressive in the march for development.[21]

Western paradigms did not recognize that the final aim of economic pursuit is the development of man—not the Promethean man of secular humanism who relentlessly seeks to conquer, but rather man as envisaged by the great traditions of East and West.[22] The solution, Anwar maintained, was to define a new paradigm that would be properly rooted in local traditions and not simply be blind borrowing from the West. He developed this new paradigm on two levels, one specifically Islamic and the other Asian.

Anwar's Islamic paradigm was different from the programs and approaches advocated by many Islamist groups. It did not start with advocating the implementation of Islamic law as defined in medieval Muslim society. He rejected the more conservative Muslim approach to tradition, which advocated emulation or following (*taqlid*) of the precedents set by previous generations. Instead, he advocated informed independent analysis, or *ijtihad*. In Anwar's view, Islam is essentially a pragmatic religion whose real strength and dynamism is in the continuing revitalization provided by *ijtihad*.[23]

Anwar's priorities were economic and social justice rather than the imposition of an Islamic state and law:

> The proponents of the imposition of Muslim laws or the establishment of an Islamic state are confined to the periphery. . . . [Southeast Asian Muslims] would rather strive to improve the welfare of the women and children in their midst than spend their days elaborately defining the nature and institutions of the ideal Islamic state. They do not believe it makes one less a Muslim to promote economic growth, to master the information revolution and to demand justice for women.[24]

This new paradigm was not to be exclusively Islamic but constructed more broadly and indigenously in "Asian values" to respond to the realities of religious and ethnic pluralism in Malaysia and in Southeast Asia. However, Anwar emphasized that he did:

not follow a policy of discarding the West. We are not anti-West. We have strong views against some Western attitudes and policies. We believe in engagement between the East and the West.[25]

Rather, a crucial part of the new paradigm would be the establishment of a new consciousness of Asian values, so that "Asia could take the lead in engaging the West in continuous dialogue."[26]

The keystone of this new paradigm would be a cultural renaissance that would provide the foundation for giving a more meaningful role to traditional concepts and values in the society of the future. Recognizing that this would involve a dangerous balancing of the affirmation of separate identities with a sense of the universal human community, Anwar noted the need for constant effort to avoid falling into the traps of religious fanaticism and ethnocentrism in the revival of the grand civilizational traditions of Asia. In addition, local cultures must be defended against homogenization due to the impact of globalization. He also developed a special conceptualization of pluralism to understand how to balance the global and local elements of contemporary affairs.

Transcending Tolerance toward a Global Convivencia

Anwar's understanding of pluralism starts from the recognition of the reality of diversity in human society and the pluralistic context of Malaysia:

> Nations can actually grow and prosper by accepting the fact of cultural diversity, strengthening themselves by learning about their differences as well as by reinforcing the values they share in common. Malaysia is a case in point. It can justifiably claim to be Asia in microcosm—a country with a truly diverse population in terms of ethnicity, culture, and faith. Admittedly this has not come about by choice. One might even say that we were forced by circumstances and history to become a nation, not by dissolving our respective identities and loyalties, but by transcending them.[27]

Toleration of differences is, in Anwar's view, an important starting point, but only a beginning. Diversity is not simply a challenge but represents a major positive resource for Malaysia in particular and for Asians of all religious and ethnic backgrounds in general. People need to transcend their differences but not eliminate them.

Transcending tolerance is thus a crucial part of this new paradigm. Going beyond mere tolerance is not just virtuous, but is, in the long run, a necessity for human survival. The strength of democracy rests upon the existence of diversity. Authoritarian regimes, according to Anwar, forget "that dissent is also a true barometer of the democracy we uphold. A case can be easily made, not for mere tolerance, but rather for the active nurturing of alternative views."[28] In this context, pluralism becomes an essential foundation for a strong democracy and, even more, it is a necessary part of a healthy and dynamic society. Lack of diversity becomes a weakness.

Anwar believed that this acceptance of pluralism that transcends tolerance is a clearly Islamic position. In a speech on civilizational dialogue, he cited the verse in the Qur'an that states: "Oh mankind! Verily we have created you all from a male and a female, and have made you into nations and tribes that you may come to know one another."[29] Thus, constructively recognizing the implications of this divine revelation involves both affirmation of distinctiveness and global humanity:

> We believe that a revitalization of tradition, with all its cultural and intellectual richness, is the most effective countervailing force against religious fanaticism and ethnocentrism. In the context of Islam, this process of revitalization comprehends the reassertion of the values of justice (*al-adl*), tolerance (*al-tasamuh*) and compassion (*al-rahmah*). These values have enabled Muslims, throughout history, to accept diversity not merely as a fact but as an essential feature of human civilization to be celebrated. Because of diversity, man becomes richer through the impetus of the quest to know and understand one another.[30]

This creates, in Anwar's view, a context of constructive living together by diverse groups of people, both in individual societies and in the broader emerging global community. He describes this condition with a term that was developed to describe the religiously pluralistic society in the Iberian Peninsula under Muslim rule, *convivencia.* In its historical sense, and as Anwar uses it, the term

> is loosely defined as "coexistence," but carries connotations of mutual interpenetration and creative influence . . . [In Spain] it is the coexistence of the three groups [Muslims, Christians, and Jews], but only as registered collectively and consciously in the culture of any one of them.[31]

In Anwar's proposed paradigm, *convivencia* is seen as the Islamic form of pluralism, but this is a vision that is quite different from the typical Islamist programs of making a place for non-Muslims in a traditionally conceived Islamic society. Primacy is given to the values of social and economic justice and equality, which are recognized as being fundamental to other great traditions of religious faith as well as Islam. This represents a special balancing of the particular and the universal. Anwar defines it in his call for an "Asian Renaissance":

> Its societies must be prepared to transform themselves and discard the harmful residue from the past—tribalism, narrow-mindedness and fanaticism. It is not the case that Asia must lose its identity, but it must renew its commitment to core values such as justice, virtue and compassion, that are in themselves universal. Creativity, imagination, and courage is [*sic*] needed to translate these values into reality.[32]

This pluralist vision becomes the key to Anwar's understanding of the future global role for Islam and for Asia. It is the foundation of his call for civilizational dialogue.

In 1993, Huntington popularized the notion of "the clash of civilizations" and set the terms of much discussion and debate in the 1990s.[33] Although Huntington's analysis was global in its coverage, it concentrated attention on the relations between Islam and the West, and did so in a way that emphasized stark contrasts:

> The problem for Islam . . . is the West, a different civilization whose people are convinced of the universality of their culture and believe that their superior, if declining, power imposes on them the obligation to extend that culture. These are the basic ingredients that fuel conflict between Islam and the West.[34]

Anwar, like many Muslim intellectuals as well as analysts in the West, rejected the clash of civilizations paradigm. He argued that

> the psyches are different, the cultures are different. Many things about America I like to emulate. But I don't need to be an American. . . . We should be modern; we should be democratic. We should not condone corruption or oppression in any form, or deny basic rights. . . . But don't tell me that democracy and freedom can only be preached by some countries and political leaders in the West.[35]

Both as an intellectual and as a political leader, Anwar joined with others who called for an emphasis on civilizational dialogue rather than clash. He identified common positions of advocacy that had emerged in the encounter between the West and "the civilizations of the East." He noted that the intelligentsia of the East faced the choice of whether to remain loyal to one's traditions or to depart for a way of life perceived as superior. They generally fall into two categories. There are those who forswore everything from the West because of their passionate and tenacious hold on everything from their own traditions. And then there were those who, overwhelmed by the dazzling light of Western civilization, became renegades to condemn their own.[36]

Both of these types of intellectuals, he maintained, had essentially accepted Huntington's fundamental premise of profound and unbridgeable differences between civilizations. Instead he argued for an authentic process of synthesis. The rediscovery of tradition in cultural rebirth

> must inevitably involve a synthesis with other cultures, including those from the West. Genuine renaissance would not be possible without our rediscovery, reaffirmation and renewed commitment with the universals within our culture.[37]

Civilizational dialogue is the necessary framework for Anwar's conceptualization of pluralism:

> For us, the divine imperative as expressed in the Qur'an is unambiguous. Humanity has been created to form tribes, races and nations, whose differences in physical characteristics, languages and modes of thought are but the means for the purpose of *lita'arafu*—"getting to know one another."[38]

In a world of dangerous confrontations, civilizational dialogue is a necessity for human survival and progress. However, this dialogue "must be an encounter among equals, between cherished ideals and values that will serve to challenge our pride and end our prejudices."[39] Old imperialist attitudes of the civilizing mission and fundamentalist rejections of the West as an enemy are not appropriate and only threaten human survival. But civilizational dialogue is a means to a goal, not the goal itself:

> Dialogue has become an imperative at a time when the world has shrunk into a global village. For it is a pre-condition for the establishment of a *convivencia,* a harmonious and enriching experience of living together among people of diverse religions and cultures.[40]

This means that the "primary motif of civilizational dialogue must be a global *convivencia.*"[41]

Mohammad Khatami: The Dialogue of Civilizations

The Islamic revolution in Iran is one of the major events of the Islamic revival of the late twentieth century and has become for many people the symbol of that resurgence. The occupation of the U.S. embassy in Tehran by revolutionary militants and the support that the action received identified the new Islamic Republic of Iran in many peoples' minds as a militant state. The frequent demonstrations chanting slogans like "death to America" and the identification of the United States as the Great Satan confirmed the revolutionary movement and the government as being dedicated to a jihad vision of world affairs. The process of demonization was mutual, with Iran becoming one of the prototypical "rogue states" in U.S. policy formulations by the 1990s. The conflict between the United States and the Islamic Republic became, for many, the classic case of the more general global clash of civilizations in the late twentieth century.

Although this image continues to persist, there have been significant changes in the policy realities. In one of the remarkable developments of the late 1990s, the newly elected president of the Islamic Republic of Iran, Khatami, stated in his inaugural speech to the Islamic Consultative Assembly on 4 August 1997 that "in our world, dialogue among civilizations is an absolute imperative."[42] President Khatami has become one of the major advocates for the dialogue of civilizations in the contemporary world. While he articulates it within the framework of the Iranian revolutionary tradition, his position represents a distinctive new phase in both the evolution of the Islamic resurgence and the debate about the clash of civilizations.

Khatami is in many ways a typical member of the Islamic scholarly elite associated with the revolution in Iran. He was born in 1943 to a family of distinguished scholars. He received a traditional education and was associated with the Ayatollah Khomeini through both his family and his studies. He speaks Arabic, English, and German in addition to Farsi and spent a short period of time as head of an Islamic center in Hamburg, Germany. As a young student and scholar he was identified with the opposition to the Shah and, following the revolution, was elected to the national assembly. From 1982 until 1992 he served as minister of culture and Islamic guidance, and in that position encouraged the development of the film industry in Iran and became an advocate of limiting censorship of the press and other media. As a result of pressure by conservatives advocating more restrictive policies, he had to resign from this ministerial position.

As a middle-level cleric of some political prominence, Khatami was able to run for president of the republic in 1997, and he won a landslide victory. His major opponent, Ali Akbar Nateq-Nouri, represented the conservative religious establishment that had assumed real political power in the Islamic Republic in the later years of Ayatollah Khomeini's life and in the early 1990s. The 1997 presidential election campaign provided an important opportunity for presenting jihadist and pro-dialogue views of world affairs. Nateq-Nouri represented the militant, jihadist view of the world that set the tone for the first decade of the Islamic Republic. In his campaign, he took "a hard stand against the West" and "was faithful to the Islamist approach which rejects all aspects of Western life as materialist and decadent."[43] In contrast, in interviews during the campaign, Khatami said, "I think the West has a superb civilization which has influenced all parts of the world," and noted that "having a deep knowledge of the West has always been very important to me."[44]

In the months following his election, Khatami defined a new stage in the relations between Iran and the United States, and in doing so, articulated a distinctive approach to relations between Islam and the West. The old-fashioned jihad/clash of civilizations perspective presented relatively stark alternatives of victory or defeat in the struggle among civilizations to establish dominance and to maintain an authentic identity in the face of foreign cultural attacks. The alternative view of the interaction of civilizations saw dialogue and exchange as leading to increasing similarity and global multicultural homogeneity. Khatami put forward a view that combined a relatively jihadist defense of Islamic identity and values with a call for civilizational dialogue by which all societies could benefit through the exchange of information and ideas. This emerging perspective advocates a position that goes beyond the thinking of both old-fashioned "fundamentalists" and old-fashioned modernizers.

In the late 1990s, the balancing of the jihad and dialogue dimensions of this approach often took the form of alternating statements and indirect debates between the newly elected president, Khatami, and Ayatollah Khamenei, who was Khomeini's successor as Supreme Guide of the Islamic Republic. A major conference in Tehran in December 1997, for example, was opened by a keynote address by Khamenei in which he outlined the jihadist charges against the "global arrogance" of the United States, and then provided the forum in which Khatami called for "a thoughtful dialogue" with the United States and a broader dialogue among civilizations.[45] Soon after, Khatami made a major gesture toward civilizational dialogue. He provided a long interview with Christiane Amanpour of the Cable News Network (CNN), which was broadcast over American television as well as globally.[46] In this discussion, he elaborated on his earlier call for "thoughtful dialogue." He again argued that Western civilization and the United States were worthy of respect, noting the experience of the Pilgrims at Plymouth as an important event in affirming religious freedom, and the importance of the example of Abraham Lincoln. The interview became a major symbol of advocacy for civilizational dialogue.

In the interview, Khatami also took strong positions criticizing Western policies, especially those of the United States, speaking of a U.S. flawed policy of domination. This position was more strongly stated by Khamenei in a Friday sermon the following week that presented the jihadist, antidialogue position. Khamenei said, "The regime of the United States is the enemy of the Islamic Republic. They are the enemy of your Islam." He added, however,

> I listened very carefully to that [CNN] interview and I have to say that all of Iran's principal positions about relations with the United States and Israel were being expressed very well. He addressed all the matters that needed to be mentioned.[47]

A few days later, Khatami repeated his strong criticism of American policy, saying that in its policies of sanctions the United States sought "to impose their own domestic law on the world . . . [but the] world will not tolerate a master any more—not only will we not tolerate a master, neither will the world."[48]

Many observers at the time saw these two lines of thought as reflecting a power struggle between the newly elected president and the Supreme Guide or as representing a major contradiction within Khatami's own thought. One observer said that Khamenei's remarks reflect his "deepening power struggle with moderates,"[49] while another said that Khatami's later remarks critical of the United States were "sharply different in tone from his recent public statements"; the *New York Times* headline proclaimed, "President Switches Tune on U.S."[50] In the following years, however, it became clear that the strong affirmation of the principles of the Islamic revolution and critique of U.S. policy would be maintained, along with emphatic advocacy of the dialogue of civilizations in general and improved Iranian-U.S. relations in particular.

The Dialogic Creation of a New (Islamic) Civilization

Khatami has combined the two dimensions together into a broader synthesis that goes beyond the conflicting rhetorics of the old jihadist perspective and "modernizing dialogue" discourse. While the conflicts of the 1980s have not been resolved, Khatami worked in the final years of the 1990s to articulate a new framework for conceptualizing the emerging global context in ways that could continue to affirm special particular identities, but in the context of a dialogue rather than a clash of civilizations. One of his early books, *Az Donya-ye Shahr ta Shahr-e Donya* [From the City-World to the World City], involved a survey of a number of Western philosophers, with some emphasis on Plato and Aristotle. He wrote: "No intellectual who studies philosophy and politics can deprive himself of these two sources."[51] The heart of Khatami's perspective is the conviction that Muslims must learn from the successes and achievements of the West if the Islamic community is to itself succeed. Khatami's reframing of the issues is quite clear. He argues that

> we must concede that the incompatibility of modern civilization with our tradition-bound civilization is one of the most important causes of the crisis in our society. What is to be done? Should we insist on re-maining immersed in our tradition, or should we melt fully into Western civilization? Or is there another way of removing this contradiction?[52]

Much of his thought and work is aimed at defining this alternative way of responding to the crisis. Looking at the past, he notes that "the sad experience of the Westoxicated and the tradition-bound is before us, and we must learn from their mistakes so that we do not repeat them."[53] The constructive alternative is to use both the experience of Western modernity and the resources of tradition to create a con-structive program for the future:

> Tomorrow is a time when humanity transcends today's civilization, and those who get there sooner will be those who are familiar with the past and focus on the future, not the rigidly tradition-bound, nor the super-ficially modern who understand only the facade of today's civilization.[54]

The reform program that Khatami gradually began to put in place fol-lowing his election in 1997 is built on this conceptualization of a syn-thesis that is neither tradition-bound jihad nor acquiescent dialogue. These policies were legitimized through Khatami's broad vision of in-tercivilizational relations, in which specific bilateral relations between Iran and the United States are only a small part.

In Khatami's view of long-term global relations, civilizations are constantly changing and evolving. They are not fixed entities. In this view, one sees the West as the latest but not the ultimate human civilization, which, like all other human artifacts, is tentative and susceptible to decay. . . . Civilizations change and there is no such thing as an ultimate and eternal civilization.[55]

This does not imply that one can ignore the West, but neither does it mean that it is necessary to adopt a complete program of Westernization. Instead, it proposes that all peoples should learn from each other in a dialogue of civilizations in order for the next phase of civilizations to emerge. In this world historical perspective:

Civilizations rise and fall. . . . Unless they are completely unaware of each other's existence, civilizations ordinarily affect and transform one another. . . . Give-and-take among civilizations is the norm of history. . . . Thus "new" civilizations are never new in the true sense, for they always feed on the work of previous civilizations, appropriating and digesting all that fits their needs, dispensing with all that does not.[56]

At the beginning of the twenty-first century, there is again need for the creation of a new civilization.

Khatami's call for dialogue must be seen within the context of this worldview. This is not a proposal for more liberal toleration. People in the West also tend to assume that "dialogue" means that eventually the non-Western peoples will see the advantages of Western civilization and become more Westernized. This conceptualization leads to an almost complete misunderstanding of Khatami's vision of dialogue. Dialogue transcends a militant vision of jihad and provides a way to avoid destructive conflict. It also is a long-term policy alternative of learning in order to strengthen civilizations as they evolve in constant change. Dialogue with the West, in this perspective, becomes an important way of strengthening Islam, because, as the West itself evolves and possibly declines, there is the opportunity for Islam to regain its position as the leading progressive world civilization. Dialogue is not a passive policy of accommodation; it is a competitive strategy for strengthening and transforming Islamic civilization and possibly the whole global context of clash and dialogue. It is in this context that Khatami argues that Iranians can think of their revolution as giving rise to a new civilization only if they are able to absorb the good qualities of the West while rejecting its negative aspects. If that can be done, then the coming new great civilization will be Islamic.

In this long-term interpretation of international relations, the "clash of civilizations" becomes an active interaction and dialogue among competitive civilizations. Khatami reflects an important new interpretation of the foundations of international relations in the twenty-first century. It represents a perspective that is significantly different from those of both Western analysts like Samuel Huntington and old-style Islamic advocates of militant jihad like Qutb and, more recently, Usama bin Ladin.

Abdurrahman Wahid: Cosmopolitan Islam and Global Diversity

In October 1999, Wahid, leader of Nahdatul Ulama [Renaissance of Religious Scholars], the biggest Islamic organization in the world's largest Muslim country, became the first elected president in Indonesian history.[57] Nahdatul Ulama (NU) is a predominantly conservative, rural-based sociocultural organization with some 35 million members headed by a man best described as a modern, urban liberal Muslim intellectual. Wahid, popularly known as Gus Dur, is an intellectual/activist whose admirers and detractors have included modernists and traditionalists alike. For decades he has held the role of religious leader and social/political reformer; his activism has been based upon an independent-mindedness and pragmatism that have generated and informed new paradigms and conceptualizations of religion and development. Head of Indonesia's largest Islamic organization, he nevertheless has staunchly warned against those Islamic reformers who would reassert Islam's role in politics and against the dangers of fundamentalism. Both as an intellectual/activist and then as president, he supports an Indonesian state that reflects and respects Indonesia's multireligious and multiethnic society and traditions.

After completing his studies in the pesantren (Islamic boarding schools) and state educational systems, Wahid traveled to the Arab world and Europe for higher studies. At Al-Azhar University, Cairo (1964–66), and then at the Arts Faculty of the University of Baghdad (1966–70), he studied Arabic literature and culture as well as European philosophy and social thought. During that time, his studies and experiences led to his conviction that Islam had to be reinterpreted (*ijtihad*), that change in Islamic teachings was necessary to bring it into conformity with modern science and knowledge.

After completing his studies, Wahid occupied a variety of positions in the pesantren network, including dean at the Hasyim Asyari (Hasan al-Ashari) University (1972–74) and secretary-general of the Pesantren Tebuireng in Jombang (1974–80). He joined with others in creating the Committee for the Development of Pesantrens to revitalize the pesantren religious educational system through expanding its economic base and impact. Networking with other pesantrens, they persuaded government agencies to fund development projects, from those for clean water and energy to mathematics and technology projects. Moving to Jakarta in 1977, Wahid became active in intellectual and religious circles, participating in forums with prominent progressive Muslim thinkers as well as with non-Muslims. He quickly emerged as a public intellectual and national commentator on current events, visible in national and international meetings, the media, and the press.

In many ways, Wahid appears an enigma. He is neither a conservative traditionalist nor an Islamic modernist. A liberal thinker, he is leader of the largest traditionally based Islamic organization. An innovative intellectual with the air of a lay professional or intellectual, he presided over an association of *ulama,* religious scholars, whose organization, NU, had been founded in 1926 to defend the interests of traditional Islam and counter the threat of modernism. Bridging the worlds of traditional Islamic scholarship and "modern" thought, he espoused a reformist intellectual synthesis and social agenda that distinguished between unchanging religious doctrines or laws and legitimate accommodation to social change. This ideal was reflected in his comments on an independent-minded pesantren religious leader (*kiai*) who could be inflexible on some religious issues but accommodating in many other social situations:

> The answer lies with the ability of Kiai Ali to discern between issues which are of essential importance to religion and those which are not; the ability to arrive at an accommodation with the demands of the day without forfeiting the original persona that is the source of the profoundest religious values.[58]

Wahid is among a generation of Islamic neomodernists (including Nurcholish Madjid, Jalalludin Rakmat, Dewan Rahardjo, and Amien Rais) who advocate a progressive Islam, one that is democratic, pluralistic, and tolerant. In contrast to those who have advocated the Islamization or re-Islamization of Indonesian society, Wahid emphasizes the Indonesianization, the indigenization, or contextualization (*pribumisasi*) of Islam. He alludes to the blending of religion and culture, Islamic belief and values, with local culture:

> The source of Islam is revelation which bears its own norms. Due to its normative character, it tends to be permanent. Culture, on the other hand, is a creation of human beings and therefore develops in accordance with social changes. This, however, does not prevent the manifestation of religious life in the form of culture.[59]

There are three pillars of Wahid's thought and activism: (1) a cosmopolitan Islam, the product of his conviction that Islam must be creatively and at times substantively reinterpreted or reformulated in order to be responsive to the demands of modern life; (2) the belief that Indonesian Islam must reflect and respond to its diverse religious and ethnic history and communities; and (3) the conviction that in the Indonesian context, Islam should not be the state religion but rather an inclusive religious, democratic, pluralistic force.

A Response to Legal-formalism and Fundamentalism: The Southeast Asian Exception

Wahid believes that contemporary Muslims have two choices or paths: to pursue a more traditional, statically legal-formalistic Islam or to reclaim and refashion a more dynamic cosmopolitan, universal, pluralistic worldview. The universalism of Islam is reflected in its monotheism (*tawhid*, oneness of God), law (*fiqh*), and ethics (*akhlaq*). These result in Islam's universal concern for human dignity:

> The principles of being equal before the law, of protection of society from despotic powers, of the maintenance of the rights of the weak and of the limitation of the authority of political power are reflections of Islamic concern with human dignity.[60]

In contrast, Islamic legalism is the product of the past but based upon a distorted historical reality. Islamic history reveals the movement or transition from dynamism to legal formalism as Islam became institutionalized primarily through law. The early tendency to formalize and institutionalize Islam's message produced a rigid, oppressive reality.

Idealizing Islam as a social system seeks to impose and implement past Islamic law albeit superficially on the present with little concern for change and cultural pluralism, generating a fortress mentality that proves socially disruptive.[61] This comprehensive reassertion of Islam as a total way of life, which increasingly has taken the form of an "Islamic fundamentalism," runs the risk of degenerating into a religious sectarianism that alienates other national groups and becomes a separatist movement.[62]

In contrast to many "fundamentalists" today, Wahid rejects the notion that Islam should form the basis for the nation-state's political or legal system.[63] He regards the enshrining of Islamic principles in law as a Middle Eastern tradition, alien to Indonesia.[64] Instead, he believes that Indonesian Muslims should apply a moderate, tolerant brand of

Islam to their daily lives in a society where "a Muslim and a non-Muslim are the same" in a state in which religion and politics are separate.[65]

Wahid rejects legal-formalism or fundamentalism as an aberration and a major obstacle to Islamic reform and to Islam's response to global change.[66] The concept of the Muslim as simply a subject of the law must be broadened to that of a multifaceted Muslim and a dynamic Islamic tradition. This requires a transformation based on fundamental values such as free will and the right of all Muslims, both laity and religious scholars (*ulama*) to "perpetual reinterpretation" (*ijtihad*) of the Qur'an and tradition of the Prophet in light of "ever-changing human situations."[67] This process will produce a dynamic (rather than statically legalistic) cosmopolitan Islam more suited to and capable of responding to the diverse realities of modern life.

The cornerstone of Wahid's worldview is pluralism, the diversity of peoples and civilizations that form the context of modern life. The new global outlook of cosmopolitan Islam is one that recognizes the need for a substantial reformulation of "existing civilizations," that is, institutional as well as spiritual frameworks of moral and human behavior. The challenge for contemporary Muslims is to articulate and preserve an authentic identity informed by their Islamic heritage but open to the cosmopolitan realities of a global environment:

> to find an identity that will develop a sense of belonging to Islam, but at the same time still retain a sense of belonging to a larger and wider association with groups motivated by world ideologies, other faiths and global concerns.[68]

This outlook responds to universal basic rights and the recognition of and respect for other faiths, ideologies, and cultures, and absorbs the best that modern science and technology have to offer.[69]

Cosmopolitan Islam, Wahid believes, produces a more flexible formulation of Islam, whose pluralism and tolerance are more appropriate to the modern realities of Indonesia. He has practiced what he preaches. He was the first official figure to publicly denounce the riots of 1996, in which most of the participants were NU members. In addition to advocating tolerance toward Christians, he called for official recognition of Confucianism as a religion in Indonesia.[70] But his political pluralism seemed to test the limits of many Muslims when, in mid-1994, he visited Israel and called for establishing relations with that state. He further aggravated traditionalist Muslims and the *ulama* (many of them members of NU) when he criticized, as meddling in politics, the Indonesian Council of Ulemas for their call for Muslims to vote for parties with Muslim candidates. Moreover, he insisted that the Indonesian government should be a secular coalition rather than a coalition of Islamic parties.[71]

Like Anwar, Wahid sees Southeast Asian Muslims as sharing many common problems of Muslims throughout much of the Islamic world but facing them in their quite distinctively diverse and pluralistic context. Indonesia, in particular, with its 3,000 islands, is a vast collection of religious and cultural groups. It is significantly influenced by the pre-Islamic, Hindu-Buddhist legacy and diverse Islamic orientations of its peoples: the militant conservatism of the Muslims of Acheh, the more nominal, syncretistic approach of Java, and the more militant brands of contemporary Islamic activism. Throughout the years, Wahid has championed the belief that Indonesia can and must provide an example that counters the stereotypes of Islam and Muslim states as radical, antimodern, antidemocratic, and intolerant:

> All that the West sees in Islam is radicalism and its incompatibility with modern, open, democratic politics. Indonesia, however, has the opportunity to show that politics based on confession—as it is in Algeria and Iran—is not the only way. Not only can modernity and open politics exist in a Muslim-majority society, as it can here in Indonesia, but it can be nurtured so that democracy can flourish well in Islam.[72]

The relationship of Islam to the nation-state has been a major issue for modern Muslims. In the several decades since national independence, a cross section of Muslim countries have struggled with issues of political legitimacy, national identity/unity, and the relationship of religion to national development in a world in which the presuppositions of development and modernization theory presumed a Western, secular path. Wahid identifies many issues and realities in nation building: the need to create national integration in the face of communalism, to establish the rule of law, and to develop viable economic frameworks for the equitable distribution of wealth. At the same time, he maintains that many governments rely on sociopolitical engineering, authoritarianism, political suppression, and violence to impose their vision. Governments that rely on social control, rather than consultation, and increasingly employ violence and repression create a climate that contributes to radicalization and violence against the state. Thus, Islamic movements are faced with "the choice of following either a radical approach or a gradual response in their struggle for social justice, equal treatment before the law and freedom of expression."[73]

Wahid believes that in the postindependence period, the Southeast Asian experience contrasts with much of the Muslim world. Many Muslims initially opposed modern nationalism and continue to debate the compatibility of Islam and nationalism. However, in Southeast Asia what clearly emerged from the independence movement was an acceptance of the nation-state, and the recognition by the majority in Indonesia and Malaysia of the bond between Islam and nationalism. Over the years political parties and organizations continued to play an "informal" role in society, while social organizations flourished in Indonesia and Malaysia. In contrast to many parts of the Muslim world where the resurgence of Islam has been primarily political, Wahid argues that the movement for greater Islamization of society in Southeast Asia has been occurring for some time and that it has been primarily cultural rather than political. In Indonesia, organizations like the Muhammadiya developed a network of more than 15,000 schools as well as hospitals and clinics; while NU, in addition to its pesantren educational system, also turned some 7,000 pesantrens across Indonesia to development projects.

Political Engagement: Social Justice and Democratization

Central to Wahid's cosmopolitan Islamic worldview and work is his bottom-up strategy and thus significant involvement in development projects. His ideology is the product of diverse religious and cultural currents: e.g., his Indonesian Islamic background and experience, the influence of Muslim thinkers and activists in the broader Muslim world such as Egypt's Hasan Hanafi and Iran's Ali Shariati, his direct experience with liberation theology in Latin America. These had a significant impact upon his view of Islam and its role in the world as well as of religion and Third World development in general.

Influenced by liberation theology's notion of "conscientization," Wahid speaks of the need for Muslims to develop a "new conscience," one that responds to the dire social realities of the majority. Thus, his cosmopolitan Islam includes a pronounced emphasis on the relationship of religion to development and to social justice: "Social justice should be made a religious as well as a political paradigm."[74]

The antithesis to cosmopolitan Islam is portrayed by fundamentalism. Wahid distinguishes between militant Islamic movements and fanatics or fundamentalists. Islamic movements draw their strength from the extent to which religion informs and transforms their ideology and activities. They are concerned with fundamental issues of self-identity but accept and work within the social and political system. Many combine modern education with a conscious reappropriation and reformulation of a religiously informed identity to respond to the failures and problems of the modern nation-state:

> As long as those efforts constitute attempts to reiterate Islamic values, without totally abandoning the process of modernization in the whole region, it is impossible to apply the label Fundamentalism to them.[75]

In contrast, fundamentalists are a minority of extremists or fanatics who reject the very idea of a social and political framework. They oppose not just a specific government but the very idea of the nation-state itself. They are small and sporadic movements, often confused with the majority of Islamically oriented but more mainstream youth. Though they challenge and disrupt the system from time to time, Wahid believes that they continue to have only local significance and are incapable of developing nationally or regionally.[76]

Wahid maintains that most governments close their eyes to a fundamental social issue of development when they reduce national problems solely to political, socioeconomic, and technical factors. The failure of governments to address deep-seated issues of the relationship of faith to national identity/ideology and institution building contributes to greater instability, "risking the dangers of massive social explosions."[77] Marriages of convenience are short-lived; long-lasting creative solutions are needed to determine the relationship of religion and the state.

The politics of the 1990s proved a challenge that often put Wahid at odds with the government, the military, and fellow Muslim intellectuals and politicians alike. President Suharto in the 1990s broadened his base by appealing to Islam, introducing new legislation and programs on religious education and religious courts and approving the creation of the Association for Indonesian Muslim Intellectuals (ICMI), an organization of intellectuals and government officials that included Nurcholish Madjid, a prominent intellectual and leader of Paramedina, a reformist organization; and Amien Rais, a U.S.-trained political scientist and head of the Muhammadiyah. In contrast, Wahid charged that the ICMI's agenda to create an Indonesian society in a 90 percent Muslim-majority country infused with Islamic values would reconfessionalize Indonesian politics, undermine national unity and religious/political pluralism, and contribute to sectarian strife. He regarded the creation of an Islamic society in Indonesia as "treason against the constitution because it will make non-Muslims second class citizens."[78]

To counter ICMI, Wahid joined 45 other intellectuals and created the Forum for Democracy, which provided a platform to promote his secular democratic vision. This was based upon Pancasila, the political philosophy that recognizes the equality of all religions and advocates separation of religion and the state as the sole national ideology. Because religious tolerance is a prerequisite for democratization, he argued that only nonpolitical, pluralistic, Indonesianized Islam recognizes the equality of all citizens necessary for the promotion of true democracy in a Muslim-majority society. Wahid warned that ICMI's Islamization of Indonesian society would mean inequality, second-class citizenship for minorities, and religious fanaticism. At the same time, he charged that Suharto's New Order had been secular but not democratic, dependent on a military-derived vision of an "integralistic secularism" lacking separation of powers, a system of checks and balances, and the independence of civil society from state control.[79]

Balancing his role as an Islamic leader/scholar and chairman of NU with that of a progressive reformer and political leader required compromise and shifting alliances, often seeming to move from one marriage of convenience to another. At times a strong critic of Suharto's military-backed government, Wahid was also willing to make substantial compromises. Nowhere was political pragmatism more pronounced than in the late 1990s, when Wahid willingly worked closely with both Megawati, former president Sukarno's daughter, who opposed Suharto, and Tutu, Suharto's daughter, who was a potential vice presidential nominee. In the aftermath of national elections, he continued to move easily among contending political leaders and forces: state officials, the military, and the opposition—at one point calling for a trio to lead the country (Megawati, who had garnered the most votes, Amien Rais, and himself), at others distancing himself from Megawati. In the end, Wahid, a compromise candidate between B. J. Habibie and Megawati, was elected president of Indonesia by the parliament and Megawati was appointed vice president in October 1999. Wahid's presidency reflected his flexible, and often unpredictable, approach to politics. Although he was forced from office in 2001 by the parliament that had elected him, he succeeded in reducing the political influence of the military and maintaining the democratic momentum. His nonjihadist approach meant that the transition of power to Megawati Sukarnoputri was peaceful, despite reports that thousands of Wahid's followers were prepared to declare jihad and march on the capital.[80]

In the months following the destruction of the World Trade Center in New York, it became clear that there were in Indonesia a number of well-armed, if small, militant Islamist groups with ties to international jihadist groups. In the context of Indonesia's efforts to move beyond the legacy of military authoritarianism, Wahid's vision of a more cosmopolitan and pluralist Islam gains significance in the struggle to determine the shape of Indonesia's future.

Conclusion

The context of international relations has been experiencing significant transformations. At the beginning of the twenty-first century, many older slogans, ideologies, and paradigms that had shaped conceptual frameworks have been discredited or replaced. The collapse of the Soviet Union and the end of the Cold War have prompted many to look for and identify "new global threats," new enemies, and sources of global conflict. For some, "Islamic fundamentalism" or Political Islam became the "next threat." The violent acts and militant rhetoric of extremists fueled visions of clashes of civilizations, concerns of Muslim jihads against the West, and global terrorism. In fact, the realities of Muslim politics reflect a far more complex and dynamic reality. Voices of conflict and confrontation are accompanied in significant ways by those of dialogue and cooperation.

The resurgence of religion and ethnicity, and of religious and ethnic nationalism, has been global in scope. Contemporary Islam and Muslim politics have reflected these realities, from the emergence of new Islamic republics to the proliferation of Islamic movements and opposition politics. Relations between Islam and the West, in particular between the United States and major Muslim countries, demonstrate a dramatic process of conflict and change. Islamic visions of militant jihads and Western visions of the clash of civilizations face new realities. By the 1990s, the diversity of Political Islam became apparent. Alongside a militant minority of extremist voices and terrorist organizations, one could see the mainstreaming and institutionalization of Islamic political and social activism. From Cairo to Jakarta, Islamically inspired schools, medical clinics and hospitals, social services, and financial institutions proliferated. In electoral politics, Islamic candidates and parties demonstrated their ability to participate within the system and provide a political alternative to entrenched regimes. Islamic activists were elected mayors and parliamentarians, they served in cabinets, and became speakers of national assemblies, prime ministers, and presidents. At the beginning of the twenty-first century, it was possible to argue that "the future of Islamic activism" was with "movements that are willing to exercise tolerance and adopt pluralism as both tactics and ideals."[81] In recent years, "Many Islamic movements . . . have eschewed violence and terrorism. Alongside the terrorist trail of unholy wars, there exists a democratic track record of Islamically oriented candidates . . .The performance of Islamist groups in national and municipal elections defied the predictions of those who insisted that Islamic movements were unrepresentative and would not attract voters."[82]

An important type of Muslim leader-intellectual became prominent, playing a significant role in Muslim reconceptualizations of religion and international relations. People like Anwar in Malaysia, Khatami in Iran, and Wahid in Indonesia have been and are in positions to articulate and sometimes to implement new concepts and paradigms in domestic and international politics. All demonstrate that there is no essentialist or monolithic Islam or Muslim society. All may share a common faith, at times articulate an Islamically inspired worldview, and use Islam as a source of legitimacy and mobilization. Still, their visions, goals, and strategies are shaped as much by specific historical and sociopolitical contexts as by faith.

It has been convenient for some in the West and in the Muslim world alike to selectively view contemporary Islam and Muslim politics through the prism of "militant Islamic fundamentalism" and to speak of historic conflicts between Islam and the West. However, at the dawn of a new millennium, Islamic activist-intellectuals are breaking new paths in domestic and international politics that emphasize engagement and dialogue, diversity and pluralism. President Khatami and his supporters have swept Iranian elections on such issues; at the same time, Khatami has broken new ground in the politics of the Islamic Republic of Iran by calling for a dialogue of civilizations. Anwar and Wahid in differing ways have articulated and pursued pluralistic paths of development emphasizing cultural coexistence and cooperation rather than conflict. Anwar's primary focus on an Islamic paradigm as leader of ABIM became broadened and situated in later years within his vision of an Asian renaissance and an emphasis on shared Asian values. He rejected an international relations based upon a clash of civilizations and instead emphasized *convivencia,* a realism based not only upon shared beliefs or values but national and regional interests. Wahid, as leader of possibly the largest Islamic organization in the world and then as president of the largest Muslim-majority country, has been a persistent champion of a liberal Islam. His cosmopolitan Islam is inclusive rather than exclusive; it promotes Islamic faith and identity within the Muslim community but religious and political pluralism in domestic politics, as well as a vision of international relations that is based upon cooperation and mutual interests rather than conflict.

The terrorism of 11 September highlighted the significance of the struggle within the Muslim world between the violent jihadist vision and the visions of pluralism and dialogue. Any effective "war on terrorism" must recognize this diversity and not transform the legitimate war on terrorism into a clash of civilizations that gives little recognition or support to the advocates of pluralism and dialogue. In the long term, "as Islamic history makes abundantly clear, mainstream Islam, in law and theology as well as in practice, in the end has always rejected or marginalized extremists and terrorists, from the Kharijites and Assassins to contemporary radical movements such as al-Qaeda."[83]

The reconceptualizations of Islam and activist politics of Khatami, Anwar, and Wahid reveal and reflect differing responses to their diverse political and cultural contexts. They challenge those who see the world of the early twenty-first century in polarities, either confrontation-and-conflict or dialogue-and-cooperation, to appreciate the limitations and failures of old paradigms. Ultimately, they demonstrate the need and ability to develop paradigms for governance and policy that are sensitive to the importance of religion and culture in domestic and international affairs.

Notes

This article utilizes our longer study, *Makers of Contemporary Islam* (New York: Oxford University Press, 2001).

1. James N. Rosenau, *Turbulence in World Politics: A Theory of Change and Continuity* (Princeton, NJ: Princeton University Press, 1990), 10.
2. Scott M. Thomas, in this volume, 23.
3. Peter L. Berger, "The Desecularization of the World: A Global Overview," in *The Desecularization of the World: Resurgent Religion and World Politics,* ed. Peter L. Berger (Washington, D.C.: Ethics and Public Policy Center, 1999), 2.
4. Rosenau, *Turbulence,* 6.
5. Sayyid Qutb, *Ma'alim fi al-Tariq* (Cairo: Dar al-Shuruq, n.d.), 116.
6. Ibid., 130.
7. Ibid., 117.
8. John L. Esposito, *Unholy War: Terror in the Name of Islam* (New York: Oxford University Press, 2002), p. 8.
9. Khaled Abou El Fadl, "Moderate Muslims Under Seige," *New York Times,* 1 July 2002.
10. S. N. Eisenstadt, "The Reconstruction of Religious Arenas in the Framework of Multiple Modernities," *Millennium: Journal of International*

Studies 29, no. 3 (2000): 593. For an expansion of this analysis, see John Obert Voll, "The Mistaken Identification of 'The West' with 'Modernity,'" *The American Journal of Islamic Social Sciences* 13, no. 1 (1966): 1–12.

11. Andreas Hasenclever and Volker Rittberger, in this volume, 115.

12. K. Das, "Chipping Away at Extremism," *Far Eastern Economic Review*, 8 February 1980, 10.

13. See, for example, Judith Nagata, "Religious Ideology and Social Change: The Islamic Revival in Malaysia," *Pacific Affairs* 53, no. 3 (1980): 425, and Fred R. von der Mehden, "Malaysia in 1980: Signals to Watch," *Asian Survey* 21, no. 2 (1981): 246.

14. Ian Johnson, "How Malaysia's Rulers Devoured Each Other and Much They Built," *The Wall Street Journal,* 30 October 1998, 1.

15. See, for example, Editorial, "Malaysia on Trial," *New York Times,* 4 November 1998 [http://archives.nytimes.com/archives/] (14 November 2000).

16. For a discussion of these broader developments in the Malaysian political context, see John L. Esposito and John O. Voll, *Islam and Democracy* (New York: Oxford University Press, 1996), chap. 6.

17. Zainah Anwar, *Islamic Revivalism in Malaysia* (Selangor: Pelanduk Publications, 1987), 13.

18. Kamaruddin Muhammad Nur quoted in Anwar, *Islamic Revivalism,* 20.

19. Anwar Ibrahim, *The Asian Renaissance* (Singapore: Times Books International, 1996), 74. See also Anwar Ibrahim, "Development, Values, and Changing Political Ideas," *Sojourn: Social Issues in Southeast Asia* 1, no. 1 (1986): 2.

20. Anwar, *Asian Renaissance,* 74.

21. Anwar, "Development, Values," 1.

22. Anwar, *Asian Renaissance,* 81.

23. Address by Anwar Ibrahim at the Ismail Faruqi Award Presentation Ceremony, International Islamic University, Malaysia, 28 February 1996.

24. Anwar Ibrahim, "The Ardent Moderates," *Time,* 23 September 1996, 24.

25. Anwar Ibrahim, "We Believe in Engagement Between the East and the West," interview in *The Diplomat,* 15 February 1996, 18.

26. Anwar, *Asian Renaissance,* 100.

27. Ibid., 24.

28. Anwar, *Asian Renaissance,* 58.

29. Surah 49:13. The translation is as it was presented in the text of Anwar Ibrahim, "Islam and Confucianism," opening address at the International Seminar on Islam and Confucianism: A Civilizational Dialogue, Kuala Lumpur, Malaysia, 13 March 1995.

30. Anwar, "Islam and Confucianism."

31. Thomas F. Glick, "Convivencia: An Introductory Note," in *Convivencia: Jews, Muslims and Christians in Medieval Spain,* ed. Vivian B.

Mann, Thomas F. Glick, and Jerrilyn D. Dodds (New York: George Braziller, 1992), 1–2.

32. Anwar, *The Asian Renaissance,* 30.
33. Samuel P. Huntington, "The Clash of Civilizations," *Foreign Affairs* 72, no. 3 (1993): 22–47.
34. Samuel P. Huntington, *The Clash of Civilizations and the Remaking of World Order* (New York: Simon and Schuster, 1996), 217–18.
35. Joyce M. Davis, *Between Jihad and Salaam: Profiles in Islam* (New York: St. Martin's Press, 1997), 309.
36. Anwar Ibrahim, "The Need for Civilizational Dialogue," speech given in Washington D.C., 6 October 1994 and printed as Occasional Paper for the Center for Muslim-Christian Understanding, Georgetown University, Washington D.C., 4.
37. Anwar Ibrahim, "Jose Rizal: Humanist and Renaissance," Address to the International Conference on Jose Rizal, Kuala Lumpur, 3 October 1995.
38. Anwar, "The Need for Civilizational Dialogue," 5.
39. Anwar, *The Asian Renaissance,* 45.
40. Anwar, "The Need for Civilizational Dialogue," 5.
41. Anwar, *The Asian Renaissance,* 45.
42. Mohammad Khatami, *Islam, Liberty, and Development* (Binghamton, NY: Institute of Global Cultural Studies, Binghamton University, 1998), 150.
43. "Islam and the Ballot Box," *The Economist,* 31 May 1997, 41.
44. Ibid.
45. An interesting contemporary analysis of the significance of the new approach is Saul Bakhash, "From Iran, an Understated Overture," *Washington Post,* 18 December 1997, A27.
46. The interview received extensive coverage in the news media. See Elaine Sciolino, "Seeking to Open a Door to U.S., Iranian Proposes Cultural Ties," *New York Times,* 8 January 1998 [http://archives.ny-times.com/archives/] (14 November 2000); Barton Gellman, "Iranian Leader Urges Exchanges with U.S.," *Washington Post,* 8 January 1998, A01; and "A Whisper in the Wolf's Ear," *The Economist,* 10 January 1998, 37.
47. John Lancaster, "Head Iranian Cleric Rejects Talks with U.S.," *Washington Post,* 17 January 1998, A18.
48. Elaine Sciolino, "At Khomeini's Tomb, Iran's President Switches Tune on U.S.," *New York Times,* 20 January 1998 [http://archives.ny-times.com/archives/] (14 November 2000).
49. Lancaster, "Head Iranian Cleric," A18.
50. Sciolino, "At Khomeini's Tomb."
51. Elaine Sciolino, "The Mullah Who Charmed Iran Is Struggling to Change It," *New York Times,* 1 February 1998 [http://archives.ny-times.com/archives/] (14 November 2000).
52. Khatami, *Islam, Liberty and Development,* 24.

53. Ibid., 29.
54. Ibid., 36.
55. Ibid., 28, 30.
56. Ibid., 49–50.
57. Eighty-seven per cent of Indonesia's population of 220 million people are Muslim.
58. Greg Barton, "The Liberal, Progressive Roots of Abdurrahman Wahid's Thought," in *Traditional Islam and Modernity in Indonesia,* eds. Greg Barton, Greg Fealy, and Nahdatul Ulama (Monash: Monash Asia Institute, 1996), 213.
59. Abdurrahman Wahid as quoted in Mujiburrahman, "Islam and Politics in Indonesia: The Political Thought of Abdurrahman Wahid," *Journal of Islam and Christian-Muslim Relations* 10, no. 3 (1999): 342.
60. Ibid., 342.
61. Abdurrahman Wahid, interview, "Islam in Indonesia: Where To," *Inside Indonesia,* 8 October 1986, 3.
62. Abdurrahman Wahid, "Islam, Nonviolence and National Transformation: A Preliminary Overview From Historical Perspectives," unpublished, February 1986, 3.
63. Wahid, "Islam in Indonesia," 3.
64. "An Islamic Awakening," *The Economist,* 17 April 1993, 14–15.
65. Recently Wahid replied to a journalist: "Yes, I have enemies. But it is important that I do the right things," *Business Times* (Singapore), 24 March 1999, 48.
66. Abdurrahman Wahid, "Reflections on the Need for a Concept of Man in Islam," Memorandum to the Rector of the U. N. University, 1 May 1983, (unpublished), 3.
67. Ibid.
68. Wahid, "Islam, Nonviolence, and National Transformation," 4.
69. Wahid, "Reflections on the Need for a Concept of Man in Islam," 4.
70. "Government Stance on Confucianism Criticized," *Jakarta Post,* 13 August 1996, 5.
71. "Gus Dur's Party Sitting Pretty after Indon Polls," *New Straits Times,* 10 June 1999, 4.
72. Douglas E. Rampage, "Democratization, Religious Tolerance, and Pancasila: The Political Thought of Abdurrahman Wahid," in *Nahdatul Ulama,* 227.
73. Wahid, "Islam, Nonviolence, and National Transformation," 3.
74. Abdurrahman Wahid, "Cultural Diversity and Religious Unity in Islam: The Indonesian Experience," *Bulletin* XVII, no. 2 (1982): 256.
75. Ibid., 7.
76. Ibid., 8.
77. Abdurrahman Wahid, 'Religion, Ideology, and Development', unpublished paper supplied to the authors, 4.
78. Douglas E. Rampage, "Democratization, Religious Tolerance, and Pancasila," 241.

79. Ibid., 254.
80. See, for example, the report in Rajiv Chandrarekaran, "Village Recruits Prepare Violent Defense of Indonesian Leader," *Washington Post,* 22 April 2001.
81. Anthony Shadid, *Legacy of the Prophet: Despots, Democrats, and the New Politics of Islam* (Boulder, CO: Westview, 2001), p. 7.
82. Esposito, *Unholy War,* p. 148.
83. Esposito, *Unholy War,* p. 128.

EPILOGUE

Terry Nardin

My aim in this epilogue is to identify what seem to me to be the most important questions that emerge from this book and to express some reservations about how the other contributors answer these questions. I write as a political theorist interested in religion and international affairs, one whose outlook is decidedly secular and liberal. Three main topics stand out, roughly corresponding to the three parts of this book. Let me take them in reverse order.

The first is the place of religion in the modern world and more specifically in an international order being transformed by the forces of globalization. Is the alleged revival of religion in a secular world an atavistic reaction against a global market economy and a global culture increasingly shaped by the English language and by American commercial and popular culture? Or must we view religion, in its diverse forms, as an essential part of this new global order? What are the prospects for a productive dialogue between religions and for avoiding a "clash of civilizations" with an apocalyptic struggle between Islam and the West as its centerpiece? Will the postmodern era be postsecular as well? We ask these questions because we want to understand the place of religion in the emerging global order and especially in an ethical global order. And the motivation behind them is practical: What can we do to bring about a world in which religion is on the side of such an order and not its enemy?

This leads to the second area of concern investigated in this book: the relationship between religion and war. It is evident that this relationship must be complicated, given the diversity of things labeled "religion" and "war" and the diversity of situations in which they are brought together. Should we view religion as a perennial source of discord, sedition, and violence, and therefore as a force that must be contained for the sake of peace, order, and justice? Or is religion merely an incidental aspect of wars that have their true sources elsewhere, in national rivalries or economic frustration? In the latter view, religion can exacerbate conflict but also ameliorate it. How compelling is the argument, important in the theory of the modern state, that in claiming ultimate authority over conduct, religion potentially subverts all government except its own and must therefore be constitutionally limited or even excluded from public life? Is this argument, expressed in doctrines like the separation of church and state, a relic of the past, irrelevant to present conditions? Or is it an achievement of Western political culture that is being undermined, with catastrophic consequences, by the absorption into the global order of cultures in which this argument is either not understood or not accepted?

The third issue discussed in these pages is the significance of religion for the study of international relations. The concern here is with religion not only as an object of inquiry but as an essential element in our understanding of it. To put the question bluntly, must the study of religion itself be religious? Must theorizing, when it is about religion, in effect be theology? More broadly still, is it the case that all theory, all understanding—not only of religion, but also of morality, politics, history, nature, and art—must reflect in some way the truths of religion? Or does identifying theory with theology constitute an intrusion of religion into inquiries in which it has no proper business? If religious experience is itself a source of knowledge, will the study of international relations, when it gives religion its due, be transformed not only by an expansion of its subject matter but also in the way it understands that subject matter? What, exactly, is involved in "taking religion seriously"?

I recapitulate these questions as a way of summarizing the agenda for future inquiry and debate that this book proposes. Much of what it has to say about this agenda is sound. Religion has indeed acquired renewed significance in world politics. If it sometimes leads to conflict or fans the flames of conflicts arising from other sources, it also offers resources for resolving conflicts. And the field of international studies does need to pay attention to religion and to do so in ways appropriate to this subject matter. As Scott Thomas suggests, the field's neglect of religion has begun to look bizarre. But rather than endorse or amplify these conclusions, I want to focus on two issues concerning which discussions of religion and international affairs are apt to go astray: the relationship between religion and morality and the relationship between religion and the study of religion.

In discussing these issues, religious scholars often oppose the insights of religious experience to Enlightenment rationalism, in some

cases bolstering a brief for religion by drawing on postmodern antira-
tionalism. At the same time, they rely on Enlightenment values—on
critical rationality and an ethic of pluralism, mutual respect, and authentic dialogue—to distinguish defensible from indefensible religious views. They reasonably contest simplistic and hostile
understandings of religion. But to call these understandings "Enlightenment" understandings, as some do, is to offer an equally simplistic
view of the Enlightenment and the complex perspectives on religion
that spring from it. These include not only the historical and comparative study of religion but also the enlightened forms of religious faith
espoused in this book.

Religion and Morality

A pervasive assumption in discussions of religion is that religion is intrinsically moral. But there are reasons to doubt this assumption.
Common sense suggests that religious practices can be immoral and
religious beliefs false. A moment's reflection is sufficient to establish
that the scope of religion is more inclusive than that of morality. A
moral system, whatever its principles may be, is concerned to pre-
scribe human conduct. Religion, as a system of belief, is concerned
with many things besides conduct. It purports to explain the origin of
the universe and the place of human beings in it. It competes with history and science in explaining events. It postulates powers that make
things happen and that can be influenced by ritual, prayer, or other behavior. In so far as religion is seen as a way for human beings to get
what they want, its significance is instrumental, not moral. Asking a
god to supply one's needs or to destroy one's enemies is an exercise in
prudence, not morality. Most religions provide moral guidance, and
their principles often converge with those that can be defended on
other grounds. But sometimes the guidance a religion provides is erroneous, either because the premises on which its precepts rest are mistaken or because they have been misinterpreted. The relationship
between religion and morality is a complicated one marked by stark
differences as well as by agreement.

People identify religion and morality because they want to reconcile their religious beliefs with moral conclusions arrived at independently of those beliefs. But defining religion in such a way as to
reconcile its claims with those of morality merely results in circularity.
To avoid this circularity and the confusions it generates, we must distinguish religion and morality as systems of belief and conduct. Some
religions do just this. In Christian societies, for example, there long

ago emerged an understanding of morality as a set of principles binding on all rational beings, principles that could be discovered not only by faith but also by reason. Aquinas and his school held that, besides the laws of conduct revealed by God, there is an independently discoverable natural law—a moral law that human beings can discover for themselves by the exercise of reason. For Grotius and other seventeenth- and eighteenth-century Protestant moralists, this natural law constitutes a "thin," or minimum, morality—one that can be distinguished from the "thick" morality of Christianity. As Grotius put it, Christian morality imposes "a greater degree of moral perfection" than does natural law. Jewish and Muslim thinkers, too, distinguished the duties of the faithful from the duties that are binding on all human beings. There are many today who are engaged in efforts, by means of comparative inquiry and interreligious dialogue, to identify a common "global ethic" resting on what John Rawls and Hans Küng call an "overlapping consensus" among diverse moral and religious traditions. They join Grotius, Kant, and other moral philosophers in distinguishing a rationally based common morality from the religious traditions in which it has been historically embedded, for these traditions contain much that is religiously specific and distinguishable from this common morality.

Sometimes, however, religions teach doctrines and practices that are not morally justifiable according to the precepts of natural law or common morality. Slavery, torture, conquest, terrorism, and genocide have all found warrant in religious traditions, but such practices have no place in natural law, or, even more conclusively, in Kantian morality understood as a system of precepts based on a fundamental principle of respect. Morality, so understood, must condemn any action or practice that fails to respect human beings as rational beings equally entitled to think and choose. When religion and morality clash, it is religion that must give way if its claim to be moral is to be sustained.

Writers on religion implicitly acknowledge this conclusion when they distinguish faiths that are "tolerant," "inclusivist," "progressive," or "humane" from those that are not. Since, clearly, some kind of moral test is being applied here, the distinction implies a gap between religion and morality. All we can say, then, is that religion has a moral potential that it sometimes fails to realize. When the failure is dramatic, as in the case of at least some kinds of religious fundamentalism, it is necessary to emphasize this potential. This leads to a genre of writing represented by John Esposito and John Voll in their account of how, in contrast to the advocates of jihad against the non-Muslim world, certain politically engaged Muslim intellectuals have urged pluralism, coexistence, and dialogue with other religions and with secular moral and political perspectives. These examples suggest that Islam is not univocal and that a humane, tolerant, and intellectually open Islam is possible. It suggests that Muslims can join the adherents of other faiths in identifying shared moral principles to define a common global ethic. But it also recognizes that there are variants of Islamic tradition that are hostile to these interpretations, and that Islam and morality are not synonymous. Similar tensions can be found in other religions.

Why, then, insist that religion is indispensable in creating a morally defensible global order? The argument is essentially pragmatic. When the confusions that arise from equating religion and morality have been sorted out, that argument can be seen to rest not on the (false) premise that religion is inherently moral but on the reasonable presumption that the effort to articulate a global ethic cannot succeed unless that ethic resonates with the moral teachings of the world's major religions. Unless there is some basis for that global ethic within these religions, their adherents will have no motive to accommodate it. As Scott Thomas puts it, "the Grotian legacy" of separating morality from religion has reduced "the thick practices of international relations embedded in the social traditions of the world religions and civilizations to thin practices (as procedural rules)" and thereby undermined "the social bond" that secured their observance in international society. The problem, then, is to find a way of recruiting religion to support the thin, or minimal, morality that is necessary for a pluralist world order. Religion is necessary, in this view, to motivate people to treat one another according to the precepts of a common morality.

That the significance of religious experience is essentially pragmatic is reinforced by Fred Dallmayr's discussion of spirituality, though we must read that discussion against the grain to reach that conclusion, for it is one he would surely disagree with. Spirituality, Dallmayr suggests, is a frame of mind in which the believer leaves the self-centered world of ordinary experience and enters a realm in which the self participates in something larger and truer than everyday life. Spirituality, in this sense, is an experience of transcendence in which the boundaries between the mundane and the divine, between self and not-self, dissolve. In Christianity and Islam this transcendent spirituality involves being at one with God. It takes two main forms: gnostic ("esoteric-intellectual") spirituality and *agape* ("erotic-mystical") spirituality.

Dallmayr distinguishes spirituality from both "reason" and "will." The distinction between spirituality and reason (*logos,* speech or argument) is clear enough, given the close identification of spirituality not only with gnosis (knowledge of reality arrived at not by discussion or reasoning but by intuitive or mystical insight, perhaps achieved by prayer, meditation, or hallucinogens) and also with *agape* (love or care, which is an emotion, a disposition, not a cognitive faculty). But spirituality, so defined, is closer to "will" than Dallmayr realizes because the significance of gnosis is practical as well as intellectual. Gnosis, I would argue, is more than esoteric-intellectual spirituality. Its significance is not merely cognitive. An esoteric practice that unites its practitioners with the divine *makes real* to them what, by reason alone, they can know only externally. It makes present what is distant, visible what is invisible, and, in doing so, brings it into the human world of choice and action. Even when a religious faith invites us to retreat from "the world" and its affairs, it is inviting us to choose and act—to reject consumerism, for example. And if gnosis has practical implications, so of course does *agape.* Love implies action, not mere contemplation. For Christians, the meaning of *agape* spirituality is a love for Jesus that is also, in Dallmayr's words, "a loving engagement with fellow humans and their sufferings." To love thy neighbor as thyself is to act on that love, respecting others and assisting them when they need assistance that you are in a position to provide. Both gnosis and *agape,* then, motivate us to act, and they do so in proportion to our success in achieving the kinds of spirituality they represent.

The assumption that spirituality necessarily motivates people to act *morally* is, however, unwarranted. What spirituality motivates is action, and action can be either moral or immoral. Religiously inspired action can be misguided or partisan, and spirituality can be an excuse for immorality. A believer who dies for his fellows is not necessarily acting morally if he dies in an unjust war. Those who stress the motivating power of religion must recognize that it can motivate just about anything. Tyrants and terrorists know that religion is motivating. Those who argue that religion is necessary to motivate support for "humane global governance" are offering a latter-day version of the case for "civil religion" made by Machiavelli, Hobbes, and Rousseau. Like these philosophers, they adopt an instrumental attitude toward religion that emphasizes its political utility rather than its intrinsic truth or moral value. Religion is needed to sustain the "virtue" required for global citizenship.

If it is a mistake to equate religion with morality, it is also a mistake to equate the secular with immorality. Religion can contribute to imagining an ethical global order and it can motivate people to support such an order. But does it follow, as Richard Falk suggests, that secular thought is necessarily impoverished and that only religion can fill the gap left by the "exhaustion of . . . the secular project"? Can it be more than vacuously true to assert, as Falk does, that efforts to promote human rights and global democracy are "religiously inspired"? He may be right that such efforts cannot succeed without mobilizing religious energies. But the problem with *that,* as the philosophers of civil religion well understood, is keeping those energies within moral bounds.

What emerges from the book's discussion of the relationship between religion and morality, then, is that religion has two moral personas. The first I would call "enlightened" religion—a label I choose to counter endemic religious hostility to the eighteenth-century European Enlightenment. Enlightened religion is tolerant of other faiths. It is open to interreligious dialogue and to accommodating secular ideas and institutions. It can, for these reasons, contribute to the project of connecting the secular and liberal ethic of Europe and America (expressed in ideas like natural law, human rights, and the rule of law) with the ethical outlooks of religious communities throughout the world. The other persona, that of "exclusivist," "intolerant," "inhumane," "regressive," or "securitized" religion, is antirational and antiliberal. It is the enemy of enlightened religion. I find it telling that scholars who argue that religion can make a positive contribution to international affairs must recruit Enlightenment rationality and morality to their side in choosing between the religious alternatives they have identified.

Religion and Theory

What are the implications of a new awareness of the importance of religion in international affairs for the study of international relations? Does it require revision of accepted modes of International Relations theory? Do we need new interpretive categories and analytical frameworks? Is it really the case, as some of my fellow contributors suggest, that proper attention to religion might revolutionize International Relations theory? If their arguments are sound, taking religion seriously has implications not only for what International Relations scholars study but for how they study it.

The claim that International Relations theory must reflect as well as study religion is asserted most explicitly by Vendulka Kubálková, who argues that if international political theory is to take religion into account, it must become an "international political theology." Theology—literally, the study or theory (*logy*) of the gods or God (*theo*)—is the activity of reasoning systematically about religious objects, the effort to establish rational coherence within a world of religious ideas. It is an inquiry that, like any other, has truth as its goal and its criterion. And, like any other inquiry, it rests on certain premises that determine the kind of inquiry it is. The premises of a theology are religious premises. Theology begins with certain articles of faith and works out their implications to generate a systematic doctrine that may depart in significant ways from the naive understanding of the ordinary believer. But it does not question those articles of faith. It aspires, in short, to a theoretical understanding of religion while grounding itself in religious assumptions. For this reason theology has been condemned as circular and self-validating, but that accusation might be made against any inquiry, for every inquiry rests on premises it does not challenge. No inquiry can get under way without making assumptions. Theology, then, is inquiry into religious questions that rests on religious premises.

It comes as a surprise to discover that Kubálková does not use the word "theology" in this way. "Theology," she writes, refers to "the systematic study of discourses [that seek] a response, transcendental *or secular,* to the human need for meaning" (emphasis added). In other words, any inquiry that is concerned with meaning—any hermeneutic inquiry—is a 'theology.' The argument seems to be this: Because religion is a matter of meaning, and theology deals with religion, theology deals with meaning. Political theory, when it shakes off the prejudices of positivist social science, also deals with meaning. Political theory is therefore theological, even when it is not concerned with religion or based on religious premises.

That there is a logical fallacy here is evident. The argument Kubálková really wants to make, in my judgment, and in which she is joined by other contributors, is not illogical, but it has nothing to do with theology. It is simply that because religion involves meaning, it cannot be studied by the methods of positivist social science, for these methods exclude the element of meaning. Positivist social science imitates the natural sciences, which deal with objects treated as manifestations of natural processes, not as expressions of mind. To understand mind and its products—the ideas our thinking generates and uses—we must adopt an approach that does not ignore the world of mind, which is a world of meanings. The appropriate method for studying religion in its various manifestations—as a system of beliefs, a set of doctrines, precepts, or rituals, an institution, a kind of experience, or a way of life—is therefore hermeneutic. But this does not mean that the study of religion must itself be religious. Hermeneutics may have originated in efforts to interpret scripture but it long ago outgrew its original mission to separate the word of God from the all too human words of the corrupted historical texts in which that word is embedded. The effort to find the divine message in historically contingent scriptures was, in fact, a decisive step toward the Enlightenment view of religion as a human construct—one that is as open, and as vulnerable, to objective historical, anthropological, and philosophical scrutiny as any other human construct.

Embracing a latter-day version of this Enlightenment insight, Kubálková identifies hermeneutic approaches to understanding human conduct with "constructivism." Religions, she observes, are social constructs, complex webs of social meaning, and these meanings must be understood before they can be explained. (Kubálková correctly observes that in the hands of some of its self-declared practitioners, constructivism has reverted to a positivist social science that must not be confused with the "rule-oriented constructivism" attentive to meaning.) But this preference for constructivism is unnecessarily limiting. As the chapters by Cecelia Lynch and several other contributors suggest, there are hermeneutic approaches besides constructivism that can illuminate religious ideas and practices. Constructivism does not exhaust the possibilities for interpretive understanding in the human sciences unless we stretch its meaning to encompass anthropology, jurisprudence, ethics, political theory, philology, literary studies, and every other kind of hermeneutic inquiry. Nor does constructivism provide ammunition for the struggle against secularism, given how well it fits with enlightened biblical criticism. It might be said to spring in part from the writings of Spinoza, Hume, and other "enlightened" students of religion. Among them was David Strauss, whose 1835 *Life of Jesus* portrayed its subject (Jesus, not Christ) as a historical figure. Applying the critical tools of German historical scholarship, Strauss treated the gospels as ordinary, and therefore partly corrupted and unreliable, historical sources. This historical picture of Jesus was converted by Ludwig Feuerbach, whose ideas influenced Marx and Engels, into a systematic critique of religion. Feuerbach's aim was to explain Christian belief by revealing it to be myth—specifically, as a confused attempt by human beings to rationalize their suffering. Theologians, he wrote, say that God has created man, but in fact it is man who has created God. Christian belief is nothing but a reflection of the human condition—an infantile projection by human beings of their fears and hopes on the imagined figure of God. Before embracing constructivism, the religious scholar would do well to see where it comes from and where it can lead.

Another point at which the effort to link hermeneutics with theology goes astray is in characterizing hermeneutic understanding as inherently subjective, a matter of empathy or imaginative reconstruction of the experience of other human beings. Interpretive social science is concerned with ideas, not psychological experiences. 'Mind' means not only the inner, private experience of individual consciousness. It also means the outer, public world of collective consciousness that is expressed in languages, customs, laws, sciences, and culture generally. When we inquire into the meaning of a poem, a law, a ritual, a gesture, a scientific theory, or any other "text," we are concerned with a mind-created object, not the psychological processes that produced that object. The object takes on a life of its own and becomes entangled in and altered by webs of meanings that are independent of the minds of the persons in whose thinking it originated. Understanding ideas does not depend on empathy—on the "insider's perspective" or "emotional identification," as Kubálková puts it—which requires us to re-create in our own minds the thoughts of those whose ideas and expressions we are studying. We are not barred from attempting empathetic reenactment of religious or other experience. But neither are we required to reenact that experience, because ideas have meanings that are distinct from the thoughts or intentions of particular persons. Those we are studying may not, in fact, understand the significance of what they are thinking or saying. The meaning of a law is not necessarily what a particular legislator, lawyer, judge, or administrator believes it to be. What it means to any individual person is an aspect of its meaning but not the whole of it. Interpretation must be distinguished from empathy because ideas depend on the shared meanings that constitute cultural practices.

It is a mistake, then, to distinguish "explanation" and "interpretation" on the grounds that interpretation, unlike explanation, is subjective. Ideas draw upon shared meanings and are in that sense intersubjective. Furthermore, what those meanings are can be ascertained by objective methods. The hermeneutic disciplines have their own intersubjective canons of inquiry and criteria for verifying hypotheses about historical events, religious practices, and other cultural objects. For this reason, we can reject the claims of poststructuralism to have demolished the possibility of objective knowledge. And if that is the case, we can also reject the suggestion, made by Derrida and endorsed here by Carsten Bagge Laustsen and Ole Wæver, that poststructuralism opens the way for a return to religion. This might be our conclusion if, after deconstructing reason, we were left with faith—irrational belief, belief that cannot be justified—as the only alternative. But the suggestion that International Relations theory can now continue only by substituting faith for reason—that it must "acknowledge its own religion"—is unduly pessimistic. It is also self-contradictory, for only by retaining its commitment to systematic reasoning can International Relations theory retain its claim to being 'theory.' Theology, after all, is systematic as well as religious. Pure faith may confer gnosis but it cannot generate a theology.

It is important to distinguish between taking religion seriously as a subject of study and treating it as a set of truths or way of life that dictates how the study of religion must proceed. Fields like the history or philosophy of science could not exist if historians or philosophers were simply to accept the self-understanding of scientists. By the same token, there must be some distance between religion and the study of religion. To say this is not to challenge religion as such, though it does challenge certain religious self-understandings. It is no more antireligious to reject the claim that all truth is ultimately religious than it is antiscientific to reject the view that science alone can yield knowledge worthy of the name. To reject such claims *is* to repudiate the foundationalism of those who think their own understanding of what is 'real' is identical with reality itself. It is to reject religious fundamentalism, certainly, but also more moderate arguments for the essentially religious character of morality and truth. It is equally to reject the uncritical faith of secular realists, social scientists, and pragmatists of all sorts that the world is what they take it to be.

The implications of these conclusions for the study of religion and international relations are straightforward. That study must give more attention to religion and it must do so in ways that take account of its manifold diversity and complexity. To do that, it will have to abandon the reductionist approaches to explaining human behavior that prevail in the discipline of International Relations and cultivate the interpretive skills of historians, anthropologists, and other students of culture. This book provides examples of such interpretive approaches and their application to international relations. The study of religion in world affairs must "listen" to the forms of religious experience it studies, avoiding the temptation to filter that experience through its own preconceived categories. But it must also avoid privileging the categories of those it studies. It cannot simply assume that religious beliefs are true, that religion must play a central role in global governance, or that a global dialogue must be a conversation among religious voices. Religion is culture but it is not the whole of culture. Cultural pluralism involves more diversity than religious pluralism. The study of religion needs not repudiate the achievements of Western liberalism, the Enlightenment, or secular modernity; doing that, even under the banner of an advanced and sophisticated postmodernism, is simply reactionary. And that repudiation, I have argued, is in any case often inauthentic. Above all, the study of religion must not confuse understanding religion with the experience of religious faith. It must distinguish religion as a subject of inquiry from the inquiries that are brought to bear on it.

Index